ROUTLEDGE LIBRARY EDITIONS: ISLAM, STATE AND SOCIETY

Volume 4

THE ISLAMIC LAW ON LAND TAX AND RENT

THE ISLAMIC LAW ON LAND TAX AND RENT

The Peasants' Loss of Property Rights as Interpreted in the Hanafite Legal Literature of the Mamluk and Ottoman Periods

BABER JOHANSEN

Routledge
Taylor & Francis Group
LONDON AND NEW YORK

First published in 1988 by Croom Helm Ltd

This edition first published in 2017
by Routledge
2 Park Square, Milton Park, Abingdon, Oxon OX14 4RN

and by Routledge
711 Third Avenue, New York, NY 10017

Routledge is an imprint of the Taylor & Francis Group, an informa business

British Library Cataloguing in Publication Data
A catalogue record for this book is available from the British Library

ISBN: 978-1-138-23270-9 (Set)
ISBN: 978-1-315-31161-6 (Set) (ebk)
ISBN: 978-1-138-23238-9 (Volume 4) (hbk)
ISBN: 978-1-138-23243-3 (Volume 4) (pbk)
ISBN: 978-1-315-31261-3 (Volume 4) (ebk)

Publisher's Note
The publisher has gone to great lengths to ensure the quality of this reprint but points out that some imperfections in the original copies may be apparent.

Disclaimer
The publisher has made every effort to trace copyright holders and would welcome correspondence from those they have been unable to trace.

THE ISLAMIC LAW ON LAND TAX AND RENT

The Peasants' Loss of Property Rights as Interpreted in the Hanafite Legal Literature of the Mamluk and Ottoman Periods

Baber Johansen

CROOM HELM
London • New York • Sydney

Croom Helm Ltd, Provident House,
Burrell Row, Beckenham, Kent BR3 1AT
Croom Helm Australia, 44-50 Waterloo Road,
North Ryde, 2113, New South Wales

Published in the USA by
Croom Helm
in association with Methuen, Inc.
29 West 35th Street
New York, NY 10001

British Library Cataloguing in Publication Data

Johansen, Baber
The Islamic law on land tax and rent:
the peasants' loss of property rights
under the Hanafite doctrine. — (Exeter
Arabic and Islamic series).
1. Real property (Islamic law)
I. Title II. Series
340.5'9 [LAW]
ISBN 0-7099-1496-2

Library of Congress Cataloging-in-Publication Data

Johansen, Baber.
The Islamic law on land tax and rent: the peasants' loss of property rights under the Hanafite doctrine/Baber Johansen.
p. cm. — (Exeter Arabic and Islamic series)
Bibliography: p.
Includes index.
ISBN 0-7099-1496-2
1. Real property tax (Islamic law) — History. 2. Rent (Islamic law) — History. 3. Landlord and tenant (Islamic law) — History. 4. Hanafis — History. I. Title. II. Series.
LAW <ISLAM 7 Joha 1988>
346.04'3'088297 — dc 19
[342.643088297] 87-30491
CIP

Printed and bound in Great Britain by
Billing & Sons Ltd, Worcester

Contents

Preface vii
Acknowledgements ix
Notes on Transcription x
Preliminary Remarks 1

1. The Birth of the Kharāj Payer 7
2. The Contract of Tenancy (Ijāra): The 'Commodification' of the Productive Use of Land 25
3. The Share-cropping Contract (al-Muzāra^{c}a): Combining Dependent Labour with the Means of Production 51
4. The 'Death of the Proprietors' 80
5. The Ottoman Muftis' New Doctrine on Tax and Rent 98
6. Summary and Conclusion 122

Bibliography 126
Name Index 132
Subject Index 134

To the memory of my brothers
Anatol, Angelus and Peter

Preface

Habent sua fata libelli. The present essay was never meant to become a book. It was a contribution to a stimulating symposium on Islamic law organised by Aziz Al-Azmeh at Exeter University. As my subject I had chosen one aspect of the important changes that occurred in the Hanafite jurists' doctrine on agricultural relations of production after the tenth century. I wanted to write an essay that demonstrated the importance of a new legal category and the way in which this legal category changed the classical doctrine of Hanafite law. Therefore, I felt justified in neglecting other important changes in the Hanafite doctrine on the agricultural relations of production, such as the new legal ordinances on the social and economic status of the peasants, the new forms of tenancy contracts and the importance of investment with regard to tenancy rights. I felt free to neglect the details of the historical transmission of the new legal category I was describing. And I did not analyse the social and economic conditions in Central Asia that, from the tenth to twelfth centuries, led Hanafite jurists in that part of the world to develop the elements of the new doctrine that I am analysing in this book. I hope to be able to integrate all these neglected elements in a book on the development of the Hanafite doctrine on relations of production in agriculture and to publish such a book within the next three years.

What I wanted to present for publication was originally a long essay. But analysing the legal categories turned out to be impossible without at least discussing some of their implications for the process of economic reasoning. The text grew in complexity and length. At that stage of the writing process Aziz Al-Azmeh's constant commitment to publish even a very long essay was truly reassuring. When he finally took the initiative to suggest publication as a book, I asked the advice of some of my close friends and colleagues and gratefully accepted the offer. I can only hope that the reader will find sufficient justification for this decision in the text of the book.

I should like to thank my colleague, Fritz Steppat, for his careful reading of the text and his encouragement to publish it as a book. I enjoyed and found very helpful the long discussions I had with Abdellah Hammoudi. Jamil M. Abun-Nasr has discussed patiently, and with genuine friendly interest, many aspects of the first draft. I am also grateful for having had the chance to present an outline of the present book in a seminar on Agriculture in the Middle East held jointly with Fritz Steppat, Engin Akarli, Abdellah Hammoudi and Peter v. Sivers at the Institute of Islamic Studies at the Freie Universität Berlin. I owe much to A.L. Udovitch's diligent reading of the text, his valuable suggestions and his encouragement.

Margaret Rausch has carefully read and corrected the manuscript. Renate Heveker has patiently and cheerfully typed and retyped the various drafts.

The remaining mistakes are all mine.

Berlin, 9th March 1987

Acknowledgements

I wish to express my thanks to Mr Ronald Buckley for meticulous editorial assistance in the preparation of this book, and to Mrs Sheila Westcott for the preparation of the final typescript with her usual patience and competence.

Aziz Al-Azmeh

Notes on Transcription

The following signs are used in the transliteration of Arabic letters:

Arabic letter	*Transliteration*
Hamza	a, i or u at the beginning of a word. In the middle and at the end of a word, the sign is used to indicate the glott stop.
Bāʾ	b
Tāʾ	t
Thāʾ	th (to be pronounced like th in thought)
Ǧīm	j
Ḥāʾ	h
Khāʾ	kh (to be pronounced like the ch in Loch)
Dāl	d
Dhāl	dh (pronounced like th in this)
Rāʾ	r
Zāy	z
Sīn	s
Shīn	sh
Ṣād	ṣ (emphatic s)
Ḍād	ḍ (emphatic d)
Ṭāʾ	ṭ (emphatic t)
Ẓāʾ	ẓ (emphatic z)
ʿAin	ʿ (a strong guttural produced in the throat)
Ghain	gh (similar to the first r in French parler)
Fāʾ	f
Qāf	q (emphatic k)
Kāf	k
Lām	l
Mīm	m
Nūn	n
Wāw	w
Yāʾ	y

Long vowels are expressed by the signs ā, ī and ū.

Book titles, single words and half sentences are simply transliterated, i.e. the transliteration reproduces the Arabic letters and not their phonetic value. Whole sentences are transcribed. The transcription, in their case, reproduces the phonetic changes that occur when sentences are spoken. Arabic words that have a common English form (e.g. Medina, mufti, Iraq) are neither transliterated nor transcribed.

Preliminary Remarks

DID ISLAMIC LAW CHANGE?

The three scholars who — in this century — have contributed most to our understanding of the history and structure of Islamic law are unanimous in supporting the view that no thoroughgoing changes occurred in Islamic law after the tenth century. According to Joseph Schacht[1] and Noel J. Coulson,[2] the *corpus juris* of the Muslim jurists was developed during the 'formative period' of Islamic law extending until the middle of the ninth or the begining of the tenth century. Chafik Chehata speaks of a 'pre-classical period' of Islamic law that comprises the eighth to the tenth centuries and in which the *corpus juris musulman* reached its final stage of development.[3] He shares with Schacht and Coulson the view that the legal ordinances of Islamic law were fully developed in this period and underwent only minor changes in the following periods.[4] He calls this period the 'pre-classical period' of Hanafite law because the most systematic and coherent forms of reasoning that underlie the various legal ordinances and establish their unity and cohesion as a legal system were developed only in the 'classical period' of Hanafite law, i.e. from the tenth to the twelfth centuries.[5] Chehata's penetrating analysis of the development of the systematic and coherent forms of reasoning of Hanafite jurists in the 'classical period' has, indeed, added much to our understanding of the structure of Hanafite law.[6]

However, the reader obtains from the works of those eminent scholars the impression that after the earliest ('formative' or 'pre-classical') period of Islamic law, its legal ordinances (its *corpus juris* or 'positive law') remained unchanged. Insofar as changes in legal reasoning are acknowledged, it is said that they 'affected neither the established decisions of positive law nor the classical doctrine of *uṣūl al-fiqh*'.[7] Schacht, Chehata and Coulson do not deny that the decisions of the muftis throughout the centuries added new material to the *corpus juris* of Islamic law. But — with the notable exception of Coulson — they seem to be convinced that any changes which occurred after the tenth century dealt with only minor matters of detail. Coulson states that '... in the field of civil transactions forces inherent in Islamic society had brought about considerable modifications of the strict classical doctrine'[8] and he stresses the importance of the muftis for this development.

In this essay, I hope to be able to demonstrate, with special reference to the development of Hanafite law in the Mamluk and Ottoman periods, that changes in the legal doctrine were not restricted to civil transactions, but also concerned the public law. Interrelated key concepts of the Hanafite law such as property, rent and the taxation of arable lands underwent thoroughgoing changes in the Mamluk and Ottoman periods. The results of these changes are well documented in the Syrian and Egyptian *fatāwā* from the sixteenth to nineteenth centuries. In this essay I cannot go into the details of the historical development of these legal doctrines. I shall be very satisfied indeed, if, by comparing the legal doctrine of the pre-classical and classical periods with the legal opinions of the Ottoman jurists, I can demonstrate the structural changes that occurred between the tenth and sixteenth centuries. But I am persuaded that closer scrutiny of the stages of development of the new legal doctrines on tax and rent will prove the crucial role played by the muftis of Central Asia and of Egypt and Syria in the formation of the new doctrines, a formation that seems to have taken place gradually between the tenth and fifteenth centuries.

HOW ARE WE TO STUDY CHANGE WITHIN ISLAMIC LAW?

Udovitch recently suggested that

> The traditional terms of the discussion of medieval Islamic land tenure along the continuum of absolute state ownership as opposed to private ownership cannot adequately accommodate the many varieties of land tenure we encounter in the medieval Middle East. Any new definition of the terms of this discussion will have to concede an overall state claim (although not necessarily ownership) in terms of revenue and taxation while taking into account different types of control and internal organisation of agricultural lands, such as private ownership of small or large estates, communal or tribal ownership, and direct state control.[9]

Islamic law certainly lends itself to such an approach. Tax and rent are interrelated key concepts of the Hanafite law that cannot be studied independently of each other. The system of taxation largely determines the margin that is left for the appropriation of the rent. The doctrine on tax and rent largely determines the conception of landed property. In the Hanafite doctrine on tax and rent, changes of individual legal ordinances and structural changes in the relationship between tax and rent occurred in the period between the tenth and sixteenth centuries. These changes led to a redefinition of the concept of landed property. In order to demonstrate the importance of these changes, I have to begin with a detailed description of the Hanafite concept of tax and rent as developed in the pre-classical and classical periods of Hanafite law. I shall restrict this discussion to those forms of the land tax (i.e. *kharāj waẓīfa* and *kharāj muqāsama*) and to those contracts of tenancy (i.e. *ijāra* and *muzāraʿa*) most important in a cereal-growing agriculture.[10]

The Middle East is an area of which Issawi says that 'practically all the cultivated area in the region, since time immemorial, has been planted to cereals'.[11] The importance of the cereal-growing agriculture is well reflected in the terms of the Hanafite contracts of tenancy (*ijāra*) and share-cropping (*muzāraʿa*). These contracts were evidently developed with a view to regulating the relations of production in an agriculture based on the tillage of open fields. Because of the emphasis placed on cereal production, control of the fields where it was grown has been and still remains a constant cause of contention between the central and provincial administration of the state, private proprietors, *waqf* administrators, state officials, army officers and peasant cultivators. The relationship between the contending parties was, of course, largely determined by the political and economic power of the respective parties and by the state protection they enjoyed. But the relationship between these classes, groups and institutions was not solely determined by their respective political and economic power. It was also regulated through legal norms developed by the administration of the Muslim state and by Muslim jurists. The social and cultural traditions of the Near East,[12] as well as the political practice of the administration of the Muslim state,[13] provided the raw material for these legal norms. But insofar as the Muslim jurists moulded these legal ordinances into coherent and systematic legal doctrines on tax and rent, the systematic character of these doctrines as well as their inner cohesion should be regarded as the jurists' intellectual achievement.

In this essay I shall try to compare the Hanafite doctrine of the pre-classical and classical periods with its post-classical homologues. I shall argue that in its early and classical periods, Hanafite law was a factor that protected peasant ownership of landed property against the state's claim to ownership of the peasants' landed property — but not against exploitation through tax and rent. Hanafite law is based on the idea that it is the individual owner of property who is the prototype of the legal person and that exchange relations between individual proprietors are the most important subject matter of the law.[14] This basic idea also determines the Hanafite legal doctrine on tax and rent. In the early and classical periods of Hanafite law the jurists developed a system of legal ordinances that were — in principle — equally applicable to all forms of ownership of landed property. It is only after the tenth century that new conceptions of tax and rent were developed that clearly differentiated between peasant holdings on the one hand and the landed property of the wealthy and powerful class of rentiers on the other hand. In order to protect the economic interests of this class of rentiers, new forms of law were developed and the law of the 'old jurists' (*al-mutaqaddimūn*) was dismissed in favour of 'the choice of the modern jurists' (*ikhtiyār al-muta'akh-khirīn*).

NOTES

1. Joseph Schacht, *An Introduction to Islamic Law* (Clarendon Press, Oxford, 1964), p. 70; Schacht, *The Origins of Muhammadan Jurisprudence* (Clarendon Press, Oxford, 1950), p. 329.
2. N.J. Coulson, *A History of Islamic Law* (Edinburgh University Press, Edinburgh, 1964), pp. 75, 80-5.
3. Chafik Chehata, *Etudes de droit musulman* (Presses Universitaires de France, Paris, 1971), Vol. l, p. 17. See also Ya'akov Meron, 'The Development of Legal Thought in Hanafi Texts', *Studia Islamica*, 30, pp. 73-118.
4. Chehata, *Etudes*, p. 17:

> *Les compilations du IIe Siècle clôturent une évolution antérieure: elles fixent, pour l'histoire, le droit musulman. Depuis, l'histoire du droit musulman va se confondre avec la doctrine musulmane. Le corpus iuris musulman n'évoluera plus au cours des siècles.*

5. Ibid., pp. 17-27. See also Meron, 'Legal Thought', pp. 73-98; Schacht, *Introduction*, pp. 71-2, also realised that the legal doctrine in the classical and the post-classical periods (according to Chehata's periodisation scheme, which I use) was not the same as in the formative period of Islamic law. See Meron, 'Legal Thought', p. 91.

6. Chehata, *Etudes*, *passim*; Chehata, *Théorie générale de l'obligation en droit musulman hanéfite* (Librairi Dalloz, Paris, 1969), *passim*; Meron, 'Legal Thought', *passim*.

7. Schacht, *Introduction, p. 72. See also p. 75; Chehata, Etudes*, vol. 1, p. 24: '*A l'intérieur de chacune de ces écoles tout au long de la période classique, des justifications ont été données aux solutions déjà admises et des solutions ont été fournies à quelques cas nouveaux*'. As far as the 'post-classical period' (twelfth to nineteenth centuries) is concerned, Chehata, ibid., states:

> *Mais l'on constate dés la fin du VIe siecle que la littérature juridique va consister principalement à gloser soit á commenter les ouvrages classiques ... Ce qui ne les empêchera pas parfois d'émettre des opinions nouvelles. Ils se retranchent alors derrière une opinion attribuée aux fondateurs ...*

He adds on p. 25:

> *...il leur arrive, malgré tout, d'adopter des solutions nouvelles par la voie d'analogie. La fermeture de la porte de l'effort n'a jamais été, dans ces limites, un handicap. Mais il faut avouer que ces limites son plutôt étroites ...*

In a similar vein Schacht, *Introduction*, pp. 71-2, states that muftis and commentators contributed to the *corpus juris* of Islamic law. For a balanced summary of this discussion see Meron, 'Legal Thought', pp. 90-1.

8. Coulson, *Islamic Law*, p. 148, see pp. 140-2; it is important to note that Coulson admits important changes in 'the domain of public, and particularly criminal, law' but he does not seem to see any relationship between the change of interrelated key concepts of the public (e.g. fiscal) and the civil law (e.g. rent).

9. A.L. Udovitch, 'Technology, Land Tenure and Plural Society: Aspects of Continuity in the Agricultural History of the Pre-Modern Middle East', in Udovitch (ed.), *The Islamic Middle East 700-1900. Studies in Economic and Social History*. (The Darwin Press Inc., Princeton, 1981), p. 20; see Charles Issawi, *An Economic History of the Middle East and North Africa* (Methuen, New York, 1982), p. 135 on the 'basic pattern' of Near Eastern agriculture.

10. Claude Cahen, 'Le régime des impôts dans le Fayyūm ayyubide', *Arabica*, 3 (1956), p. 14.

11. Issawi, *Economic History*, p. 118; see Cahen, *Der Islam I. Vom Ursprung bis zu den Anfängen des Osmanenreiches* (Fischer Taschenbuch Verlag, Frankfurt am Main, 1969), p. 146.

12. Michael G. Morony, 'Landholding in Seventh-Century Iraq:

Late Sasanian and Early Islamic Patterns', in Udovitch (ed), *The Islamic Middle East*, pp. 135-75, stresses the importance of pre-Islamic traditions as decisive factors for the organisation of agriculture in the early Islamic period.

13. Schacht, *Origins*, pp. 190 ff.

14. Baber Johansen, 'Secular and Religious Elements in Hanafite Law — Function and Limits of the Absolute Character of Government Authority', in Ernest Gellner and Jean-Claude Vatin (eds), *Islam et politique au maghreb* (Centre National de la Recherche Scientifique, Paris, 1981), pp. 281-303.

1

The Birth of the Kharāj Payer

1. WHAT IS KHARĀJ?

The basic legal principle that governs the Hanafite position on taxation is summarised in the following sentence ascribed to Abū Ḥanīfa:

> In contrast to all other commodities, the productive lands in our territory are never exempted from taxation. This taxation consists either of *kharāj* or of *ᶜushr* (*al-arāḍi n-nāmiyatu lā takhlū ᶜan waẓīfat ⁱⁿ fī dārinā wa-l-waẓīfatᵘ imma l-kharāju awi l-ᶜushr*).[1]

Whereas European feudalism recognised the maxim '*Nulle terre sans seigneur*', the Hanafite jurists adhered to the principle '*Nulle terre sans taxe*'.[2] The right of the state to tax all landed property was never questioned by the Hanafite jurists. It is, therefore, not coincidental that the first known Hanafite book of law is Abū Yūsuf's *Kitāb al-kharāj*, the 'Book on the Land-tax'. Hanafite jurists recognised only two legitimate forms of taxes to be levied on landed property: *ᶜushr* and *kharāj*. It is well known and generally acknowledged that *ᶜushr* is a tax on the landed property of Muslims. What is not well known and certainly not generally acknowledged by scholars is that according to Hanafite law not only *ᶜushr* but also *kharāj* are taxes payable by the proprietors of landed property. It is difficult to explain why this aspect of *kharāj* as a tax on private landed property is not generally acknowledged by Western scholars. For nearly 200 years, specialists in the field have tried to draw attention to the fact that *kharāj* is a tax payable by the private proprietor of landed property. Some 170 years ago, von Hammer was the first to draw attention to this fact.[3] He was followed by Belin in the second half of the nineteenth century.[4] Seventy years ago, Aghnides clearly stated that *kharāj* proves ownership of property in Hanafite law,[5] a fact of which Gibb and Bowen reminded us some 20 years ago.[6] European historians, especially those concerned with the economic and social history of the Near and the Middle East, do not seem to accept this point of view. Even outstanding scholars such as Becker[7] and, in his earlier works, Claude Cahen[8] state that *the* Islamic law defines *kharāj* as a tax the payment of which implies acknowledging state-held title of ownership to the lands concerned.[9] This is not the position of the Hanafites, although it is held by other Sunnī schools of Islamic law. Western scholars have often been confused by the divergence of legal opinions on this question, as they tend to underestimate the differences between the Sunnī schools of law. Some scholars, therefore, simply pass over certain information in the Hanafite texts that they study. Some years ago, Paul Forand, in his essay on the Sawād lands of Iraq, drew extensively on the work of an early Hanafite jurist in order to describe the juridical status of the inhabitants of the Sawād lands without indicating that the jurist whom he quotes unequivocally states that the lands of the Sawād are the property of their owners if they pay *kharāj* on them.[10] Other Western scholars try to reconcile the Orientalist understanding of Islamic law with their Hanafite texts. In a recently published important study on the pre-Islamic traditions relating to agriculture in Iraq and their influence on the Muslim reorganisation of the relations of production in agriculture, Morony points out that the Hanafite jurist Sarakhsī considers *kharāj* lands as the private property of the tax payers. Morony then adds that with regard to *kharāj* 'in fact al-Shāfiʿī's interpretation was preferred by the legal scholars thus contributing to the van Berchem thesis ...'[11] This holds true for Western scholars. Hanafite jurists continued to prefer the tradition of their own school.

For the argument I shall develop in this essay, it is important to provide an accurate description of the Hanafite legal position on *kharāj* by presenting statements on this question by authoritative eighth- to nineteenth-century Hanafite scholars. Abū Yūsuf, writing in the eighth century, declares that land assigned through *iqṭāʿ* becomes the private property of the assignee who has to pay *kharāj*[12] and that *kharāj* also has to be paid on reclaimed *mawāt* lands, since, in this case, the cultivator becomes the proprietor. The fact that in this case the cultivator and proprietor has to pay *kharāj*[13] shows that private property is subject to *kharāj*. The rule that in a contract of share-cropping (*muzāraᶜa*) the proprietor is required to pay *kharāj*[14] would indicate the same. Abū Yūsuf's companion, Shaibānī, declared it licit for Muslims to buy *kharāj* lands from non-Muslim subjects of the Muslim government,[15] even for strictly commercial purposes.[16] These legal opinions of early Hanafite jurists are not whimsical juridical abstractions. In his penetrating analysis of the development of the theory of *faiʾ*, Schmucker points out that not only were there legal opinions to this effect but these legal traditions reflected the historical practice of private appropriation of *kharāj* lands in Iraq.[17] According to Schmucker, the Sawād lands of Iraq were left in the hands of the inhabitants of the Sawād who could freely dispose of them. Only crown lands (*ṣawāfī*) fell under immediate state control.[18] The Hanafite legal position on *kharāj* supports the ensuing rights of the owners of *kharāj* lands. In the ninth century, the Hanafite jurist, Khaṣṣāf, writing in Iraq, sanctioned the transformation of *kharāj* lands into *waqf* on the grounds that 'the lands of *kharāj* belong to their proprietors' (*li-anna arḍa l-kharāji li-mālikīhā*).[19] In another context he states, 'It is *kharāj* land and is owned by those who hold it' (*wa-hiya arḍu kharājⁱⁿ wa-hiya milkᵘⁿ li-arbābihā*).[20] In a similar vein, the Egyptian-born jurist Ṭaḥāwī explained at the beginning of the tenth century: 'The *kharāj* lands are private property. Their sale and donation is permissible, so is their transformation into *waqf*. The rules of inheritance apply to them as to all other goods' (*wa-araḍu l-kharāji mamlūkātᵘⁿ yajūzu baiᶜuhunna wa-hibatuhunna wa-waqfuhunna yajrī fīha l-mawārīthu kamā yajrī fīmā siwāhunna*).[21] At the beginning of the eleventh century the Iraqi author, Qudūrī, stated: 'The lands of the Sawād are the property of their inhabitants who may sell them and dispose of them [as they wish]' (*wa-arḍu s-sawādi mamlūkatᵘⁿ li-ahlihā: yajūzi baiᶜuhum lahā wa-taṣarrufuhum fīhā*).[22] The eleventh-century Transoxanian author, Sarakhsī, reported that the companions of the Prophet paid *kharāj*. He concluded from this that the payment of *kharāj* cannot be regarded as a humiliation for a Muslim. After explaining the procedure for the levying of *kharāj*, he says the buyer of *kharāj* lands will have to pay the *kharāj* on them.[23] Sarakhsī makes it clear that *kharāj* has one basic characteristic in common with the rent, i.e. that it is paid as a requital for the fact that it lies within the cultivator's power to put the land to use. 'The *kharāj*', he says, 'falls due in consideration of [the fact that] it is possible to put [his land] to use'.[24] But he also makes it clear that the obligation of paying the *kharāj* arises only for the owner of landed property: 'The reason for which *kharāj* falls due is the [existence of] private property of the land that is put to use'.[25] The twelfth-century Transoxanian author Marghīnānī declared that the lands of the Sawād of Iraq and those of Syria (Shām) are *kharāj* lands and that they are the property of their owners.[26] He is supported in this legal opinion by the fifteenth-century commentator of his work, the Egyptian jurist, Ibn al-Humām.[27] Continuing the same legal tradition the sixteenth-century Egyptian mufti, Ibn Nujaim, states: 'The Hanafite Imams, may God have mercy on them, are unanimously of the opinion that if the Imam conquers a country and recognises its inhabitants' rights [as proprietors] to it and imposes the *kharāj* on its lands, then the inhabitants enjoy the right of private property with regard to the lands. All forms by which they dispose [of them] such as sale, donation, testamentary bequest, leasing, lending and transformation into *waqf* are valid, regardless of whether the disposing person remains an unbeliever or becomes a Muslim' (*thumma ttafaqa aʾimmatu l-Ḥanafīyati, raḥima llāhu ʿanhum, ʿalā anna l-imāma idhā fataḥa baladat^an^ wa-aqarra ahlahā ʿalaihā wa-waḍaʿa l-kharāja ʿalā l-arāḍī fa-innahum yamlikūna l-araḍīya wa-taṣiḥḥu minhum sāʾiru t-taṣarrufāti min baiʿ^in^ wa-hibat^in^ wa-waṣīyat^in^ wa-waqf^in^ sawāʾ^an^ kāna l-mutaṣarrifu bāqiy^an^ ʿalā kufrihi au aslam*).[28] Similar statements can be found in the Syrian *fatāwā* of the seventeenth and eighteenth centuries[29] as well as in the works of other jurists of the Ottoman period.[30] The last significant instance of the Hanafite jurists adhering to this legal tradition consists of Article 2 § 4 of the Ottoman *Land Code* of 1858 which states:

> *Les terres mulk ou de propriété privée sont de quatre sortes:*
> ...
> 4. *Celles dites 'kharadjié', qui à la même époque* [i.e. the period of conquest by a Muslim ruler as explained in paragraph 3 of the same article] *ont été laissées et confirmées dans la possession des indigènes ... La pleine propriété de la*

terre mulk appartient au propriétaire, elle se transmet par voie d'héritage, comme tout autre bien; et les dispositions de la loi telle que la mise en vakouf, le gage ou hypothèque,[31] *la donation, la préemption (choufa) lui sont applicables. Toute terre 'uchrié' ou 'khar. .djié', au decès sans héritier de son propriétaire, fait retour au domaine public (Beit ul-Māl) et devient ainsi 'miri'.*[32]

This paragraph is based on the position of the Hanafite school of law according to which the payment of *kharāj* proves property rights. This legal opinion was maintained for a thousand years. For this reason the authors of the Ottoman *Land Code* could conclude this pararaph with the following statement: '*Les législations et la procédure relatives à ces quatre sortes de terres mulk, se trouvant dans les livres de la jurisprudence religieuse (fiqh), ne seront pas traitées ici*'.[33]

2. HOW DOES ONE ACQUIRE OWNERSHIP OF LANDED PROPERTY?

The discussion of the problems connected with the legal doctrine of *kharāj* by Hanafite scholars shows that the jurists considered ownership of landed property to be acquired in one of the following ways:

(a) Through the Imam's confirmation of the primordial rights of the agriculturists at the time of the conquest. The example usually given of this kind of primordial property right is that of the peasants of the Sawād of Iraq who proved their rights as owners of landed property by having paid *kharāj* on it.[34] As Schmucker has shown, in large parts of the Sawād the property rights of the inhabitants were confirmed by the Muslim authorities after the conquest. There is historical evidence proving that these lands were bought and sold.[35] According to Morony, it is quite probable that peasant cultivators became proprietors of some of these lands.[36] The Muslim conquest must in fact have led to a partial emancipation of the peasants. Hanafite law supports this emancipation. By transforming land into a commodity and the land tax into a proof of property, the Hanafite legal position on *kharāj* stands in the way of the attempt to consider the peasant as

a serf bound to the soil;
(b) Through the channels of commodity exchange, i.e. through sale, pre-emption (*shufʿa*), donation, bequest[37] and inheritance.[38] According to the jurists, even the landed private property of the Imam should be acquired in this way;
(c) Through the Imam's assignment of waste lands (*mawāt*) to private persons who are obliged to reclaim these lands. Through reclamation these lands become private property on which either *kharāj* or *ʿushr* must be paid;[39]
(d) Through the assignment of arable lands to private proprietors by the Imam. Consequently, these lands become private landed property on which *ʿushr*[40] or *kharāj*[41] must be paid.

Lands acquired in one of the four ways mentioned above are considered private property on which either *kharāj* or *ʿushr* must be paid. Since only owners of landed property can transform their lands into *waqf*, *kharāj* or *ʿushr* must also be paid on *waqf* lands as these are lands previously recognised as private property.[42] That is to say, on all forms of landed property not owned by the state, *kharāj* or *ʿushr* must be paid. To judge from the casual descriptions given by the jurists, they seem to think of *iqṭāʿ* (assignment) and *waqf* as typical examples of big estates cultivated through the employment of slaves and of salaried labour.[43] A non-Muslim always has to pay *kharāj* on his landed property. A Muslim has to pay *kharāj* on *kharāj* land if he acquires *kharāj* land through the channels described under b, c, and d or if he converts to Islam. A Muslim has to pay *ʿushr* on his landed property if the Muslim ruler assigns conquered lands to him or if he acquires *ʿushr* land through the mechanisms described under b, c and d. *ʿUshr*, therefore, is always related to the religious status of the proprietor, whereas *kharāj* tends to become a land tax without religious connotations.

3. NOT EVERY GRANT OR POSSESSION IS TAXABLE OWNERSHIP OF LANDED PROPERTY

Only two kinds of legal claims to arable lands did not entail the payment of the land tax. These two claims were also not accepted as a basis for transforming lands into *waqf* because these claims did not constitute ownership rights. The first of these two claims consisted of the assignment by the Imam of the taxes on arable lands to state officials, army officers or other favourites of his. Schmucker has pointed out that individual cases of this kind of *iqṭāʿ* already existed in the seventh century.[44] In the ninth century, this form of tax assignment was a well-known practice, as the following description by the Iraqi jurist Khaṣṣāf shows. Khaṣṣāf tells one of his students:

> If the Sultan assigns something belonging to the public treasury (*bait al-māl*) to a person, that person is not allowed to transfer it into a *waqf*.

The student asks: 'How can he assign a claim of the public treasury [to a third person]?' to which Khaṣṣāf answers:

> This is land that belongs to a [private] person and on which *kharāj* must be paid. It is the property of the people who hold it (*wa-hiya milk*^{un} *li-arbābihā*). The Sultan takes from them half of what God makes the arable land yield. He assigns part of that half that he takes for the public treasury by telling a person: I grant you four-fifths of it [i.e. of the *kharāj*] and you are obliged to pay one-fifth of it to the public treasury [i.e. one-tenth of the whole produce of the land] (*wa-idhā aqṭaʿa s-sulṭānu insān*^{an} *shaiʾ*^{an} *min ḥaqqi baiti l-māli lam yajuz waqfuhu li-dhālika. qultu: wa-kaifa yuqṭiʿu shaiʾ*^{an} *min ḥaqqi baiti l-māl? qāla: hādhihī arḍ*^{un} *li-insān*^{in} *wa-hiya arḍu kharāj*^{in} *wa-hiya milk*^{un} *li-arbābihā. fa-s-sulṭānu yaʾkhudhu minhumu n-niṣfa mimmā yukhriju llāhu ʿazza wa-jalla min arḍi z-zarʿi fa-aqṭaʿa s-sulṭānu min hādha n-niṣfi lladhī yaʾkhudhuhu li-baiti l-māli baʿḍahu fa-yaqūlu li-man aqṭaʿahu qad aqṭaʿtuka min hādha n-niṣfi arbaʿata akhmāsihi wa-jaʿaltu ʿalaika khumsahu li-baiti l-māli wa-huwa l-ʿushru min jamīʿi mā tukhriju l-arḍ*).[45]

Such an assignment cannot be the basis for the transforming of land into *waqf*, because it does not constitute private property and because what the assignee pays is not regarded as the *kharāj* of his property. It is the proprietor of the land who pays the *kharāj* and who therefore is solely entitled to transform his landed property into *waqf*.

The other group of persons who are not allowed to transform their rights on arable lands into *waqf* are the peasants tilling lands appropriated by the ruler. These peasants are not regarded as proprietors of the land. The dues they pay to the ruler are not regarded as taxes, but rather as a kind of rent. The peasants cultivating estates appropriated by the ruler are regarded as merely share-croppers, devoid of ownership rights. The student who transmits the legal opinions of Khaṣṣāf reports the following:

> I said: what do you say about the lands of the *ḥauz*? If a person transforms part of it into *waqf*, is that legally permissible? He said: the *ḥauz* is something that the Sultan takes possession of (*ḥāzahu*). He brings the share-croppers (*muzāriʿūn*) to it, so that they may cultivate it. In this way they become farm-hands (*akara*) of the Sultan, whom he may oust at any time he pleases (*qultu: fa-mā taqūlu fī arḍi l-ḥauzi yūqifu insān*^{un} *minhā shaiʾ*^{an} *hal yajūz? qāla: al-ḥauzu huwa shaiʾ*^{un} *qad ḥāzahu s-sulṭānu wa-adkhala fīhi muzāriʿīna yaʿmurūnahā fa-innamā hum akarat*^{un} *fī dhālika li-s-sulṭāni lahu an yukhrijahum min dhālika matā shāʾa fa-in waqafa aḥad*^{un} *min hāʾulāʾi l-muzāriʿīna shaiʾ*^{an} *min arḍi l-ḥauzi lam yajuz*).[46]

The dues of these peasants are not considered taxes. The peasants do not enjoy proprietary rights with regard to the land that they till. Their legal status is much worse than that of the *kharāj*-paying proprietors. The example of the farm-hands (*akara*) on the *arḍ al-ḥauz* shows the importance of a clear differentiation between tax and rent for the preservation of the peasant's landed property. Whenever the government or its representatives regard the peasants' dues as rent, they also tend to regard the peasants as evictable tenants or as serfs bound to the soil.

To the best of my knowledge, the jurists of the early and classical periods of Hanafite law do not inform us on the origins of *arḍ al-ḥauz*. But in the light of the development of this term in the juridical literature of the Mamluk period, it seems reasonable to relate it to the jurists' discussion of the problems that result from the *kharāj* payer's flight (*hurūb*) from his village, from his incapacity to pay the taxes and till the soil and finally from his death without legal heirs. All these are topics already discussed in the early and classical periods. The jurists agree that in all such cases the Imam is entitled to take care of the cultivation of the land. He may cultivate it by paying hired labourers from the public treasury or by farming it out in a contract of share-cropping (*muzāraᶜa*) or tenancy (*ijāra*). According to jurists from the tenth and twelfth centuries,[47] he may also sell it. But this sequestration of the land does not — in the first three cases — annihilate the property rights of the former owners. The Imam is merely entitled to the *kharāj*. If he obtains any 'surplus' through the contracts of share-cropping or tenancy or through the sale of the land, he is legally bound to give this 'surplus' to the former proprietors. The former proprietors maintain very precarious property rights, the state takes responsibility for the cultivation of the lands and the new peasant cultivators enjoy a very uncertain status as evictable share-croppers. It is only in the case of the *kharāj* payer who dies without legal heirs that the public treasury enjoys full and unrestricted ownership of the lands.

4. DOES THE TENANT OR THE LESSOR PAY THE TAX?

Even in the pre-classical and classical periods of Hanafite law, the legal maxim that the payment of the land tax proves ownership rights on arable lands is in one respect problematic, namely in that the jurists are tempted to shift the burden of taxation from the lessor to the tenant. Different forms of land tax do not, in the Hanafite law, represent the same kind of obligation. The *kharāj waẓīfa* (or *kharāj muwaẓẓaf*) is a fixed sum of money whose amount depends on the size and the quality of the land.[48] It is furthermore a personal obligation[49] and must, therefore, be paid by the owners.[50] *ᶜUshr* and *kharāj muqāsama* consist of a fixed percentage of the crop and are considered obligations *in re*.[51] Early Hanafite jurists like Abū Yūsuf consider the *kharāj muqāsama* the most equitable form of taxation.[52] Other jurists report that the peasants of the Sawād asked for the introduction of this kind of taxation. But Makoto Shimizu has persuasively argued that the *kharāj muqāsama* in the Sawād of Baghdad was introduced by the government in order to monopolise the grain trade of that province and use its profits for the construction of Baghdad.[53] The founder of the Hanafite school of law, Abū Ḥanīfa, insisted that the same rules should apply both to the monetary land tax and to the taxes in kind. According to Abū Ḥanīfa, in a contract of tenancy (*ijāra*) it is always the proprietor who pays the *kharāj*, be it *muwaẓẓaf* or *muqāsama*, i.e. a fixed sum of money or a percentage of the crop.[54] But his disciples in the eighth and ninth centuries tended to shift the tax burden from the lessor to the tenant.[55] Abū Yūsuf, writing in the eighth century, decided that the tenant in a contract of tenancy (*ijāra*) or of share-cropping (*muzāraᶜa*) has to pay the *ᶜushr*.[56] His companion Shaibānī made the tenant pay the *ᶜushr* and the *kharāj muqāsama*.[57] According to this legal reasoning, the lessor of the land must always pay the *kharāj muwaẓẓaf*, but not the *kharāj muqāsama*.

There is no reason to doubt that in the short run the new doctrine introduced by Abū Yūsuf and Shaibānī worked in favour of the landowners: shifting the tax burden to someone else's shoulders is always an appealing proposition. It also seems that in Iraq, originally, *kharāj muqāsama* was mainly levied on crown lands around Kūfa that the Caliph ᶜUthmān granted to members of the Meccan aristocracy, whereas the *kharāj muwaẓẓaf* was mainly levied on the lands of the *dahāqīn* and the early Muslim invaders. The legal ordinances making the tenant pay the *kharāj muqāsama* did, therefore, work in favour of the old Arab aristocracy.[58] According to Cahen, the levying of *kharāj muqāsama* remained restricted to the Sawād of Baghdad until well into the tenth century. Only when tax assignments (*iqṭāᶜ*) were generally used to compensate army officers for their services, did the *kharāj muqāsama* become a generalised form of taxation.[59] In the pre-classical period, therefore, *kharāj* was largely identified with *kharāj muwaẓẓaf*, *kharāj muqāsama* remaining a form of taxation that was applied to privileged owners. In the long run, such a privileged form of taxation might have endangered the landowner's title of ownership of landed property. If it were the tenant who paid the tax, it would have been perfectly reasonable for the state to levy it on him directly, in which case the owner would have lost his position as an intermediary between the state and the tenant and would have had no justification for receiving a share of the crop. There is no reason to believe that the jurists of the eighth and ninth centuries were not aware of this danger. If they wanted to support the interests of the lessor, as I believe they did, their legal reasoning only makes sense if it presupposes that the tenant was obliged to pay his tax to the lessor.[60] Be that as it may, to judge from the legal ordinances, the tenant who leased land on which the tax was levied as a percentage of the crop faced a much greater burden than the tenant who leased land on which a monetary land tax was levied.[61] In the first case, the tenant paid his rent plus the tax, whereas in the second case the tenant only paid the rent.

It seems, however, that this new doctrine on the tenant's obligation of paying the *kharāj muqāsama* met with resistance in the Hanafite school and that neither the doctrine of Abū Ḥanīfa nor that of his immediate disciples became the prevalent legal opinion of the Hanafite school. Until well into the twelfth century it was left to the discretion of the individual jurists as to which legal opinion to adopt.[62]

5. THE CLASSICAL HANAFITE DOCTRINE ON LAND TAX SUPPORTS PEASANT OWNERSHIP OF LANDED PROPERTY

The works of Cahen[63] and Ashtor[64] show that peasant proprietors did play a major role in the agriculture of the Near and the Middle East until at least the end of the tenth century. Side by side with the smallholdings of peasants, large estates were found to be held by assignees (*muqṭaᶜs*) or transformed into *auqāf* (s. *waqf*) whose labour force consisted of slaves, share-croppers and salaried workers.[65] In addition, we find state lands along with a peculiar category of sequestrated and state-controlled lands, the *arḍ al-ḥauz*, of which the cultivators were only farmhands whereas the former proprietors of the lands still claimed very precarious ownership rights. The lines of demarcation between these different forms of landed property must, by necessity, always have been rather vague. The struggle for control over the produce of the arable lands ensued between a variety of groups, classes and institutions and the relationship between the different forms of property of arable lands can best be understood as the result of a permanent struggle between these groups, classes and institutions. In this struggle, with whom did the Hanafite jurists side? There is no easy answer to this question. A clear partisanship for ownership rights of cultivating peasants cannot be discerned in their legal doctrine on tax and rent. It seems certain, though, that the basic elements giving systematic unity and inner coherence to this legal doctrine protect the peasants against attempts to consider them serfs or to define their status as that of being attached to the soil. These basic elements are the following:

(a) in principle land is considered a commodity like all other commodities;
(b) in contrast to other, urban, commodities, productive land is never exempt from taxation. Taxation is general and embraces all productive lands;
(c) the payment of the land tax proves the ownership of property rights. This is a principle that must have worked in favour of existing property rights of the peasants. The Hanafite legal doctrine, by establishing the basic idea that a land tax is payable only for landed property, enables the jurists to develop a clear criterion of distinction between tax and rent and allows them to unite (at least as far as *kharāj muwaẓẓaf* is concerned) taxation of all kinds of landed property into one set of basic rules. It does not, in this respect, differentiate between the smallholdings of the peasant proprietors and the big estates of the wealthy and powerful landlords. Cahen has pointed out that *kharāj* was mainly levied on peasants' smallholdings.[66] If this is true, then the legal doctrine of the Hanafite school of law must have worked in favour of the property rights of the peasants.
(d) the most important element of the Hanafite doctrine working in favour of peasant ownership is the conception that the peasant population regained their primordial property rights through the Imam's confirmation of these rights and through their payment of *kharāj* (see section 2(a)). Ownership of landed property does not depend on religion, or on whether or not the lands were conquered by force or obtained under the terms of a treaty. These questions remain important with regard to the distinction between *kharāj* and *ᶜushr*, but under the Hanafite law this difference in taxation does not denote a distinction between ownership or possession of landed property. With regard to the Sawād lands of Iraq, Hanafite jurists stated time and again that the Imam confirmed the existence of primordial rights of the peasants and by the same token imposed the *kharāj* upon them. Through this confirmation of their primordial rights, the peasants became the legal owners of their landed property. Three sources of landed property ownership are thus established in Hanafite law: (i) the

primordial rights of the peasants as confirmed by the state, (ii) the grants of land effected by the Imam (including *mawāt* lands) and (iii) the commodity exchange (including testamentary bequest and inheritance). The first two sources feed equally into the third source.

These are factors that clearly work against an attempt to treat the peasant as a serf and to define his status as that of being attached to the soil. But the Hanafite legal doctrine clearly does not protect the peasant cultivator against exploitation through tax and rent. The jurists allow for a very high percentage, up to 50 percent, as the percentage of the crop that should be levied as *kharāj*. If such a tax burden is to be paid in addition to the rent — as is the case with *kharāj muqāsama* — it clearly overtaxes the peasant's economic resources. His property will fall prey to tax and rent, and it will either end up in the *arḍ al-ḥauz* or as part of the property of his landlord.

It would appear that the Hanafite legal doctrine of the land tax was best suited for an agriculture that was integrated in a market economy with a monetary circuit and fixed monetary land tax (*kharāj muwaẓẓaf*). It was within this framework that its basic tenets could be most coherently applied. Wherever taxation in kind (*kharāj muqāsama*) allowed the shifting of the tax burden to the shoulders of the tenant, the system could not but work in favour of landlordism. When *kharāj muqāsama* became a general form of taxation in the Middle East, the Hanafite doctrine may have worked in the interest of big landownership of all those strata of society whose living depended on their capacity to transform their titles to arable land into rent-yielding property.

NOTES

1. Sarakhsī, *Kitāb al-Mabsūṭ*, reprint edn (Beirut, n.d.), vol. 3, p. 6. For the Ottoman reformulation of this basic principle see Ibn ᶜĀbidīn, *Radd al-Muḥtār ᶜalā ad-Durr al-Mukhtār. Sharḥ Tanwīr al-Abṣār fī Fiqh Madhhab al-Imām al-Aᶜẓam Abī Ḥanīfa an-Nuᶜmān* (Cairo, 1307 A.H.), vol. 2, p. 54. Here it is *al-arḍ* al-muᶜ add li-l-istighlāl which is never exempt from taxation.

2. Abū Yūsuf Yaᶜqūb, *Kitāb al Kharāj*, tr. E. Fagnan as *Le livre de l'impôt foncier* (Librairie Orientaliste paul Geuthner, Paris 1921), p. 91:

> *Je ne suis pas d'avis qu'il* [the Imam] *laisse une terre, sans la donner en fief car cela sert à l'accroissement de la prospérité du pays et augmente le Kharâdj. Et c'est là à mes yeux ... le but à poursuivre dans l'attribution des fiefs.*

The assignment of lands serves as a means to procure revenue in form of taxes. In the Hanafite context 'Nulle terre sans seigneur' is only a means to realise the state of 'Nulle terre sans taxe'.

3. Joseph von Hammer, *Des Osmanischen Reiches Staatsverfassung und Staatsverwaltung dargestellt aus den Quellen seiner Grundgesetze* (Vienna, 1815 reprint edn Georg Olms Verlagsbuchhandlung, Hildesheim, 1963), vol. 1, p. 344.

4. M. Belin, 'Etudes sur la propriété foncière en pays musulmans, et spécialement en Turquie (rite hanéfite)', *Journal Asiatique* (August 1861-May 1862), see 1861, pp. 409, 427; February-March 1862, p. 193, sec. 297; April-May 1862, p. 272, sec. 383.2. Belin tries to establish a compromise between the Muslim schools of law and considers the *mīrī* tax as *kharāj* and connects it with the Malikite and Shafiᶜite concept of *waqf*. In this way he establishes two kinds of *kharāj*, one that establishes property rights and one that does not establish proprietory rights.

5. N.P. Aghnides, *Mohammedan Theories of Finance* (AMS Press, New York, 1916), pp. 364-5.

6. H.A.R. Gibb and Harold Bowen, *Islamic Society and the West. A Study of the Impact of Western Civilisation on Moslem Culture in the Near East* (Oxford University Press, London, 1950), vol. 1, pt. 1, pp. 166, 252, n. 3.

7. C.H. Becker, *Islamstudien. Vom Werden und Wesen der islamischen Welt* (Quelle und Meyer Leipzig, 1924, reprint edn Georg Olms Verlagbuchhandlung, Hildesheim, 1967), vol. 1, p. 229.

8. This holds true only for older works of Claude Cahen, such as *Der Islam I., Vom Ursprung bis zuden Anfängen des Osmanenreiches* (Fischer Taschenbuch Verlag, Frankfurt am Main, 1969), pp. 46, 108, 149. For a slightly modified version see Cahen, 'Contribution à l'étude des impôts dans l'Egypte médiévale', *Journal of the Economic and Social History of the Orient*, 5 (1962), p. 273, where it is said that '... *dans la conception arabe primitive, le kharadj est une espèce de loyer payé par le cultivateur non-musulman en reconnaissance de l'éminente propriété de la communauté musulmane*'. But in his contribution to the article 'Kharādj' in the *Encyclopaedia of Islam* (New Edition,.E.J. Brill, Leiden, 1978), vol. 4, pp. 1030-31 Cahen states: 'Some general principles emerge from amongst the particular practices. The first is the guaranteeing of their lands to all proprietors — at this time non-Muslim — in such a way as to ensure their value. They paid taxes on these lands ...' And in Claude Cahen, Yūsuf Rāghib and Muṣṭafā Anouar Taher, 'L'achat et le waqf d'un grand domaine egyptien par le vizier fatimide Ṭalāi b. Ruzzīk — contribution à une publication des waqfs egyptiens médiévaux', *Annales Islamologiques*, vol. 14 (1978), p. 76, the authors state: '*En Egypte les cultivateurs, mêmes s'ils sont en fait metayers/ muzāriᶜūn, sont juridiquement des propriétaires ayant comme tels à*

payer le Kharādj, qu'ils versent en l'occurrence au fermier'.

9. This is the accepted opinion among Western scholars, e.g. John Ruedy, *Land Policy in Colonial Algeria, The Origins of the Rural Public Domain* (University of California, Los Angeles, 1967), p. 3; Robert H. Eisenman, *Islamic Law in Palestine and Israel* (E.J. Brill, Leiden, 1978), pp. 54-5.

10. Paul G. Forand, 'The Status of the Land and Inhabitants of the Sawād during the First Two Centuries of Islam', *Journal of the Economic and Social History of the Orient*, 14 (1971), pp. 25-37. The Hanafite jurist in question is Khaṣṣāf. See below for his position on the property rights of the Kharāj payer.

11. Morony, 'Landholding in Seventh-Century Iraq: 'Late Sasanian and Early Islamic Patterns' in Udovitch (ed.) *The Islamic Middle East 700-1900. Studies in Economic and Social History* (Princeton, 1981), p. 154.

12. Abū Yūsuf, *Kitāb al-Kharāj*, pp. 58, 59-60, 61-2.

13. Ibid., pp. 65, 66.

14. Ibid., pp. 90, 91.

15. Shaibānī, *Kitāb al-Aṣl*, (Hyderabad, 1969), vol. 2, pp. 143, 164.

16. Ibid., pp. 143, 159; see ibid., pp. 118, 164.

17. Werner Schmucker, *Untersuchungen zu einigen wichtigen bodenrechtlichen Konsequenzen der islamischen Eroberungsbwegungen* (Orientalisches Seminar, Bonn, 1972), pp. 102, 126. It can therefore come as no surprise that al-Azdī, *Kitāb al-Amwāl* (Cairo, 1968), pp. 119-21, shows that, in the ninth century, not a few non-Hanafite jurists considered the sale and bequest of *kharāj*-lands to be permissible. See also Morony, 'Landholding', p. 162.

18. Schmucker, *Untersuchungen*, pp. 124, 125, 127, 132-3, 145, 147, 160-1, 162, 166-7, 169, 177.

19. al-Khaṣṣāf, *Kitāb Aḥkām al-Auqāf* (Cairo, 1322 A.H./1904 A.D.), p. 34.

20. Ibid., p. 35.

21. Ṭaḥāwī, *Mukhtaṣar* (Cairo, 1370 A.H.), p. 135; see also p. 285.

22. al-Qudūrī, *al-Kitāb*, printed on the margin of ᶜAbd al-Ghanī al-Ghanīmī ad-Dimashqī al-Maidānī, *al-Lubāb fī Sharḥ al-Kitāb* (reprint edn Beirut, 1400 A.H./1980 A.D.), vol. 4, p. 138.

23. Sarakhsī, *Mabsūṭ*, vol. 10, pp. 83-4; vol. 3, pp. 47, 48.

24. Ibid., vol. 3, p. 48: '*Wa-qad bayyannā anna wujūba l-kharāji bi-ʿtibāri t-tamakkuni mina l-intifāᶜ*'; see also pp. 46-7.

25. Ibid., p. 50: '*li-anna sababa wujūbi l-kharāji milku l-arḍi l-muntafaᶜi bihā*; see also ibid., pp. 5, 46, 47.

26. al-Marghīnānī, *al-Hidāya, Sharḥ Bidāyatiʾal l-Mubtadiʾ*, printed on the margin of Ibn al-Humām, *Sharḥ Fatḥ al-Qadīr* (Cairo, 1356 A.H.), vol. 4, p. 359: '*wa-arḍu s-sawādi mamlūkatᵘⁿ li-ahlihā yajūzu baiʿuhum lahā wa-taṣarrufuhum fīhā*'.

27. Ibn al-Humām, *Sharḥ Fatḥ al-Qadīr*, vol. 4, p. 359.

28. Zain b. Nujaim, *at-Tuḥfa al-Marḍīya fī al-Arāḍī al-Miṣrīya*, ms. Berlin We 1724, fol.132b. I am obliged to the Staatsbibliothek Berlin

for the permission to use the manuscript.

29. Ramlī, *Kitāb al-Fatāwā al-Khairīya li-Naf' al-Barrīya* (Bulaq, 1300 A.H., reprint edn Beirut, 1974), vol. 1, pp. 98, 215; vol. 2, pp. 13, 154; Ibn ᶜĀbidīn, *al-ᶜUqūd ad-Durrīya fī Tanqīḥ al-Fatāwā al-Ḥāmidīya* (2nd edn Bulaq, 1300 A.H., reprint 2nd edn Beirut, n.d.), vol. 1, pp. 182-3. This book is an abridged edition of the *fatāwā* of the eighteenth century Damascene mufti Ḥāmid ibn ᶜAbd ar-Raḥmān al-ᶜImādī, edited by Ibn ᶜĀbidīn.

30. Ibn ᶜAbidīn, *Radd al-Muḥtār*, vol. 2, p. 54; vol. 3, pp. 277-81, 287; Ḍamād Afandī, *Majma' al-Anhur fī Sharḥ Multaqā al-Abḥur* (Dār Iḥyā' at-Turāth al-ᶜArabi, 1316 A.H., reprint edn n.d.), vol. 1, p. 663; '*wa-arḍu s-sawādi mamlūkat*[un] *li-ahlihā ᶜindanā yajūzu bai' uhum lahā wa-taṣarrufuhum fīhā li-annahā mamlūkat*[un] *lahum*'; al-Ḥaṣkafī, *Durr al-Muntaqā fī Sharḥ al-Multaqā* (printed on the margin of Ḍamād Afandī, ibid), vol. 1, p. 663:

> *wa-arḍu s-sawādi wa-kullu mā futiḥa ᶜanwat*[an] *wa-uqirra ahluhū ᶜalaihi au ṣūliḥū wa-wuḍiᶜa l-kharāju ᶜalā arāḍīhim fa-hiya mamlūkat*[un] *li-ahlihā yajūzu bai' uhum wa-taṣarrufuhum fīhā ᶜindanā muṭlaq*[an] *kahibat*[in] *wa-waṣīyat*[in] *wa-ijārat*[in] *wa-waqf*[in] *wa-tūrathu 'anhum ilā an lā yabqā minhum aḥad.*

31. It is, indeed, well known that the *hypothèque* is not an institution of Islamic law, whereas the pawn is.

32. George Young, *Corps de droit Ottoman* (Clarendon Press, Oxford, 1906), vol. 6, pp. 45-6; see Belin, 'Etudes', April-May 1862, ch. 11, sec. 2, pp. 292-3.

33. Young, *Droit Ottoman*, p. 46; See Belin, 'Etudes', April-May 1862, ch. 11, sec. 2, p. 294.

34. Ṭaḥāwī, *Mukhtaṣar*, p. 258; Qudūrī, *al-Kitāb*, vol. 4, p. 139; Sarakhsī, *Mabsūṭ*, vol. 10, pp. 15-6; Samarqandī, *Tuḥfat al-Fuqahā'*, (Damascus, n.d., vol.1, p. 657; Marghīnānī, *al-Hidāya*, vol. 4, pp. 304-5, 359; Ibn al-Humām, *Sharḥ Fatḥ al-Qadīr*, vol. 4, pp. 304-5, 359; Ibn Nujaim, *Tuḥfa*, fol. 1326; al-Ḥaṣkafī, *ad-Durr al-Mukhtār Sharḥ Tanwir al-Abṣār* (printed on the margin of Ibn ᶜĀbidīn, *Radd al-Muḥtār*), vol. 3, p. 227; Ibn ᶜAbidīn, *Radd al-Muḥtār*, vol. 3, p. 227. For the historical background to this legal reasoning see Schmucker, *Untersuchungen*, pp. 119, 127, and Morony's reference to Balādhurī in Morony, 'Landholding', p. 159.

35. Schmucker, *Untersuchungen*, pp. 126-7. 129, 147, 162, 166-7, 169, 177, 193 (see also above, note 18).

36. Morony, 'Landholding', pp. 150 and 152 for the *milk* of former *dahāqīn* and pp. 157, 165 for forms of peasant property.

37. Shaibāni, *Kitāb al-Aṣl*, vol. 2, pp. 143, 159, 164; see also p. 118; Schmucker, *Untersuchungen*, as quoted in note 35 above. al-Azdī, *al-Amwāl*, pp. 119-21; Ṭaḥāwī, *Mukhtaṣar*, p. 135; Qudūrī, *al-Kitāb*, vol. 4, pp. 138-9.

38. Ṭaḥāwī, *Mukhtaṣar*, p. 135; Ibn Nujaim, *al-Tuḥfa*, fol. 132b; Young, *Droit Ottoman*, vol. 6, pp. 45-6.

39. Abū Yūsuf, *Kitāb al Kharāj*, pp. 58, 65-6; Khaṣṣāf, *Kitāb Aḥkām*

al-Awqāf, pp. 34-5.

40. Abū Yūsuf, *Kitāb al-Kharāj*, p. 58, 59-60.

41. Ibid., pp. 58, 59-60, 62.

42. Khaṣṣaf, *Kitāb Aḥkām al-Auqāf*, pp. 34-5; Ṭaḥāwī, *Mukhtaṣar*, p. 137; Qudūrī, *al-Kitāb*, vol. 2, p. 182; Sarakhsī, *Mabsūṭ*, vol. 12, p. 45; Baber Johansen, 'Amwāl Ẓāhira and Amwāl Bāṭina. Town and countryside as reflected in the Tax System of the Hanafite School', in Wadad al-Qāḍī (ed.), *Studia Arabica et Islamica. Festschrift for Iḥsān ʿAbbās on his Sixtieth Birthday* (American University of Beirut, Beirut, 1981), p. 257. This legal ordinance was in fact applied by the fiscal administration until well into the Fatimid period. See Janine Sourdel-Thomine and Dominique Sourdel, 'Biens fonciers constitués waqf en Syrie Fatimide pour une famille de šarīfs Damascains', in *Journal of the Economic and Social History of the Orient*, 15 (1972), pp. 283-4, 294.

43. Khaṣṣāf, *Kitāb Aḥkām al-Auqāf*, pp. 34-5; Ṭaḥāwī, *Mukhtaṣar*, p. 137; Qudūrī, *al-Kitāb*, vol. 2, p. 182; Sarakhsī, *Mabsūṭ*, vol. 12, p. 45. For the historical importance of slave work in Muslim agriculture see Mohamed Talbi, 'Law and Economy in Ifrīqiya (Tunisia) in the Third Islamic Century: Agriculture and the Role of Slaves in the Country's Economy', in Udovitch (ed.), *The Islamic Middle East*, pp. 214-17, 235. See also Morony, 'Landholding', pp. 141, 142, 148, 164, 165 and Udovitch, *The Islamic Middle East*, p. 21.

44. Schmucker, *Untersuchungen*, p. 142.

45. Khaṣṣāf, *Kitāb Aḥkām al-Auqaf*, p. 35.

46. Ibid.

47. Ṭaḥāwī, *Mukhtaṣar*, p. 295; Qāḍīkhān, *Kitāb al-Fatāwā al-Khānīya* (Cairo, 1282 A.H.), vol. 3, p. 617.

48. Abū Yūsuf, *Kitāb al-Kharāj*, pp. 36, 37, 38; Ṭaḥāwī, *Mukhtaṣar*, p. 294; Qudūri, *al-Kitāb*, vol. 4, pp. 141-2; Sarakhsī, *Mabsūṭ*, vol. 3, p. 51. In principle, this standard of evaluation resembles the *ʿibra* as practised in most of the fiscal administrations of the Near East. See Claude Cahen, 'Le regime des impôts dans le Fayyūm ayyūbide', *Arabica* 3 (1956), p. 12; and Heinz Halm, *Ägypten nach den mamlukischen Lehensregistern*, vol. 1, *Oberägypten und das Fayyum* (Dr. Ludwig Reichert Verlag, Wiesbaden, 1979), pp. 7-8, 40-2.

49. Johansen, 'Amwāl Ẓahira', p. 259, n. 99.

50. Sarakhsi, *Mabsūṭ*, vol. 16, p. 41; Samarqandī, *Tuḥfat al-Fuqahāʾ*, vol. 1, part 2, p. 663; Qāḍīkhān, *Kitāb al-Fatāwā*, vol. 3, p. 618.

51. Johansen, 'Amwāl Ẓāhira', p. 259, n. 98.

52. Abū Yūsuf, *Kitāb al-Kharāj*, pp. 76-7.

53. Makoto Shimizu, 'Les finances publiques de l'etat abbaside', *Der Islam*, 42 (1966), pp. 20-2.

54. Sarakhsī, *Sharḥ Kitāb as-Siyar al-Kabīr* ed. Ṣalāḥ ad-Dīn Munajjid (Cairo, 1971), vol. 5, p. 2247, ns. 4473, 4474.

55. Sarakhsī, *Mabsūṭ*, vol. 16, p. 41.

56. Abū Yūsuf, *Kitāb al-Kharāj*, pp. 90-1.

57. Sarakhsī, *Sharḥ Kitāb as-Siyar*, vol. 5, p. 2247, n. 4473; Qāḍīkhān, *Kitāb al-Fatāwā*, vol. 3, p. 618.

58. Morony, 'Landholding', pp. 158-9.

59. Claude Cahen, 'Fiscalité, propriété, antagonismes sociaux en Haute-Mésopotamie au temps des premiers ᶜAbbāsides d'après Denys de Tell-Mahré', *Arabica*, 1 (1954), pp. 144-5. For the late medieval situation see Cahen's two articles quoted above, note 8.

60. This is what actually happened; see Cahen, 'Le waqf d'un grand domaine egyptien', quoted above, note 8.

61. For the different degrees of the integration of agriculture in the market economy see E. Ashtor, *A Social and Economic History of the Near East in the Middle Ages* (Collins, London, 1976), pp. 157-8; Andrew M. Watson, 'A Medieval Green Revolution: New Crops and Farming Techniques in the Early Islamic World', in Udovitch (ed.), *The Islamic Middle East*, pp. 47-8.

62. Compare for example the position of Qāḍīkhān, *Kitāb al-Fatāwā*, vol. 3, pp. 617-8, with that of Sarakhsī, *Mabsūṭ*, vol. 16, p. 41, vol. 23, p. 35-6, and Samarqandī, *Tuḥfat al-Fuqahā*ᵓ, vol. 2, pp. 662-3 and Ṭaḥāwī, *Mukhtaṣar*, p. 133.

63. Cahen, *Der Islam I*, pp. 154-5; Cahen, 'Fiscalité', pp. 151-2.

64. Ashtor, *A Social and Economic History*, pp. 38, 156, 159.

65. See above, note 43.

66. Cahen, *Der Islam I*, p. 108.

2

The Contract of Tenancy (Ijāra): The 'Commodification of the Productive Use of Land

1. THREE CONTRACTS IN ONE

The most important legal institution that contributes towards transforming the possession of arable lands into rent-yielding property is the contract of tenancy (*ijāra*). It derives its name from the terms *ajr* or *ujra* (rent, salary).[1] This type of contract is used for a variety of economic purposes. It represents, as Schacht has shown, a combination of three formerly separate transactions, i.e. *kirāʾ*, the renting of real property (corresponding to the *locatio conductio rei*), *ijāra*, the hiring of salaried labour (*locatio conductio operarum*) and *juʿl* (*locatio conductio operis/Werkvertrag*). This combination of three formerly separate transactions into one type of contract was most probably effected during the first Islamic century.[2] Its origin partly explains the complex character of the contract of *ijāra*. But there is a more important reason for the complex character of this contract. Under the contract of *ijāra*, labour and the productive use of land are 'commodified' — to use a modern sociological neologism. This process of 'reification' of human activities adds to the complexity of the contract. Its complicated structure may explain the fact that we do not have, in Western literature, any detailed and comprehensive analysis of the contract of *ijāra* according to Hanafite law.[3] The following pages are not intended to give such a comprehensive and detailed analysis. They are restricted to the legal ordinances concerning the renting of arable lands. Even with regard to the 'contract of tenancy' it is not my intention to give a detailed and comprehensive analysis of all legal ordinances. My contribution is meant to explain the relationship between the contractual and the non-contractual elements in a legal relationship of tenancy.

2. A CONTRACT FOR THE LEASING OF FIELDS

Through the 'contract of tenancy' (*ijāra*), fields are let to tenant farmers. The contract implies transferring the use of arable lands (*arḍ baiḍā*ʾ,[4] *terre nue*, as the jurists say) from the lessor to the tenant in return for the payment of rent. The jurists define the growing of cereals — together with the planting of trees and the construction of buildings — as the *raison d'être* of the contract of tenancy.[5] But from their discussion it is clear that summer crops[6] such as cucurbitaceous fruits, sugar cane and others may also be legitimately grown under a contract of tenancy.[7] Under Hanafite law it is not permissible to rent a garden in order to consume the fruits growing in it. Such a tenancy is called a 'tenancy of consumption' (*ijārat al-istihlāk*), because through it the tenant consumes part of the rented object, whereas under a contract of tenancy (*ijāra*), he is only entitled to make use of the rented object.[8] For the same reason, Hanafite jurists consider the farming out of pastures or canals to be prohibited.[9] It is, however, considered to be permissible to use the rented land (*sāḥa*) in order to plant trees or an orchard on it.[10] The tenant enjoys the usufruct of the land in so far as the fruits are the result of his own labour and investment. In principle, gardens, plantations and pastures are, therefore, excluded from the realm of tenancy. The contract is valid with regard to arable lands on which plants and trees are not already grown. It is a legal institution that concerns agriculture practised on fields. It serves the purpose of putting arable lands to productive use in such a way as to preserve their substance and increase the revenue derived from them.[11] The contract is apparently best suited to growing crops that can be sown and harvested within a term of a year, but is also admissible for other types of crops[12] and for longer periods.[13]

3. A BILATERAL CONTRACT

A contract of tenancy is valid if the partners specify (a) the arable lands that are the object of the contract of tenancy,[14] (b) the crops that the tenant intends to grow on these lands,[15] (c) the duration of the contract,[16] and (d) the rent to be paid by the tenant.[17]

The contract of tenancy is construed by the jurists as a

bilateral contract[18] serving as a means for the exchange of commodities and meant to fit into a monetary economy that follows the rules of a market system. The basic characteristics of all bilateral, synallagmatic contracts are established by analogy to the contract of sale, that is, considered to be the model of all bilateral and commutative contracts. In a bilateral contract one commodity (*māl mutaqawwim*) is exchanged for another commodity. The receiving of the commodity sold engenders the obligation to pay an equivalent.[19] In the contract of tenancy, the rent is considered to be an equivalent for another commodity. This commodity consists of the *tamlīk al-manāfiʿ*, i.e. of the transfer of property rights with regard to the usufruct of specified lands through the growing of specified crops during a specified period of time. In the eighth and ninth centuries some jurists would admit only a monetary indication of rent in a contract of *ijāra*. Hanafite jurists of the ninth century, such as Khaṣṣāf, assert that Abū Yūsuf and Shaibānī held this legal opinion.[20] But Khaṣṣāf's younger contemporary, Ṭabarī, relates that most of the jurists of the eighth and ninth centuries, including Abū Yūsuf and Shaibānī, admitted the fixing of the rent in the form of money or commodities.[21] From other sources it is quite clear that Hanafite jurists of the pre-classical and classical periods of Hanafite law accepted not only money and commodities but even services as a legally admissible form of rent. Whatever the form of the rent, it always functions as an equivalent for the *tamlīk al-manāfiʿ*, for the transfer of property rights with regard to the use of specified lands.

4. RESISTANCE AGAINST THE CONTRACT

The jurists' definition of rent as an equivalent in an exchange of commodities transforms the productive use of land into a commodity. This idea met with strong resistance in religious circles. The eleventh-century Hanafite jurist Sarakhsī reports that Abū Ḥanīfa based his refusal to accept the principle of share-cropping (*muzāraʿa*) on the strength of a *ḥadith* stating that the owner of arable land who is not willing or able to till his land should draw no revenue from it. The Prophet is reported as saying: 'Till it or grant it free of charge to your brother (*izraʿ hā au imnaḥhā akhāka*)'.[22] Sarakhsī informs us that pious religious circles used the same *ḥadīth* to refute the religious legitimacy of the contract of tenancy (*ijāra*), As in many other cases, the jurists dismissed the religious opposition to their economic conceptions as stemming from 'stubbornly ignorant' people. As Sakakhsī puts it, only 'some of the stubbornly ignorant (*mutaʿassifa*) hold that it is not permissible to give arable land in tenancy for gold or silver for the purpose of having it cultivated . . .'[23]

The religious opposition to considering the productive use of land as a commodity resulted from a social and economic order, in which — to use the succinct categories applied by Abdellah Hammoudi to the irrigation system of the Ḍrā valley in southern Morocco — the ownership or the use of land and water was a 'relationship' and not a 'substance'. To quote Hammoudi:

> Nothing, then, is more abstract or more mysterious than a share of water and, consequently, ownership of a share. If by substance is meant any quantity delimited in terms of known area or volume, such as a defined or measured plot of land, it should be clear that what an individual owns is not a substance. All he has in his hands — as distinct from a substance — is a relationship that is evaluated in relation to other users over time . . . this relationship permits him to obtain water to irrigate his lands.[24]

It should be understood that Hammoudi analyses the irrigation system of the Ḍrā valley in Morocco in the nineteenth and twentieth centuries. It is my contention that the results which Hammoudi obtains from his analysis shed light on the way in which the Eastern Muslim world of the pre-classical and classical periods of Hanafite law perceived the productive use of land.

5. THE 'COMMODIFICATION' OF THE PRODUCTIVE USE OF LAND

In the society of the jurists of the pre-classical and classical periods of Hanafite law, the productive use of land is not conceived of as a substance that could be bought and sold, but rather as a relationship. When the jurists set out to transform this relationship into a substance, into a measurable commodity, they met not only with religious opposition but also with great difficulties of a technical juridical nature. They faced three main difficulties: (a) how to transform the productive use of arable land into a commodity, (b) how to legitimise this transformation in terms of the Hanafite legal system and (c) how to measure the commodity value of the productive use of the arable land. I should like to describe in some detail how the jurists handled these difficulties.

(a) How can the productive use of arable lands be defined as a commodity? Commodities are things that can be accumulated and stored until times of need, according to the Hanafite definition.[25] Obviously neither human labour nor the productive use of arable lands through human labour can be easily subsumed under such a definition. It is difficult to accumulate and store work and the productive use of land. The Hanafite definition of commodity reflects the situation of an economy in which no general demand for salaried work exists. It also reflects the values of a peasant economy based on subsistence production in which work and the productive use of land are not considered commodities. Finally, it should fit smoothly into the labour relations on large estates that are not integrated into a market economy.

Under all these conditions, the productive use of arable lands is — to use Hammoudi's categories — a 'relationship', not a 'substance' nor a quantifiable commodity. In the terms of the Hanafite jurists, the 'use [of land and of human labour] is a contingency that does not have a sequence in time' (*li-anna l-manāfiʿa aʿraḍ^un la tabqā waqtain*).[26] For this reason, the use cannot be regarded as a commodity:

> ... the use is not a commodity representing a commodity value (*māl mutaqawwim*) and is not, therefore, warranted against damage, like wine and animals not ritually slaughtered. The explanation for this is that the quality of commodity is only established of a thing that can be accumulated. And the accumulation is the conservation of a thing and its storage for times of need. The use does not last in time [literally: does not last for two different times, i.e. is not storable and cannot be accumulated].[27] Rather, it is a contingency which fades away in the same way as it left the realm of nothingness into the realm of existence. No one can imagine

> its accumulation and, therefore, it does not represent a commodity value for the creditor and the heirs (... *anna l-manfaʿata laisat bi-mālin mutaqauwimin falā tuḍmanu bi-l-itlāfi ka-l-khamri wa-l-mayta. Wa-bāyanuhu anna ṣifata l-māliyati li-sh-shaiʾi innamā tathbutu bi-t-tamauwul. Wa-t-tamauwulu ṣiyānatu sh-shaiʾi wa-ddikhāruhu li-waqti l-ḥāja. Wa-l-manāfiʿu lā tabqā qauwiyīn* [sic!! That is to say: *waqtain*] *wa-lākinnahā aʿrāḍun kamā takhruju min ḥaiyizi l-ʿadmi ilā ḥaiyizi l-wujūdi tatalāshā fa-lā yataṣauwaru fīha t-tamauwul. wa-li-hādhā lā yataqauwamu fī ḥaqqi l-ghuramāʾi wa-l-waratha*).[28]

Through the contract of *ijāra* this basic refusal to view work and the productive use of land as commodities had to be integrated into a legal system that is closely related to the rules of market exchange of commodities. The 'contingency' that had 'no sequence in time' and subsequently could neither be stored nor accumulated, had to be turned into a 'substance', a 'commodity' representing a calculable commodity value. This transubstantiation is performed through the contract of tenancy (*ijāra*). As Sarakhsī puts it: 'It is through the contract [i.e. of *ijāra*] that the quality of enjoying safeguards and representing commodity value are legally established with regard to the use' (*fa-ammā bi-l-ʿaqdi yathbutu li-l-manfaʿati ḥukmu l-iḥrāzi wa-t-taqawwumi sharʿan*).[29] He adds that with regard to this problem, the contract of *ijāra* contradicts the analogy of the contract of sale and he underlines the fact that liability to pay the rent can, therefore, only arise from a contract, not from a delict (*ʿudwān*).[30]

(b) How can this transformation of a relationship, of a passing contingency, into a substance, a commodity, be legitimised in terms of the Hanafite legal system? The contract of tenancy transforms the productive use of land into a commodity. But this commodity only comes into existence after the contract of tenancy has been concluded. The contract of tenancy, therefore, contradicts the basic rule of the contract of sale according to which nothing may be legally sold that is not in existence and at the disposal of the seller at the time of the sale. Many Hanafite jurists of the classical period admitted that on the basis of strict analogy to this fundamental rule, the contract of *ijāra* should not be considered permissible.[31] They overcame this legal difficulty by appealing to the principle of *istiḥsān*, i.e.

of admitting for practical purposes legal solutions that openly contradicted conclusions drawn on the basis of analogical reasoning from the basic rules of the Hanafite legal system.[32] They justified the solution of *istiḥsān* by pointing out that the contract of *ijāra* responded to a general economic need.[33]

(c) The fact that the partners to the contract demonstrate their willingness to consider the productive use of land as a commodity and to assign a commodity value to it in the contract, transforms the use of land into a commodity. The rent is considered its equivalent, performing the same function as the price in the contract of sale.[34] In a valid contract of tenancy, the rent is always fixed through contractual agreement. It is then called 'the contractually fixed rent' (*al-ajr al-musammā* or *al-badal al-musammā*) or simply 'that which is fixed' (*al-musammā*).[35] But the rent is fixed at the time when the contract is concluded. At this time the equivalent of the rent, i.e. the productive use of the land, does not yet exist. And the jurists are very precise in stressing the fact that the obligation to pay the rent does not result from the contract itself, but from the fact that it is possible for the tenant to use the land under a contract of tenancy.[36] This 'possibility of making use of the rented property' (*at-tamakkun min al-intifāᶜ*)[37] is the commodity that is sold under a valid contract of tenancy. Whether the tenant actually uses the land is not important. The tenant's obligation to pay the rent results from the fact that it is possible for him to use the land. Therefore, the obligation to pay the rent begins upon the lessor's conveyance (*taslīm*) of the land to the tenant and not upon concluding the contract.[38] Unless the partners agree in the contract that the rent should be paid in advance or at the end of the period of tenancy, the rent, in principle, falls due at regular intervals during the period of the contract of tenancy.[39] The tenant is obliged to pay the rent as long as it lies within his power to use the land. The tenant's obligation to pay the rent ends as soon as it is no longer possible for him to use the land, regardless of whether this situation is the result of a defect in the rented property, *force majeure* or unauthorised use by a third person (*ghaṣb*).[40] In other words, by concluding the contract the use of the land is transformed into a commodity. But it is the time during which it is possible for the tenant to use the land that determines the size of the commodity for which the tenant has to pay rent.

The jurists express this relationship between rent and use

with a stock phrase, saying '... the rent is appropriated in accordance with the appropriation of the use: hour by hour' (*li-anna l-ujrata tumlaku ʿalā ḥasabi milki l-manāfiʿi sāʿat*^{an} *fa-sāʿat*^{un}).[41] Sarakhsī states that the time is the measure and the yardstick for the use much as the dry measure (*kail*) and the weight (*wazn*) are measures for other commodities.[42] The jurists speak of the contract of tenancy (*ijāra*) as consisting of 'several contracts which are concluded anew each time that the usufruct is realised' (*anna-l-ijārata ʿuqūd*^{un} *mutafarriqat*^{un} *yatajaddadu inʿiqāduhā bi-ḥasabi mā yaḥduthu mina l-manfaʿa*).[43] The calculation of time as an economic factor which determines the amount of the salary and rent enters into the political economy of Islamic law through the contract of *ijāra*.

6. THE CONTRACT AS A NECESSARY CONDITION FOR THE OBLIGATION TO PAY RENT

It should be clear from the discussion above that Schacht's explanation according to which 'the usufruct is, in a certain way, regarded as a thing ...'[44] is at best a useful over-simplification of a very complex relationship between contract and actual situation. It is the contract that 'commodifies' the use, turns it from a 'relationship' into a 'substance', from a 'passing contingency' into a substance with an existence in time. It is the time during which it is possible for the tenant to use the rented object that is considered the measure and yardstick of the size of the commodity. The contract is no empty formality. Quite the contrary. The obligation to pay rent only results if the productive use of arable lands is preceded by a contract. Unlawful appropriation of the land without a contract of *ijāra* or *muzāraʿa* can never give rise to the obligation to pay rent (see below on the voidable *ijāra* and on *ghaṣb*). Unless the contract of *ijāra* has been concluded on behalf of an institution or a third person, the death of one of the partners to the contract ends the relationship between tenant and lessor and may jeopardise the lessor's and the tenant's claims.[45] Finally, in a valid contract of tenancy, the rent can never exceed the 'contractually fixed rent' (*musammā*).[46]

It would appear that the element of contractual consent is much more important with regard to a tenancy relationship than with regard to sale. In the latter, the object sold is always a commodity that represents a commodity value regardless of the contract of sale. In the contract of *ijāra* the productive use of land is considered to be a commodity only if preceded by a contract. But the contract itself does not produce any obligation to pay rent if the actual 'possibility to make use' (*at-tamakkun min al-intifāᶜ*) of the land does not exist. On the other hand, the possibility to make use of the land does not create any obligation to pay rent, if it is not preceded by a contract of tenancy or share-cropping. A balanced relationship between the contract and the actual possibility to make use of the land characterises the Hanafite legal doctrine on rent during the pre-classical and classical periods of Hanafite law. It is precisely the importance of the contractual element that dwindles into insignificance in the Ottoman Hanafite doctrine on rent.

7. THE 'CONTRACTUALLY FIXED RENT' AND THE 'FAIR RENT': THE SPECIAL STATUS OF *WAQF* AND BIG ESTATES

The element of contractual consent is clearly represented through the 'contractually fixed rent' (*musammā*), the rent on which the partners to the contract agreed. But the jurists also developed a concept of rent that was independent of the intention of the contracting partners. This is the concept of the 'fair rent' (*ujrat al-mithl/ajr al-mithl*) whose amount is determined by the average market level of rents attainable for lands of comparable quality and size.[47] It is evident that, from a very early date, the jurists tried to protect certain types of properties against disadvantages which arose from the divergence of the contractually fixed rent (*musammā*) from the 'fair rent' (*ajr al-mithl*). Already in the ninth century Khaṣṣāf discussed the problems that resulted from the fact that the contractually fixed rent (*musammā*) of *waqf* land fell below the rent level of comparable lands in a way that constituted a *laesio enormis* (*ghabn fāḥish*) to the interests of the *waqf*. He decided that the lessor or the *qāḍī* should dissolve the contract of *ijāra* if the contractually fixed rent fell so far below the 'fair rent' (*ajr al-mithl*) as to constitute a *laesio enormis* with regard to the interests of the *waqf*. After the dissolution of the contract, the land should be farmed out for a rental that should not fall below the 'fair rent'.[48] If the contractually fixed rent fell so far below the 'fair rent' as to constitute a *laesio enormis* to the interests of the lessor, the contract could — under certain specified conditions — be dissolved. But as long as it was not dissolved, the tenant was under the obligation to pay only the 'contractually fixed rent' (*musammā*).[49]

Restricting the period of tenancy was another way of protecting the interests of the lessor against the dangers that result from the divergences between the contractually fixed rent and the 'fair rent'. This possibility is already discussed during the eighth century.[50] From the ninth century onwards, Hanafite jurists tried to restrict the period of tenancy with regard to *waqf* lands and big estates.[51] Some of them formally interdicted periods of more than a year, others of more than three years. Still others wanted the *qāḍī* to examine regularly the difference between the contractually fixed rentals and the 'fair rent'. This tendency seems to have developed earlier in Central Asia than in Iraq or Syria. The discussion of the permissible periods of the tenancy contracts is important because it shows the jurists' awareness of the economic problems resulting from the weight given to the contractually fixed rent, and a tendency to distinguish between different types of property.

8. THE 'VOIDABLE CONTRACT OF TENANCY' (*IJĀRA FĀSIDA*)

The importance given to the *musammā*, the 'contractually fixed rent', is also clearly discernible in the legal norms concerning the *ijāra fāsida*, the voidable contract of tenancy.[52] A contract of tenancy is voidable if one of the following items is not exactly specified in it: (a) the size, quality and location of the rented fields, (b) the use to which the arable lands should be put, (c) the duration of the tenancy and (d) the amount of the rent.[53] The contract of tenancy also becomes voidable if it contains stipulations that constitute one-sided charges to the advantage of either the tenant or the lessor.[54] A voidable contract is not without legal effects.[55] The jurists of the early and classical periods of the Hanafite law hold the legal opinion that a voidable contract is validated through the tenant's use of the arable lands. In this case, the voidable contract is a necessary condition for the obligation to pay rent.[56] Under a valid contract of tenancy, the obligation to pay rent results from the fact that it is *possible* for the tenant to make use of the arable lands. Under a voidable contract of tenancy, it is the *actual* use, i.e. the process of tilling the land and harvesting the crop, that obliges the tenant to pay the rent. The voidable contract is thus validated through the realisation of the use.

An important problem remains: what kind of rent does the tenant have to pay? Is it the 'contractually fixed rent' or the 'fair rent'? If the question was answered in strict analogy to the contract of sale, it would have to be the 'fair rent'.[57] This solution is accepted by the Hanafite jurists with regard to contracts that are considered 'voidable' because they do not contain a 'contractually fixed rent' (*musammā*).[58] Sarakhsī, the eleventh-century Transoxanian author of the *Mabsūṭ*, applies this solution to all voidable contracts of tenancy.[59] Schacht thinks that this is the general opinion of Muslim jurists.[60] But the majority of the jurists of the pre-classical and classical periods, whose works I have examined, choose a solution through *istiḥsān* and say that in no case should the rent be higher than the contractually fixed rent (*musammā*). I quote the twelfth-century jurist, Kāsānī, who summarises the solution according to *istiḥsān* in the following words:

> ... in a contract that contains the fixing (*tasmiya*) [of a rent] the rent shall not be higher than the fixed rent (*musammā*) according to our three companions [i.e. Abū Ḥanīfa, Abū Yūsuf and Shaibānī]. This is based on the fact that, according to our three companions, use (*manāfiʿ*) does not have legally acknowledged commodity value (*ghairu mutaqauwimāt^{in} sharʿ^{an}*). It acquires a commodity value only through the contract (*wa-innamā tataqauwamu bi-l-ʿaqd*) and through contractual assignment of value by the two partners to the contract (*bi-taqwīmi l-ʿāqidain*). And the two partners to the contract assigned it a value only through the contractually fixed amount (*wa-l-ʿāqidāni mā qauwamāhā illā bi-l-qadari l-musammā*). If an additional [sum] above the contractually fixed rent was made obligatory, then it would fall due without a contract (*fa-lau wajabati z-ziyādatu ʿalā l-musammā la-wajabat bilā ʿaqd*). And without contract, the use does not have any commodity value (*wa-innahā lā tataqauwamu bilāʿaqd*).[61]

To summarise: in the pre-classical and classical periods of Hanafite law, the rent to be paid under a voidable contract of tenancy is the 'contractually fixed rent', the rent that is established through contractual agreement. Only if no rent has been stipulated is the tenant under the obligation to pay the 'fair rent' which is determined on the basis of the general market level of rents. In general, under a voidable contract of tenancy the 'contractually fixed rent' serves to protect the tenant against unforeseeable claims of the lessor. Most of the jurists hold the legal opinion that under a voidable contract of tenancy, if there is a divergence between the amount of the 'contractually fixed rent' and the 'fair rent', the tenant is under the obligation to pay only the lower of the two rentals.[62] Sarakhsī is the only jurist I find who unequivocally defends the position that, under a voidable contract of tenancy (*ijāra fāsida*), the tenant is always obliged to pay the 'fair rent'. Whether this dissenting opinion represents a particular regional development, I am not able to say. Twelfth-century Hanafite authors of Central Asia such as Qāḍīkhān hold the legal opinion that the voidable contract of tenancy engenders the obligation to pay the 'fair rent' but that the 'fair rent' should not exceed the level of the 'contractually fixed rent'.[63] According to their teachings, this legal ordinance does not apply to *waqf* lands nor to orphans' landed property, i.e. landed property that is administered in the interest of the minor proprietor. If the 'contractually fixed rent' with regard to *waqf* land and orphans' landed property falls far below the level of the 'fair rent', the contract should be considered a voidable contract of tenancy (*ijāra fāsida*). In this case the tenant owes the 'fair rent' however high it may be. It is not always clear, however, whether Qāḍīkhān — contrary to the teachings of Kāsānī — considers this obligation to pay the fair rent to be retroactive.[64] Be that as it may, the majority of Hanafite jurists of the pre-classical and classical periods whose works I have studied, clearly support the validity of the 'contractually fixed rent' (*musammā*) also under a voidable contract and they use this legal ordinance in order to protect the economic interests of the tenant.

9. NO RENT WITHOUT CONTRACT: 'UNAUTHORISED USE' DOES NOT ENGENDER THE OBLIGATION TO PAY RENT

In the Hanafite legal doctrine of the pre-classical and classical periods, the tenancy relationship is clearly differentiated from the 'unauthorised use' (*ghaṣb*) of arable lands. Originally, Hanafite law defended the position that 'unauthorised use' in the legal sense of the word does not apply to landed property and that, therefore, the person who makes unauthorised use of landed property is not liable to make compensation for any damage inflicted on the landed property unless he intentionally causes these damages.[65] Shaibānī, writing in the second half of the eighth century,[66] and the ninth-century Iraqi jurist, Khaṣṣāf,[67] admitted that 'unauthorised use' of landed property is possible and engenders the user's liability to make compensation for all kinds of damage that diminish the value of the land.

This is to say that already in the pre-classical doctrine Hanafite jurists developed two conflicting opinions as to the sources of the obligation to make compensation. According to one opinion, this obligation results only when the land is intentionally used because it is presupposed that the productive use of the land will in most cases entail a loss of value of the land. According to the second opinion, the very fact that a person makes unauthorised use of the land engenders his obligation to make compensation for all damages caused to the land.[68] According to both legal opinions, the person who makes unauthorised use (*ghaṣb*) of the land, and diminishes the value of the land through the cultivation of the field, is held liable to make compensation. But if the unauthorised user leases the land to a third person and this tenant's cultivation of the soil diminishes the value of the land, the conflicting legal opinions lead to different legal decisions. According to the first opinion, it is the tenant who is held liable to make compensation because it is through his cultivation of the soil that the land's value diminishes. According to the second opinion, the landlord has the choice of making one of the two persons liable for the payment of compensation, because, from his point of view, both are making unauthorised use of his landed property.[69]

But according to both legal opinions, the unauthorised use of arable lands does not engender the obligation to pay rent. All Hanafite lawyers of the pre-classical and classical periods whose works I have studied are — with one significant exception — unanimous on this question. Those who make unauthorised use of landed property have to return the wrongfully appropriated object and to pull up the cereals or trees that they may have grown or planted. They are liable to make compensation for that which they have destroyed and for the diminution (*nuqṣān*) of the value of the land arising from their cultivation of it, on the grounds that land, being a commodity, represents a commodity value and is warranted against damage. Persons who unlawfully harvest fruits from a garden or cut down trees on plantations are liable to restore the value of the destroyed goods.[70] But the persons making unauthorised use of landed property cannot be obliged to pay rent. Without a contract of tenancy or share-cropping (*muzāraʿa*) the use does not represent a commodity value and is not warranted. Therefore, the unauthorised use (*ghaṣb*) of land does not entail the obligation to pay rent. As Kāsānī puts it: 'According to our legal method, the person who makes unauthorised use of a thing must not pay rent' (*wa-lā ujrata alā l-ghāṣibi ʿalā aṣlinā*).[71] The productive use made of arable lands does not engender the obligation to pay rent unless it is preceded by a valid or voidable contract of tenancy.[72] It does not matter, from a jurist's point of view, that the owner, through a third person's unlawful use (*ghaṣb*) of his landed property, loses the chance to lease his landed property and earn rent.

10. THE CONTRACT OF TENANCY AS AN INSTRUMENT OF SOCIAL AND ECONOMIC INTEGRATION

Throughout the early and classical periods of Hanafite law, the obligation to pay rent is viewed as arising within the framework of a contractual agreement. The use of arable land engenders the obligation to pay rent only if it is preceded by a valid or voidable contract of tenancy or of share-cropping. The fact that the obligation to pay rent presupposes a contractual agreement clearly distinguishes the rent from all kinds of taxes. The concept of rent as developed in the pre-classical and classical periods of Hanafite law clearly works in favour of the emancipation of the peasants and against all attempts to view them as serfs and to regard their rent as a kind of menial due. In addition, the Hanafite jurists clearly view the contract of tenancy as an instrument for the furthering of social and economic integration of various strata of the rural society. The tenant obtains the right to use the rented property, a right which is construed as being a form of property, for which the jurists use the term *milk al-manfaʿa*, the 'property of use'.[73] Through the contract and his work and through the payment of rent the tenant acquires the right to sell or consume the products of his labour without any interference from the lessor. Furthermore, the tenant's right of access to the market is unrestricted not only with regard to the products of his labour, but also with regard to the land that he rented. The tenant has the right to lease it to a second tenant and to charge a higher rental than the one he himself pays.[74]

In the case of a sublease, the first tenant must take the precaution of specifying the second rent in a coinage or commodity different from those with which he himself pays his rent. Otherwise, the profits he realises would be morally reprehensible though valid from a legal point of view.[75] It is also legally valid to sublet a rented object at a higher rental, if some investment into the object is effected.[76] The subtenant in turn enjoys the same rights as the first tenant. In principle, there is no legal restriction on the number of subtenants who in turn may sublease and obtain a share of the rent of the same plot of land. This legal arrangement makes speculation possible, but is also a means of social and economic integration. In principle, it creates conditions for the development of a common interest amongst the tenants and lessors sharing the rent of the same land in different proportions. Tenants and lessors are thought of as proprietors and for that reason both of them may become lessors and rentiers.

11. THE NEW CONCEPT OF RENT IN BALKH AND BUKHARA

The classical Hanafite doctrine on rent is based on the idea that use of land does not engender the obligation to pay rent, unless it is preceded by a valid or voidable contract of tenancy or share-cropping (*muzāra'a*). In everyday life, the difference between the amount of money or goods payable as rent and the amount of money or goods payable as compensation for the diminution (*nuqṣān*) of the value of the arable land may not always have been very important. In fact, we learn from the jurists that the amount of money to be paid as compensation for damage inflicted on the land during the unauthorised use could be higher than the land tax (*kharāj*).[77]

Rent and compensation were both paid for arable lands and

represented comparable values. This practical economic aspect of the problem apparently led the jurists of Balkh to reconsider the classical Hanafite differentiation between 'unauthorised use' (*ghaṣb*) of landed property and tenancy relationships (*ijāra*), between compensation and rent. Apparently there were a variety of social, economic and political reasons for this reconsideration, but I cannot deal with them in this article. The eleventh-century Transoxanian author, Sarakhsī, discusses the problem of whether it is the owner of arable lands or the person who makes unauthorised use (*ghaṣb*) of them who has to pay the land tax. He defends the position that ownership engenders the obligation to pay the land tax. His legal reasoning shows that prominent Hanafite jurists of Central Asia in the eleventh century tended to obscure the difference between 'unauthorised use' (*ghaṣb*) of landed property and the tenancy relationship (*ijāra*). Sarakhsī ascribes to Abū Ḥanīfa the legal opinion that only ownership engenders the obligation to pay the tithe (*ᶜushr*) and the land tax (*kharāj*). If someone makes unauthorised use of the landed property of a third person, he is obliged to pay a compensation to the landowner. Sarakhsī goes on to say: 'This is as if he leases the land for that amount' (*fa-kāna bi-manzilati mā lau ājara l-arḍa bi-dhālika l-qadr*). According to Abū Ḥanīfa, it is not the tenant, but the lessor who has to pay the tax. From this Sarakhsī draws the following conclusion:

> This supports the legal opinion of those of our scholars ... who hold that [the payment of the compensation for] the damage (*nuqṣān*) to the land is a recompense for its use and that the method of defining the damage (*nuqṣān*) is to compare the amount for which it could be leased before and after the cultivation (*muzarāᶜa*).[78] The difference [between the two rentals] is the damage inflicted on the land. With regard to this problem, there is a conflict [of legal opinion] among the leading scholars of Balkh. Some of them say: according to our legal reasoning the use is not warranted against damage. And the [compensation for] the diminution (*nuqṣān*) of the land value should rather be regarded as a substitute for that part of the thing which is lost. The way to know it [the diminution of the value] is to compare the prices for which it could be sold before and after its agricultural use. The difference between the two [prices] is the diminution of the value of the land (*nuqṣān*). On the basis of the answer

that he mentions here, the first legal opinion is more correct. Verily, he treated the diminution (*nuqṣān*) of the value as if it were the rent according to the legal opinion of Abū Ḥanīfa (*wa-hādhā yuqauwī qaula man yaqūlu min aṣḥābinā ... anna nuqṣāna l-arḍi ʿiwaḍᵘⁿ ʿan manfaʿatihā. Wa-inna ṭ-ṭarīqa fī maʿrifati n-nuqṣāni an yunẓara bikam tuʾjaru l-arḍu qabla l-muzaraʿati wa-baʿdahā. fa-miqdāru t-tafāwuti huwa nuqṣānu l-arḍi. wa-fī hādhā ikhtilāfᵘⁿ baina aʾimmati Balkh. fa-inna baʿḍahum yaqūlūna anna l-manfaʿataʿindanā la tuḍmanu bi-l-itlāf. wa-lākinna n-nuqṣāna fī ḥukmi badali juzʾⁱⁿ fāʾitⁱⁿ mina l-ʿain. wa-ṭarīqu maʿrifatihi an yunẓara bi-kam kānat tushtarā tilka l-arḍu qabla z-zirāʿati wa-bi-kam tushtarā baʿdahā. fa-tafāwutu mā bainahumā huwa n-nuqṣān. wa-l-qaulu l-auwalu aqrabu ila ṣ-ṣawāb, bināʾᵃⁿ ʿala l-jawābi lladhī dhakarahu hāhunā fa-innahu jaʿala n-nuqṣāna bi-manzilati l-ujrati ʿinda Abī Ḥanīfa*).[79]

From this quotation four conclusions may safely be drawn: (a) Some prominent eleventh-century Hanafite jurists of Central Asia assimilated the tenancy relationship to that of *ghaṣb*, of unauthorised use of landed property. In their legal reasoning, the payment of compensation for the diminution of the value of landed property through unauthorised use is treated as if it were a kind of rent for the productive use of landed property. The importance of the contractual framework in which the payment of rent is embedded is clearly diminished through this form of legal reasoning. (b) Such a form of legal reasoning considers the use to be a commodity that has a definable value of its own and is warranted against damage. (c) This legal opinion is ascribed to Abū Ḥanīfa because it clearly contradicts the *ẓāhir ar-riwāya*, the Hanafite legal tradition as embodied in the works of Shaibānī.[80] (d) It is also clear that this new form of legal reasoning is still considered to be a debatable issue, even among the leading scholars of Balkh.

To the best of my knowledge, Sarakhsī follows this legal reasoning only in this particular case and not in any other instance regarding the *ijāra*, the tenancy relationship. No trace of this teaching is to be found in the works of Samarqandī, Kāsānī or Bābartī, i.e. the leading Syrian and Iraqi jurists of the twelfth and fourteenth centuries. Even Hanafite authors of Central Asia, who clearly defend their own legal tradition within the Hanafite school, do not draw all the legal and logical conclusions from this new legal doctrine. The twelfth-century author, Qāḍīkhān, for example, holds the legal opinion that if a contract of tenancy concerns *waqf* lands or orphans' property and if the 'contractually fixed rent' falls far below the level of the 'fair rent', this contract should either be considered a 'voidable contract of tenancy' (*ijāra fāsida*) or an 'unauthorised use' (*ghaṣb*) of the arable lands. According to Qāḍīkhān such an 'unauthorised use' of the *waqf* land or the orphans' property engenders the obligation to pay the 'fair rent'. The voidable contract of tenancy is identified here with 'unauthorised use' and — contrary to the classical doctrine — unauthorised use (*ghaṣb*) is thought of as engendering the obligation to pay the 'fair rent'.[81]

Traces of the classical doctrine are still to be found in Qāḍīkhān's *fatāwā*.[82] It seems that Qaḍīkhān wavers between the classical Hanafite doctrine on rent and 'unauthorised use' and new legal opinions better suited to protect the interests of the *waqf* and, in general, the rentier class. He refers to leading tenth-century Hanafite jurists of Bukhara and a group of anonymous jurists who hold the legal opinion that 'unauthorised use' of *waqf* lands and the orphans' property always engenders the obligation to pay the 'fair rent'. But he also stresses the fact that this legal opinion contradicts the *ẓāhir ar-riwāya*, the embodiment of the Hanafite legal tradition.[83] In other instances of conflicting legal opinion, Qāḍīkhān informs his readers which of the legal opinions the mufti should follow.[84] In the case of 'unauthorised use' (*ghaṣb*) of *waqf* lands and orphans' property he is apparently undecided and gives no solution to the conflict between the classical doctrine and the new legal opinion.

Be that as it may, Sarakhsī's remarks on the eleventh-century Hanafite jurists of Balkh, who treat the payment of compensation as if it were a kind of rent, and Qāḍīkhān's reference to Hanafite authorities from the tenth century and to twelfth-century Hanafite jurists in Central Asia who teach that unauthorised use of *waqf* lands engenders the obligation to pay the 'fair rent', mark the beginning of a new legal doctrine concerning the tenancy relationship and the sources of the obligation to pay rent. In this new legal doctrine on rent and tenancy relationship the contractual element loses its importance. One of the main sources for the obligation to pay rent becomes the 'unauthorised use' of landed property, and the tenancy relationship of the peasants is described more and more in terms of the unequal and hierarchical relationship between tenant and lessor that, in Hanafite law, characterises the *muzāraʿa*, the contract of share-cropping.

NOTES

1. Nasafī, *Ṭalibat aṭ-Ṭalaba fi-l-Iṣtilāḥāt al-Fiqhīya* (n.p., 1311 A.H.), p. 124; al-Ghanīmī (reprint edn Beirut, 1400 A.H./1980 A.D.), *al-Lubāb fī Sharḥ al-Kitāb*, vol. 2, p. 87.

2. Joseph Schacht, *An Introduction To Islamic Law* (Clarendon Press, Oxford, 1964), pp. 20-2.

3. Ibid., p. 276 in his excellent bibliography notes only the article of Erich Pritsch and Otto Spies, 'Der islamische Werklieferungsvertrag', *Zeitschrift für vergleichende Rechtswissenschaft*, 56 (1953), pp. 47-75.

4. Abū Yūsuf, *Kitāb al-Kharāj*, Dr. E. Fagnan as *Le livre de l'impôt foncier* (Librairie Orientaliste Paul Geuthner, Paris, 1921), pp. 133, 138. See Arabic edition (Bulaq 1382 A.H.), pp. 88, 90; Ṭabarī, *Kitāb Ikhtilāf al-Fuqahā'*, 2nd edn (Beirut, n.d., reprint edn of F. Kern's edn, 1902), pp. 117, 118, 120, 122-4; Samarqandī, *Tuḥfat al-Fuqahā'* (Damascus, n.d.), vol. 2, p. 488; Khaṣṣāf, *Kitāb Aḥkām al-Awqāf* (Cairo, 1322 A.H./1904 A.D.), p. 207.

5. Ṭaḥāwī, *Mukhtaṣar* (Cairo, 1370 A.H.), p. 132; Khaṣṣāf, *Kitāb Aḥkām al-Awqāf*, p. 207; Kāsānī *Kitāb Badā'iʿ aṣ-Ṣanā'iʿ fī Tartīb ash-Sharā'iʿ*, (Cairo, 1328 A.H./1910 A.D.), vol. 4, pp. 175, 183, 188; Qudūrī, *al-Kitāb*, printed on the margin of al-Ghanīmī, *al-Lubāb fī Sharḥ al Kitāb*, vol. 4, pp. 88-9; Samarqandī, *Tuḥfat al-Fuqahā'*, vol. 2, p. 479; Marghīnānī, *al-Hidāya Sharḥ Bidāyat' al-Mubtadi'*, printed on the margin of Ibn al-Humām *Sharḥ Fatḥ al-Qadīr* (Cairo, 1356 A.H.), vol. 7, pp. 150, 166; Qāḍīzādeh, *Natā'ij al-Afkār fī Kashf ar-Rumūz wa-l-Asrār* (printed as vols 7 and 8 of Ibn al-Humām, *Sharḥ Fatḥ al-Qadīr*), vol. 7, pp. 166, 197; Sarakhsī, *Kitāb al-Mabsūṭ*, reprint edn (Beirut, n.d.), vol. 16, p. 33.

6. Summer crops deplete the soil of its fertility, see Andrew M. Watson, 'A Medieval Green Revolution: New Crops and Farming Techniques in the Early Islamic World', in A.L. Udovitch (ed.), *The Islamic Middle East 700-1900. Studies in Economic and Social History* (The Darwin Press, Princeton, 1981), pp. 40-1. They need irrigation and larger investment in terms of capital and labour, see Roger Owen, *The Middle East in the World Economy 1800-1914* (Methuen, London and New York, 1981), pp. 30-31, 32, 40-41, 43. For the most important summer crops in medieval Egypt see Claude Cahen, 'al-Makhzūmī et Ibn Mammātī sur l'agriculture egyptienne médiévale', *Annales Islamologiques*, 11 (1972), pp. 146-8. For the most important summer crops in medieval Syria see Cahen, 'Aperçu sur les impôts du sol en Syrie au moyen age', *Journal of the Economic and Social History of the Orient*, 18 (1975), part 3, pp. 236, 238, 240. The term 'summer crop' is used by Hanafite jurists, e.g. Sarakhsī, *Mabsūṭ*, vol. 23, p. 41: '*ghallat ṣaif*'.

7. The jurists often used *ruṭba* as the example for summer crops, see

Sarakhsī, ibid., vol. 17, p. 33; Kāsānī, *Badāʾiʿ aṣ-Ṣanāʾiʿ*, vol. 4, pp. 216, 223; Samarqandī, *Tuḥfat al-Fuqahāʾ*, vol. 2, p. 488; Marghīnānī, *al-Hidāya*, vol. 7, pp. 167, 173; Bābartī, *Sharḥ al-ʿInāya ʿalā al-Hidāya* (printed on the margin of Ibn al-Humām, *Sharḥ Fatḥ al-Qadīr* and Qāḍīzādeh, *Natāʾij al-Afkār*), vol. 7, pp. 167, 173; Qāḍīkhān, *Kitāb al-Fatāwā al-Khānīya* (Cairo, 1282 A.H.), vol. 3, p. 269; Ibn ʿĀbidīn, *Radd al-Muḥtār ʿalā ad-Durr al-Mukhtār. Sharḥ Tanwīr al-Abṣār fī Fiqh Madhhab al-Imām al-Aʿẓam Abī Ḥanīfa an-Nuʿman* (Cairo, 1307 A.H.), vol. 3, p. 283. *Ruṭba* is defined by Ibn ʿĀbidīn, ibid., and by Sarakhsī, *Mabsūṭ*, vol. 23, pp. 66-7 as comprising melons, cucumbers and aubergines. This coincides with Lane's definition of the term. Kāsānī, *Badāʾiʿ aṣ-Ṣanāʾiʿ*, vol. 4, pp. 216, 223 says that *ruṭba* is different from cereals in that its growth does not end after one year and that it weakens the soil much more than cereals. This idea seems to be generally employed in the jurist's discussion of *ruṭba* and other summer crops, see Marghīnānī, *al-Hidāya*, vol. 7, pp. 167, 173 and Bābartī, *Sharḥ al-ʿInāya ʿalā al-Hidāya*, printed on the margin of Ibn al-Humām, *Sharḥ Faṭh al-Qadīr* (Cairo, 1356 A.H.), vol. 7, pp. 167, 173. I find it difficult to reconcile this reasoning with my insufficient knowledge of cucurbitaceous fruits.

8. Sarakhsī, *Mabsūṭ*, vol. 16, pp. 31-3; Samarqandī, *Tuḥfat al-Fuqahāʾ*, vol. 2, p. 488; Kāsānī, *Badāʾiʿ aṣ-Ṣanāʾiʿ*, vol. 4, p. 175; Ibn Nujaim, *al-Ashbāh wan-Naẓāʾir ʿalā Madhhab Abī Ḥanīfa an-Nuʿmān* (Beirut, 1400 A.H./1980 A.D.), p. 269.

9. Samarqandī, *Tuḥfat al-Fuqahāʾ*, vol. 2, p. 488; Kāsānī, *Badāʾiʿ aṣ-Ṣanāʾiʿ*, vol. 4, p. 175; Sarakhsī, *Mabsūṭ*, vol. 16, p. 43 also providing the *ḥīla* against this prohibition; Ibn Nujaim, *al-Ashbāh*, p. 196.

10. Qudūrī, *al-Kitāb*, vol. 2, pp. 89-90; Qāḍīzādeh, *Natāʾij al-Afkār*, vol. 7, pp. 166-7; Bābartī, *Sharḥ al-ʿInāya*, vol. 7, pp. 166-7.

11. Sarakhsī, *Mabsūṭ*, vol. 16, pp. 31 explains the relationship between the rented object and the productive use made of it as one in which the realisation (*istīfāʾ*) of the productive use allows the separation of the usufruct from the rented object: '*fa-maḥallu l-ijārati manfaʿat^un tanfaṣilu ʿani l-ʿaini bi-l-istīfāʾ*'.

12. Schacht, *Introduction*, p. 155 states: '... if the crop has not yet been harvested when the lease expires, it continues for the fair rent until the crop has ripened'. This holds true for cereals (*zarʿ*). But summer crops rarely and trees never have a 'specified end' (*nihāya maʿlūma*) at a given period of the year. At the end of the specified period of tenancy, therefore, the tenant has to remove them from the ground. If this should turn out to be harmful to the land, the lessor may buy the crop or plantation — at the value they represent after being pulled out from the ground. He may also prolong the contract of tenancy. See Qudūrī, *al-Kitāb*, vol. 2, pp. 89-90; Qāḍīkhān, *Kitāb al-Fatāwā*, vol. 3, p. 269; Kāsānī, *Badāʾiʿ aṣ-Ṣanāʾiʿ*, vol. 4, pp. 222-3; Marghīnānī, *al-Hidāya*, vol. 7, p. 167; Bābartī, *Sharḥ al-ʿInāya*, vol. 7, p. 167. It is evident that the tenant who grows summer crops or plants trees will face many legal and economic conflicts at the end of the specified period of tenancy.

13. In principle, any specified period for a contract of tenancy is

considered to be valid, see Ṭaḥāwī, *Mukhtaṣar*, p. 132; Qudūrī, *al-Kitāb*, vol. 2, p. 88; Sarakhsī, *Mabsūṭ*, vol. 15, pp. 132-3, 151; Kāsānī, *Badāʾiʿ aṣ-Ṣanāʾiʿ*, vol. 4, p. 181. From the twelfth century onwards the jurists tended to limit the contract of tenancy with regard to *waqf* lands to a period of three years; see Marghīnānī, *al-Hidāya*, vol. 7, p. 150; Bābartī, *Sharḥ al-ʿInāya*, vol. 7, p. 150.

14. Sarakhsī, *Mabsūṭ*, vol. 16, p. 33: Samarqandī, *Tuḥfat al-Fuqahāʾ*, vol. 2, p. 487; Kāsānī, *Badāʾiʿ aṣ-Ṣanāʾiʿ*, vol. 4, p. 180.

15. Qudūri, *al-Kitāb*, vol. 2, p. 89; Samarqandī, *Tuḥfat al-Fuqahāʾ*, vol. 2, p. 479; Kāsānī, *Badāʾiʿ aṣ-Ṣanāʾiʿ*, vol. 4, pp. 183, 196, 213, 216; Marghīnānī, *al-Hidāya*, vol. 7, p. 166; Bābartī. *Sharḥ al-ʿInāya*, vol. 7, p. 166. With the exception of Qudūrī, all the jurists quoted in this note stress that different crops may have different effects on the soil. Kāsānī, *Badāʾiʿ aṣ-Ṣanāʾiʿ*, vol. 4, p. 216 declares it to be an act of unlawful appropriation (*ghaṣb*) if a tenant whose contract entitles him to grow cereals, grows summer crops instead.

16. Qudūrī, *al-Kitāb*, vol. 2, p. 88; Sarakhsī, *Mabsūṭ*, vol. 15, pp. 75, 132-3; Samarqandī, *Tuḥfat al-Fuqahāʾ*, vol. 2, pp. 476, 487; Kāsānī, *Badāʾiʿ aṣ-Ṣanāʾiʿ*, vol. 4, p. 181; Marghīnānī, *al-Hidāya*, vol. 7, p. 150; Bābartī, *Sharḥ al-ʿInāya*, vol. 7, p. 150.

17. Qudūrī, *al-Kitāb*, vol. 2, p. 88; Sarakhsī, *Mabsūṭ*, vol. 15, pp. 75, 76; Samarqandī, *Tuḥfat al-Fuqahāʾ*, vol. 2, pp. 476, 487; Kāsānī, *Badāʾiʿ aṣ-Ṣanāʾiʿ*, vol. 4, pp. 179, 193; Marghīnānī, *al-Hidāya*, vol. 7, pp. 147, 148; Bābartī, *Sharḥ al-ʿInāya*, vol. 7, p. 148.

18. The idea is expressed through the terms *ʿiwaḍ* or *muʿāwaḍa*, see Qudūrī, *al-Kitāb*, vol. 2, p. 88; Sarakhsī, *Mabsūṭ*, vol. 15, p. 74; Samarqandī, *Tuḥfat al-Fuqahāʾ*, vol. 2, p. 476; Kāsānī, *Badāʾiʿ aṣ-Ṣanāʾiʿ*, vol. 4, p. 179; '*al-ijāra tijāra*'; p. 201; '*ʿaqd muʿāwaḍa*'; Bābartī, *Sharḥ al-ʿInāya*, vol. 7, pp. 147, 154; Marghīnānī, *al-Hidāya*, vol. 7, p. 148: '*li-anna l-ujrata thamanu l-manfaʿati fa-taʿtabiru bi-thamani l-mabīʿ* ...'.

19. Chafik Chehata, *Droit musulman. Applications au Proche-Orient* (Librairie Dalloz, Paris, 1971), p. 138; Chehata, *Théorie générale de l'obligation en droit musulman hanéfite* (Editions Sirey, Paris, 1969), pp. 67-9, 180.

20. Khaṣṣāf, *Kitāb Aḥkām al-Awqāf*, p. 206.

21. Ṭabarī, *Ikhtilāf*, pp. 123-4.

22. Sarakhsī, *Mabsūṭ*, vol. 23, p. 12.

23. Ibid.

24. Abdellah Hammoudi, 'Substance and Relation: Water Rights and Water Distribution in the Ḍrā Valley', in Ann Elizabeth Mayer (ed.), *Property, Social Structure and Law in the Modern Middle East* (State University of New York Press, Albany, 1985), pp. 52-3.

25. Sarakhsī, *Mabsūṭ*, vol. 11, p. 79: '*wa-bayānuhu anna ṣifata l-māliyati li-sh-shaiʾi innamā yathbutu bi-t-tamauwul. Wa-t-tamauwulu ṣiyānatu sh-shaiʾi wa-ddikhāruhu li-waqti l-ḥāja*'. See also Schacht, *Introduction*, pp. 134-5.

26. Sarakhsī, *Mabsūṭ*, vol. 15, p. 74; see also vol. 11, pp. 78-9. This is a stock phrase of the Hanafite jurists in the classical and post-classical periods, see Qāḍīzādeh, *Natāʾij al-Afkār*, vol. 7, p. 395: '*wa-l-*

manāfi'u a'rāḍun lā tabqā waqtain wa-l-'ainu tabqā auqātun wa-baina mā yabqā wa-mā lā yabqā tafāwut. In a very similar vein Marghīnānī, *al-Hidāya*, vol. 7, pp. 394-5, states: '*li-annahā a'raḍun lā tabqā fa-yamlikuhā daf'an li-ḥājatihi lā baqā'a lahā wa-li-annahā lā tumāthilu l-a'yāna li-sur'ati fanā'ihā*'. See also Bābartī, *Sharḥ al-'Ināya*, vol. 7, pp. 394, 396.

27. The printed text reads: '*wa-l-manāfi' lā tabqā qauwiyīn* ...'; this is wrong from a grammatical point of view and it does not make much sense with regard to the content. I prefer to read: '*wa-l-manāfi'u lā tabqā waqtain*'. This is a stock phrase of the Hanafite jurists (see above, note 26). It is often used by Sarakhsī to describe the fact that the use does not have a reliable sequence in time, see *Mabsūṭ*, vol. 11, pp. 78, 80; vol. 15, p. 74, and also on the page from which the present quotation is taken (ibid., vol. 11, p. 79) line 10 from the bottom.

28. Sarakhsī, *Mabsūṭ*, vol. 11, p. 79; compare also vol. 16, p. 33. The fact that the use cannot be inherited is stressed by Marghīnānī, *al-Hidāya*, vol. 7, p. 220; Bābartī, *Sharḥ al-'Ināya*, vol. 7, p. 220.

29. Sarakhsī, *Mabsūṭ*, vol. 11, p. 79; compare also vol. 15, pp. 85, 94, 96; see also Kāsānī, *Badā'i' aṣ-Ṣanā'i'*, vol. 4, p. 184; '*wa-l-manāfi'u 'alā aṣlinā lā tataqauwamu illā bi-l-'aqdi ṣ-ṣaḥīḥi awi-l-fāsid*', see also p. 178; Marghīnānī, *al-Hidāya*, vol. 7, p. 175: '*wa-lanā anna l-manāfi'a lā tataqauwamu bi-nafsihā bal bi-l-'aqdi li-l-ḥāja*'; Bābartī, *Sharḥ al-'Ināya*, vol. 7, p. 175.

30. Sarakhsī, *Mabsūṭ*, vol. 11, p. 79; Kāsānī, *Badā'i' aṣ-Ṣanā'i'*, vol. 4, p. 184; Samarqandī, *Tuḥfat al-Fuqahā'*, vol. 3, p. 112.

31. Sarakhsī, *Mabsūṭ*, vol. 15, p. 74 quotes this legal opinion but differs from it. The following jurists admit that the *ijāra* does not fulfil the conditions of true analogy: Kāsānī, *Badā'i' aṣ-Ṣanā'i'*, vol. 4, p. 173; Marghīnānī, *al-Hidāya*, vol. 7, p. 147; Qāḍīzādeh, *Natā'ij al-Afkār*, vol. 7, pp. 147-8.

32. Kāsānī, *Badā'i' aṣ-Ṣanā'i'*, vol. 4, p. 173 gives the following reasoning: 'but according to our *istiḥsān*, which we base on the Holy Book, the Sunna and the Ijmā', we allow it' (i.e. the contract of tenancy). Basing the solution of *istiḥsān* on scriptural sources seems to imply that *qiyās* is mainly based on analogy to the basic rules of the Hanafite legal system and that *istiḥsān* can repeal this analogy by appealing to the *uṣūl*. In a similar vein Bābartī, *Sharḥ al-'Ināya*, vol. 7, p. 147.

33. Kāsānī, *Badā'i' aṣ-Ṣanā'i'*, vol. 4, p. 174; Marghīnānī, *al-Hidāya*, vol. 7, p. 147; Bābartī, *Sharḥ al-'Ināya*, vol. 7, p. 147.

34. It does not, in this respect, matter whether the rent consists of money, commodities or services. Qudūrī, *al-Kitāb*, vol. 2, p. 88 and Sarakhsī, *Mabsūṭ*, vol. 15, p. 137 do not mention services. Marghīnānī, *al-Hidāya*, vol. 7, pp. 148-9 states that what may not serve as a price in a contract of sale may still be a valid rent in a contract of tenancy. Bābartī, *Sharḥ al-'Ināya*, vol. 7, p. 149 and Qāḍīzādeh, *Natā'ij al-Afkār*, vol. 7, p. 149 make it clear that services are valid forms of rent.

35. Ṭaḥāwī, *Mukhtaṣar*, p. 133 still calls it *mā ājarahā*; Qudūrī, *al-Kitāb*, vol. 2, p. 98 and all jurists after him call the contractually fixed rent *musammā*; Sarakhsī, *Mabsūṭ*, vol. 15, p. 140; Kāsānī, *Badā'i' aṣ-*

Ṣanā'iʿ, vol. 4, p. 187.

36. Qudūrī, *al-Kitāb*, vol. 2, p. 96; Ṭāḥāwī, *Mukhtaṣar*, p. 128; Sarakhsī, *Mabsūṭ*, vol. 15, p. 100; Kāsānī, *Badā'iʿ aṣ-Ṣanā'iʿ*, vol. 4, pp. 201-3; Samarqandī, *Tuḥfat al-Fuqahā'*, vol. 2, p. 477.

37. Sarakhsī, *Mabsūṭ*, vol. 15, p. 160 and vol. 16, pp. 15, 16; Kāsānī, *Badā'iʿ aṣ-Ṣanā'iʿ*, vol. 4, p. 179; Marghīnānī, *al-Hidāya*, vol. 7, p. 157; Bābartī, *Sharḥ al-ʿInāya*, vol. 7, pp. 157-8, 159; Qāḍīzādeh, *Natā'ij al-Afkār*, vol. 7, p. 157.

38. Qudūrī, *al-Kitāb*, vol. 2, p. 104; Ṭāḥāwī, *Mukhtaṣar*, p. 128; Samarqandī, *Tuḥfat al-Fuqahā'*, vol. 2, p. 477; Kāsānī, *Badā'iʿ aṣ-Ṣanā'iʿ*, vol. 4, p. 204; Marghīnānī, *al-Hidāya*, vol. 7, p. 157; Bābartī, *Sharḥ al-ʿInāya*, vol. 7, p. 157.

39. Qudūrī, *al-Kitāb*, vol. 2, p. 96; Ṭaḥāwī, *Mukhtaṣar*, p. 128; Sarakhsī, *Mabsūṭ*, vol. 15, p. 108; Samarqandī, *Tuḥfat al-Fuqahā'*, vol. 2, p. 477; Kāsānī, *Badā'iʿ aṣ-Ṣanā'iʿ*, vol. 4, pp. 201-3; Marghīnānī, *al-Hidāya*, vol. 7, p. 152; Qāḍīzādeh, *Natā'ij al-Afkār*, vol. 7, pp. 152-5; Bābartī, *Sharḥ al-ʿInāya*, vol. 7, pp. 152, 154, 155. On the other hand, if the contract of *ijāra* is used to employ salaried labour, the employer pays at the end of the contractual period unless otherwise specified in the contract, see Qudūrī, *al-Kitāb*, vol. 2, pp. 96-7; Kāsānī, *Badā'iʿ aṣ-Ṣanā'iʿ*, vol. 4, p. 204.

40. On political *force majeure* see Bābartī, *Sharḥ al-ʿInāya*, vol. 7, p. 157; on natural *force majeure* Qudūrī, *al-Kitāb*, vol. 2, p. 104; Sarakhsī, *Mabsūṭ*, vol. 16, p. 6; Samarqandī, *Tuḥfat al-Fuqahā'*, vol. 2, p. 480; Kāsānī, *Badā'iʿ aṣ-Ṣanā'iʿ*, vol. 4, p. 196; on *ghaṣb* see Qudūrī, *al-Kitāb* vol. 2, p. 104; Samarqandī, *Tuḥfat al-Fuqahā'*, vol. 2, p. 480; Marghīnānī, *al-Hidāya*, vol. 7, pp. 158, 220; Bābartī, *Sharḥ al-ʿInāya*, vol. 7, pp. 157, 158, 220. Qāḍīkhān, *Kitāb al-Fatāwā*, vol. 2, p. 339 states that if *force majeure* (*āfa*) makes it impossible for the tenant to use the land before he sows the corn, no rent is due. He quotes two legal traditions concerning the tenant's obligation to pay rent if *force majeure* makes it impossible for him to use the land after the cereals are growing. These traditions are ascribed to Shaibānī. According to the first one, the tenant has to pay the full rent. According to the second, the tenant should apply to the *qāḍī* in order to seek redress. According to Qāḍīkhān, the *fatwā* should follow the following solution: the tenant pays no rent after *force majeure* made it impossible for him to use the land unless it is possible for him to grow a second crop of comparable effect on the arable land. From the cases that Qāḍīkhān discusses in this respect it is obvious that the tenant has to apply to the *qāḍī* for the dissolution of the contract. This opinion is in accordance with the legal opinion held by the other authors quoted above. See also ibid., vol. 2, pp. 287, 290.

41. Marghīnānī, *al-Hidāya*, vol. 7, p. 147; Ṭaḥāwī, *Mukhtaṣar*, p. 128: 'for every part of the time of the *ijāra* that has gone, he takes his *ujra* from him'; Samarqandī, *Tuḥfat al-Fuqahā'*, vol. 2, p. 477: '*li-anna l-ujrata tumlaku ʿalā ḥasabi milki l-manāfiʿi sāʿat*^{un}*, fa-sāʿat*^{un}'; Kāsānī, *Badā'iʿ aṣ-Ṣanā'iʿ*, vol. 4, pp. 201-2: '*fa-kāna yanbaghī an yajiba ʿalaihi taslīmu l-ujrati sāʿat*^{an} *fa-sāʿat*^{an}'; Qāḍīkhān, *Kitāb al-Fatāwa*, vol. 2, p. 280: '... *li-anna l-ijārata tanʿaqidu sāʿat*^{an} *fa-sāʿat*^{an}

ʿalā ḥasabi ḥudūthi l-manfaʿati fa-ṣaḥḥati l-ijāratu fīmā baqiya mina l-mudda . . .'; Marghīnānī, *al-Hidāya*, vol. 7, p. 159; Bābartī, *Sharḥ al-ʿInāya*, vol. 7, p. 159. Another stock phrase is: 'Truly, the use comes into being piece by piece' ('*fa-inna l-manāfiʿa kānat taḥduthu shaiʾan fa-shaiʾan*'), see Sarakhsī, *Mabsūṭ*, vol. 15, pp. 75, 132; Kāsānī, *Badāʾiʿ aṣ-Ṣanāʾiʿ*, vol. 4, pp. 179, 181, 194, 195, 201, 202; Marghīnānī, *al-Hidāya*, vol. 7, p. 154; Bābartī, *Sharḥ al-ʿInāya*, vol. 7, p. 154.

42. Sarakhsī, *Mabsūṭ*, vol. 15, pp. 96, 132; Bābartī, *Sharḥ al-ʿInāya*, vol. 8, p. 34 uses the same expression. See also Marghīnānī, *al-Hidāya*, vol. 8, p. 34 and Qāḍīkhān, *Kitāb al-Fatāwā*, vol. 3, p. 150.

43. Sarakhsī, *Mabsūṭ*, vol. 15, p. 96; Kāsānī, *Badāʾiʿ aṣ-Ṣanāʾiʿ*, vol. 4, pp. 195-6.

44. Schacht, *Introduction*, p. 134.

45. Ṭaḥāwī, *Mukhtaṣar*, p. 128; Qudūrī, *al-Kitāb*, vol. 2, p. 105; Marghīnānī, *al-Hidāya*, vol. 7, p. 220; Bābartī, *Sharḥ al-ʿInāya*, vol. 7, p. 220. Protective measures against this danger are taken by the jurists, Kāsānī, *Badāʾiʿ aṣ-Ṣanāʾiʿ*, vol. 4, pp. 222-3; Qāḍīkhān, *Kitāb al-Fatāwā*, vol. 2, p. 268, see note 12 above.

46. Under a valid contract of *ijāra* it is always the *musammā* that falls due. Only under a voidable contract of *ijāra* is it possible to pay less than the contractually fixed rent, see Khaṣṣāf, *Kitāb Aḥkām al-Awqāf*, p. 206; Ṭaḥāwī, *Mukhtaṣar*, p. 133; Qudūrī, *al-Kitāb*, vol. 2, p. 98; Sarakhsī, *Mabsūṭ*, vol. 15, pp. 85, 101, 138, 140, 149; Kāsānī, *Badāʾiʿ aṣ-Ṣanaʾiʿ*, vol. 4, p. 201. See also pp. 177, 187, 191, 195, 207, 217-8; Samarqandī, *Tuḥfat al-Fuqahāʾ* vol. 2, p. 489; Marghīnānī, *al-Hidāya*, vol. 7, p. 175; Bābartī, *Sharḥ al-ʿInāya*, vol. 7, p. 175; Qāḍīzādeh, *Natāʾij al-Afkār*, vol. 7, pp. 174-5.

47. Chehata, *Théorie générale*, p. 133; Jazīrī, *Kitāb al-Fiqh ʿalā al-Madhāhib al-Arbaʿa*, 6th edn (Beirut, n.d.), vol. 3, pp. 114, 119-20.

48. Khaṣṣāf, *Kitāb Aḥkām al-Awqāf*, p. 205.

49. Kāsānī, *Badāʾiʿ aṣ-Ṣanāʾiʿ*, vol. 4, p. 200.

50. Abū Yūsuf, *Kitāb al-Kharāj*, p. 138.

51. Khaṣṣāf, *Kitāb Aḥkām al-Awqāf*, p. 205; Sarakhsī, *Mabsūṭ*, vol. 15, pp. 132, 151; Kāsānī, *Badāʾiʿ aṣ-Ṣanāʾiʿ*, vol. 4, p. 181; Marghīnānī, *al-Hidāya*, vol. 7, p. 150; Bābartī, *Sharḥ al-ʿInāya*, vol. 7, p. 150; Qāḍīkhān, *Kitāb al-Fatāwā*, vol. 3, p. 330 gives a full list of the historical authorities which is largely reproduced in Ṭarābulsī, *al-Isʿaf fī Aḥkām al-Awqāf*, reprint edn (Beirut, 1401 A.H./1981 A.D.), p. 68. He refers among other jurists to Abū Hifṣ al-Bukhārī (ninth century), Abū Laith (died in 393 A.H./1003 A.D.) and ʿAlī as-Sughdī (eleventh century).

52. For voidable contracts see J. Chitty, *On Contracts*, 25th edn (Sweet & Maxwell, London, 1983), vol. 1 (General Principles), secs. 14-7, pp. 13-15. I owe the reference to Professor Dieter Giesen (Berlin). The term is used here in a less technical meaning to denote contracts that are not valid but also not without legal effects.

53. Samarqandī, *Tuḥfāt al-Fuqahāʾ*, vol. 2, p. 487; compare Sarakhsī, *Mabsūṭ*, vol. 16, p. 32 and Kāsānī, *Badāʾiʿ aṣ-Ṣanāʾiʿ*, vol. 4, p. 218.

54. Qudūrī, *al-Kitāb*, vol. 2, p. 95; Sarakhsī, *Mabsūṭ*, vol. 16,

pp. 34 ff; Kāsānī, *Badāʾiʿ aṣ-Ṣanāʾiʿ*, vol. 4. p. 195; Chehata, *Théorie générale*, pp. 127-8, 130-4.

55. Schacht, *Introduction*, p. 121, see also p. 163; Chehata, *Théorie générale*, pp. 127-8, 130-4; Chehata, *Etudes de droit musulman*, vol. 2: *La notion de responsabilité contractuelle. La concept de propriété* (Presses Universitaires de France, Paris, 1973), pp. 36-9.

56. Ṭaḥāwī, *Mukhtaṣar*, p. 133; Qudūrī, *al-Kitāb*, vol. 2, p. 103; Sarakhsī, *Mabsūṭ*, vol. 15, p. 104: '*fa-kamā anna l- manfaʿata tataqauwamu bi-l-ʿaqdi l-jāʾizi fa-kadhālika bi-l-ʿaqdi l-fāsid*'; see also p. 138 and vol. 11, p. 73; Samarqandī, *Tuḥfat al-Fuqahāʾ*, vol. 2, p. 489; Kāsānī, *Badāʾiʿ aṣ-Ṣanāʾiʿ*, vol. 4, pp. 177, 184: '*li-anna l-manāfiʿa ʿalā aṣli ashābinā lā tuḍmanu illā bi-l-ʿaqdi ṣ-ṣaḥiḥi awi l-fāsid*'; see also pp. 178, 195, 207, 218; Marghīnānī, *al-Hidāya*, vol. 7, p. 175; Bābartī, *Sharḥ al-ʿInāya*, vol. 7, p. 175; Qāḍīzādeh, *Natāʾij al-Afkār*, vol. 7, pp. 174-5.

57. Because the object sold is always a commodity whose value — if not established by the contractually fixed price — is established through reference to the general price level of comparable commodities.

58. Kāsānī, *Badāʾiʿ aṣ-Ṣanāʾiʿ*, vol. 4, pp. 195, 217, 218; Qāḍīzādeh, *Natāʾij al-Afkār*, vol. 7, p. 175 with reference to *adh-dhakhīra* and to the *fatāwā* of Qāḍīkhān.

59. Sarakhsī, *Mabsūṭ*, vol. 15, pp. 85, 101, 138, 140, 149.

60. Schacht, *Introduction*, p. 154.

61. Kāsānī, *Badāʾiʿ aṣ-Ṣanāʾiʿ*, vol. 4, p. 218, see ibid., p. 184; see also Qudūrī, *al-Kitāb*, vol. 2, p. 103; Samarqandī, *Tuḥfat al-Fuqahāʾ*, vol. 2, pp. 479, 489; Marghīnānī, *al-Hidāya*, vol. 7, pp. 175, 191; Bābartī, *Sharḥ al-ʿInāya*, vol. 7, pp. 175, 191.

62. Qāḍīzādeh, *Natāʾij al-Afkār*, vol. 7, pp. 174-5, 191, correctly points out that many jurists tend to assign the lower of the two rentals if there is a difference between the *musammā* and the *ujrat al-mithl.*

63. Qāḍīkhān, *Kitāb al-Fatawā*, vol. 2, pp. 276, 301.

64. Ibid., vol. 2, p. 281, vol. 3, pp. 331, 335. Whether the payment of the 'fair rent' falls due retroactively is not always clear. Vol. 2, p. 281 is not quite clear. Page 282 seems to suggest a solution following the line of Kāsānī, *Badāʾiʿ aṣ-Ṣanāʾiʿ*, see above note 49. Vol. 3, pp. 331 and 336 seems to suggest a retroactive payment of the 'fair rent'.

65. Qudūrī, *al-Kitāb*, vol. 2, p. 189; Sarakhsī, *Mabsūṭ*, vol. 15, pp. 57, 73, 74-5; Samarqandī, *Tuḥfāt al-Fuqahāʾ*, vol. 3, p. 111; Marghīnānī, *al-Hīdāya*, vol. 7, pp. 367-9; Bābartī, *Sharḥ al-ʿInāya*, vol. 7, pp. 368-9; Qāḍīzādeh, *Natāʾij al-Afkār*, vol. 7, p. 368.

66. Qudūrī, *al-Kitāb*, vol. 2, p. 189; Sarakhsī, *Mabsūṭ*, vol. 11, pp. 73-4; Samarqandī, *Tuḥfāt al-Fuqahāʾ*, vol. 3, p. 111; Marghīnānī, *al-Hidāya*, vol. 7, pp. 368-9; Bābartī, *Sharḥ al-ʿInāya*, vol. 7, pp. 368-9.

67. Khaṣṣāf, *Kitāb Aḥkām al-Awqāf*, pp. 240-3.

68. Sarakhsī, *Mabsūṭ*, vol. 11, pp. 73-6, vol. 23, p. 73; Marghīnānī, *al-Hidāya*, vol. 7, pp. 368, 369, 370; Bābartī, *Sharḥ al-ʿInāya*, vol. 7, pp. 369-70.

69. Sarakhsī, *Mabsūṭ*, vol. 15, pp. 138, 148; Kāsānī, *Badāʾiʿ aṣ-Ṣanāʾiʿ*, vol. 4, p. 187; Qāḍīkhān, *Kitāb al-Fatāwā*, vol. 3, pp. 171,

179, 180, see also vol. 2, pp. 279, 280.

70. Khaṣṣāf, *Kitāb Aḥkām al-Awqāf*, pp. 240, 241-2; Qudūrī, *al-Kitāb*, vol. 2, pp. 192-3; Sarakhsī, *Mabsūṭ*, vol. 11, pp. 49-50, 68-9; Samarqandī, *Tuḥfāt al-Fuqahā*, vol. 3, p. 111; Qāḍīzādeh, *Natā'ij al-Afkār*, vol. 7, p. 368; Kāsānī, *Badā'iᶜ aṣ-Ṣanā'iᶜ*, vol. 4, pp. 213, 216; Marghīnānī, *al-Hidāya*, vol. 7, pp. 369-70, 383-4, 388; Bābartī, *Sharḥ al-ᶜInāya*, vol. 7, pp. 369-70, 383-4, 388.

71. Kāsānī, *Badā'iᶜ aṣ-Ṣanā'iᶜ*, vol. 4, p. 213.

72. Ṭaḥāwī, *Mukhtaṣar*, p. 118; Sarakhsī, *Mabsūṭ*, vol. 11, p. 79; Samarqandī, *Tuḥfat al-Fuqahā'*, vol. 2, p. 112: '*inna l-manāfiᶜa lā tuḍmanu bil-ghaṣbi wa-l-itlāf*'; Kāsānī, *Badā'iᶜ aṣ-Ṣanā'iᶜ*, vol. 4, pp. 184, 213; Marghīnānī, *al-Hidāya*, vol. 7, pp. 173, 396; Bābartī, *Sharḥ al-ᶜInāya*, vol. 7, p. 173: '*wa-yajibu ᶜalaihi ḍamānu mā naqaṣa wa-saqaṭa l-ajru li-anna l-ajra wa-ḍ-ḍamān lā yajtamiᶜān idh al-ajru yastalzimu ᶜadma t-taᶜaddī wa-n-nuqṣānu yastalzimuhu. wa-tanāfi l-lawāzimi yadullu ᶜalā tanāfi l-malzūmāt*'. See also note 56.

73. Sarakhsī, *Mabsūṭ*, vol. 15, pp. 109, 110; Kāsānī, *Badā'iᶜ aṣ-Ṣanā'iᶜ*, vol. 4, pp. 173, 201, 218; Bābartī, *Sharḥ al-ᶜInāya*, vol. 7, pp. 147, 394; Marghīnānī, *al-Hidāyā*, vol. 7, p. 394; Qāḍīzādeh, *Natā'ij al-Afkār*, vol. 7, p. 394.

74. Kāsānī, *Badā'iᶜ aṣ-Ṣanā'iᶜ*, vol. 4, p. 206. See also Sarakhsī, *Mabsūṭ*, vol. 15, pp. 78-9.

75. Kāsānī, *Badā'iᶜ aṣ-Ṣanā'iᶜ*, vol. 4, p. 206.

76. Sarakhsī, *Mabsūṭ*, vol. 15, pp. 78-9.

77. Ibid., vol. 23, p. 100.

78. This method of calculation is ascribed by Bābartī, *Sharḥ al-ᶜInāya*, vol. 7, p. 370 to Naṣīr b. Yaḥyā, a ninth-century jurist from Balkh.

79. Sarakhsī, *Mabsūṭ*, vol. 23, p. 100.

80. For the importance of the *ẓāhir ar-riwāya* for the Hanafite legal tradition and the six books of Shaibānī as the incorporation of this *ẓāhir ar-riwāya*, see Ibn ᶜĀbidīn, *Radd al-Muḥtār*, vol. 1, pp. 51-2.

81. Qāḍīkhān, *Kitāb al-Fatāwā*, vol. 2, p. 281, see also vol. 3, pp. 331, 336. Other instances of legal reasoning that ascribe identical effects to an *ijāra fāsida* and to *ghaṣb* are ascribed to Ismāᶜīl az-Zāhid, see ibid., vol. 3, pp. 160, 168.

82. Ibid., vol. 2, pp. 267, 294: '*la ajra lahu ᶜalā l-ghāṣib*'.

83. Ibid., p. 281.

84. Ibid., pp. 270, 280, 281, 283, 296, 300, 302, 306.

3

The Share-cropping Contract (al-Muzāraʿa): Combining Dependent Labour with the Means of Production

1. A CONTRACT FOR SOWING, NOT FOR PLANTING

The *muzāraʿa* is a share-cropping contract that legally entitles proprietors to collect rent from the cultivators of their fields. It serves as a legal basis for the productive use of lands whose proprietors are not willing or able to till their land through their own work or through salaried labour or slaves. As the name suggests and as Kāsānī puts it: '... under this contract one may sow but not plant' (*li anna d-dākhila taḥta l-ʿaqdi z-zarʿu lā al-ghars*).[1] The planting of trees is regulated under a different contract, called *al-muʿāmala* or *al-musāqāt*, which differs in many respects from the share-cropping contract (*al-muzāraʿa*) and which will not detain us here because we are concerned with the legal ordinances concerning the rent that proprietors collect from the cultivators of their fields. The *muzāraʿa* contract serves mainly as a legal basis for the cultivation of cereal-producing lands, although some jurists recognise its use as the contractual basis for the collection of rent on lands producing various kinds of summer crops.[2] The share-cropping contract (*muzāraʿa*) is valid only if the lands leased are suitable to be used for the growing of crops and if no trees and plantations are already being grown on them.[3] The sprouting seed of crops (*baql*), however, is no obstacle to a valid *muzāraʿa* contract because the work of growing the crop has still to be performed.[4]

2. THE ORIGINS OF THE SHARE-CROPPING CONTRACT

As Morony and Ziaul Haque have shown, share-cropping was a well-established practice in Iraq before Islam,[5] and as a fiscal practice, it was also widely spread in the Byzantine Empire.[6] In Iraq it was mainly practised on state lands (where the difference between tax and rent was largely obscured),[7] on estates that were assigned by the rulers to private individuals[8] and on the land of religious communities.[9] Ziaul Haque has collected copious evidence for the fact that, during the first century of Islam, the *muzāraʿa* was mainly practised on lands that formed part of the public domain.[10] The writings of the jurists reflect this situation. The ninth-century Iraqi scholar, Khaṣṣāf, discusses the *muzāraʿa* as a means of cultivating the *arḍ al-ḥauz* (see 1.4 above), the estates that were assigned to private individuals by the ruler[11] and the *awqāf*, the pious foundations.[12] From the historical sources and the writings of the jurists it would appear that the contract was first used on state, *iqṭāʿ* and *waqf* lands and later found its way to other forms of landed property. This origin of the *muzāraʿa* may explain the fact that it establishes unequal and hierarchical relationships between the partners to the share-cropping contract.

3. THE OPPOSITION TO THE CONTRACT

Muzāraʿa is a share-cropping contract under whose provisions the rent is not a separate investment, but a part of the yield of agricultural production. The 'rent', therefore, never falls due before the seeds bear fruit and the corn is ripe. Apart from a share of the yield of agricultural production, the tenant is not required to pay an equivalent in money or in kind for the productive use of the land. Indeed, this form of contract does not even presuppose the existence of money. It can therefore be easily imposed on peasants conducting their economic relations within the framework of a subsistence economy.

In the eighth and early ninth centuries, the share-cropping contract (*muzāraʿa*) was strongly criticised on religious grounds. The most important argument used against this form of contract was based on an understanding of Islamic ethics and the Prophet's example which implied that a Muslim could enjoy economic benefits only from a piece of land he tilled, and not from one he could not till. This was expressed in the Prophet's saying: 'Till it or grant it free of charge to your brother' (*izraʿhā au imnaḥhā akhāka*).[13] The most prominent Muslim jurists of the eighth and early ninth centuries, such as Abū Ḥanīfa, Mālik b. Anas and Shāfiʿī, rejected the contract of the *muzāraʿa*. Abū Ḥanīfa insisted that, in accordance with the strict principle of Islamic law and ethics, no one may be made to work on the basis that his remuneration will consist of only part of the fruits of his labour.[14] He and other prominent jurists of the eighth and ninth centuries point out that the share-cropping contract (*muzāraʿa*) implies risk and gambling and is, for this reason, invalid.[15] The generation of Muslim jurists who created Islamic law as a specialised discipline and a literary genre condemned the *muzāraʿa* on the grounds that it violated religious, moral and legal principles. Mālik, Abū Ḥanīfa and Shāfiʿī made it clear that, with regard to arable lands, they considered only the contract of tenancy (*ijāra*) to be admissible.[16]

4. THE TECHNICAL LEGAL DIFFICULTIES OF THE CONTRACT

During the eighth century, the contract of *muzāraʿa* found prominent supporters among the jurists only in Iraq. Abū Yūsuf and Shaibānī as well as Thaurī (d. A.D. 778) declared it to be valid[17] and treated the Prophet's saying quoted against it as a purely moral exhortation having no legally binding character.[18] In legalising the contract of *muzāraʿa*, the Iraqi jurists faced the same difficulties as with the contract of *ijāra*: the share-cropping contract contradicted the basic principles drawn by analogical reasoning from the contract of sale, which were considered to be the basic principles of all bilateral, synallagmatic contracts. In the share-cropping contract the object sold, i.e. the productive use of arable lands and of human labour, does not exist at the time of the conclusion of the contract and is not considered to be a commodity representing a commodity value. In addition, the share-cropping contract (*muzāraʿa*) offers difficulties that do not exist with regard to the contract of tenancy (*ijāra*). At the time when the partners to a contract of tenancy conclude their agreement, the rent is existent, known and specified. It is a personal obligation that the tenant has to pay whether he tills the soil or not because it results from the fact that it is possible for him to use the land (see 2.5c and 2.6 above). Under the share-cropping contract (*muzāraʿa*), the rent is a share of the crop. It is, therefore, non-existent at the time of the conclusion of the contract. As the future yield of the agricultural labour is unknown, so is the rent. The agricultural labour may not yield any produce. The rent under the share-cropping contract (*muzāraʿa*) is an obligation *in re*, which means that, if the agricultural production does not produce a crop, there can be no claim to a rent. Therefore, at the time when the partners to a *muzāraʿa* conclude the share-cropping contract, the rent is non-existent (*maʿdūm*), unknown (*majhūl*) and may never exist.

The Hanafite jurists treat the problems that arise from considering the use of land and human labour to be commodities along the same lines as analysed above (see 2.4-10) with regard to the contract of tenancy. That is to say, that the share-cropping contract (*muzāraʿa*) transforms the use of land and labour into commodities, assigns value to them and warrants them against damage.[19] The jurists acknowledge that, with regard to the rent, the share-cropping contract contradicts all forms of analogical reasoning (*qiyās*) drawn from the basic principles of bilateral, synallagmatic contracts.[20] As in the case of the contract of tenancy (*ijāra*), they declare the share-cropping contract (*muzāraʿa*) to be valid on the basis of *istiḥsān*, i.e. of admitting for practical purposes legal solutions that openly contradict conclusions drawn on the basis of analogical reasoning from the basic rules of the Hanafite legal system. They base this *istiḥsān* on a report about the Prophet according to which he concluded a share-cropping contract with the Jewish people of the oasis of Khaibar.[21] Sarakhsī adds a practical argument: labour and the means of production may be divided among several persons and would remain idle if not combined through the share-cropping contract.[22] But the main argument which the Hanafite jurists adduce against their opponents and on which they base their *istiḥsān* is that the share-cropping contract is sanctioned by the 'recognised custom of people in all countries' (*ʿurfᵘⁿ ẓāhirᵘⁿ fī jamīʿi l-buldān*)[23] and that business practice (*taʿāmul*) is a valid reason for abandoning analogical reasoning.[24]

5. THE ADMISSIBLE COMBINATIONS OF LABOUR AND THE MEANS OF PRODUCTION

The Hanafite jurists' *istiḥsān* is based on the Prophet's example and general custom. The share-cropping contract can, therefore, only be legalised to the extent that it coincides with the Prophet's example and general business practice.[25] According to the jurists, this means that land, seed, work and cattle should be considered to be the four most important elements of the process of agricultural production and that, of these four elements, only two may legally be regarded as forming the object of the contract (*al-maʿqūd ʿalaihi*). They teach that the share-cropping contract begins as a contract of tenancy (*ijāra*) and ends as a partnership.[26] Because it begins as a special contract of tenancy based on *istiḥsān* and limited in its application to the rules set by the Prophet's example and by general business practice, the objects leased under the share-cropping contract (*muzāraʿa*) may be either land or labour. Either the labourer leases the land or the proprietor of the land leases the labourer.[27] The other two means of production, i.e. seed and cattle, may be combined with land and labour. But separately they may never become the object of a legally valid share-cropping contract.[28] Only three combinations of the four elements, that together constitute the process of agricultural production, are regarded as legally valid: (A) partner A contributes land and seed, partner B contributes work and cattle to the *muzāraʿa*, (B) partner A contributes land to the *muzāraʿa*, partner B work, cattle and seed, (C) partner A contributes work to the *muzāraʿa*, partner B land, seed and cattle.[29]

According to the jurists, in combination (A) the owner of the land and the seed hires the worker and his cattle, in combination (B) the labourer who owns seed and cattle is the leaseholder of the land, and in combination (C) the land owner who also contributes seed and cattle to the *muzāraʿa*, hires the labourer.[30] In all three cases, the share-cropping contract (*muzāraʿa*) begins as a contract of *ijāra*, in which one partner to the contract hires the use of the other partner's land or labour, and ends as a *sharika* with both of the partners sharing in the crop.

6. THE COMMERCIAL UNDERSTANDING OF THE PROCESS OF AGRICULTURAL PRODUCTION: THE TRANSFORMATION OF THE ELEMENTS OF PEASANTS' MUTUAL HELP INTO COMMODITIES

The jurists base their *istiḥsān* on the Prophet's example, general custom and the practical need for combining the means of production with labour. Their interpretation of the Prophet's example is rejected by Abū Ḥanīfa who insists that the agreement between the Prophet and the people of Khaibar was an instance of the Prophet's fiscal policy imposing the *kharāj muqāsama* on a subject population and not a model for a share-cropping contract.[31] And the very compendia of the Hanafite jurists make it clear that the reduction of the combination of labour and the means of production to only three legally valid forms is not justifiable on the grounds that the means of production would otherwise remain idle or that the general custom in all countries allows only these three legally valid forms.

In fact, Transoxanian authors like Sarakhsī and Qāḍīkhān constantly refer to other ways of combining labour with the means of production. These ways of combining labour with the means of production clearly represent the usages of a peasant society in which labour and the productive use of land were considered to be forms of mutual help and not commodities to be exchanged. The jurists explain these usages in terms of 'offering help'(*iʿāna*) or 'asking for help' (*istiʿāna*) if labour is used gratuitously,[32] of 'gratuitous lending' (*iʿāra*) if land is used free of charge,[33] and of 'gratuitous credit' (*qarḍ*) if seed is given free of charge and restored after harvesting.[34] These usages allow for the gratuitous use of land, labour and cattle but not, according to the jurists, of seed, because seed is a commodity that is consumed in the act of sowing and has to be replaced. The use of land, labour and cattle is no commodity, has no value of its own and must only be remunerated if it has become the object of a valid or voidable contract of share-cropping or tenancy. Otherwise it is regarded as 'gratuitous lending' of land or as 'offering help' through gratuitous labour. With regard to these usages, practically all combinations but not all ratios of sharing are permissible.[35] It is easy to see that these usages also lend themselves to exploitation, e.g. if the owners and administrators of large estates regard the work of peasants as gratuitous help or if a powerful man justifies his gratuitous use of peasants' land and labour as 'gratuitous lending' or help through labour. In fact, in many of the instances discussed by the jurists, the whole crop falls to one person,[36] and this may well reflect the situation of large estates and state lands.

But on the whole, there seems to be no reason to doubt that the gratuitous offering of labour, land and cattle as well as the 'credit' of seed reflect usages of a peasant society and have a social as well as an economic meaning. The share-cropping contract (*muzāraʿa*) transforms these elements of mutual help of a peasant society into commodities. It dissociates labour and the means of production from their social and political environment and meaning and treats them as purely economic elements, i.e. commodities. But the jurists also use the notions of 'offering help', 'gratuitous lending' and 'gratuitous credit' in order to declare permissible share-cropping contracts whose ratios of sharing do not follow the logic of commodity exchange and whose combination of labour and the means of production does not fit into one of the three legally valid combinations of labour and the means of production (see 3.5 above). In such instances, the usages of a peasant society are used as non-commercial elements that help to achieve a greater flexibility of the *muzāraʿa* contract.[37] By combining forms of mutual help of a peasant society with the three legally valid forms of *muzāraʿa*, the jurists declare legally permissible a great number of combinations of labour and the means of production. But they do not permit all ratios of sharing. Especially with regard to share-cropping arrangements between partners who jointly contribute some of the means of production, the jurists declare voidable all contracts whose ratio of sharing does not correspond to the distribution of the seed between the partners (see 3.8b below). By controlling the sharing of the crop, the jurists try to establish a hierarchical order among the means of production over labour. In a subtle way, they uphold their understanding of labour, seed, land and cattle as commodities in a commercialised system of exchange by controlling the sharing of the crop.

This commercial understanding of the process of agricultural production transforms the peasant into a 'proprietor' of labour and into a free partner to a contract. In those regions where, before Islam, the peasants under the share-cropping system were reduced to serfdom, the legal construction of the contract of share-cropping may have helped, as Ziaul Haque suggests,[38] to emancipate the peasant from the status of a tenant-serf.[39] To the degree that the jurists helped to spread this contract into regions that were not formerly part of a fiscal or commercial share-cropping system, this form of contract must have helped to legitimise the exploitation of the peasant's labour by those who owned or controlled the means of production. There can be little doubt, however, that Ziaul Haque is right in stressing the protective effects of a contractual system of share-cropping if compared to a fiscal or a tributary share-cropping system or a combination of both, such as was developed under Hanafite law after the tenth century.

7. UNEQUAL RELATIONS OF PRODUCTION

Under the *muzāraʿa* contract, the unequal distribution of the means of production must necessarily lead to an unequal and hierarchical relationship between the partners to the contract. The unequal relationship between the two partners resulting from combination (C) is obvious. The landless agricultural labourer or the small peasant who cannot live from his own land faces a partner who owns land, seed and cattle. Combination (B) must have worked in favour of the well-to-do peasant and wealthy landowner, who had enough cattle, seed and, according to the jurists, also salaried labourers and slaves,[40] to be able to use them as an investment in the *muzāraʿa* on peasants' land. The weaker partner in this case must have been the poor peasant having no cattle of his own. Only combination (A) allows for a balanced relationship between the two partners. In two out of the three valid combinations, the share-cropping contract creates an unequal and hierarchical relationship between the partners based on unequal access to the means of production.

8. ASSURING THE DOMINANCE OF THE MEANS OF PRODUCTION OVER LABOUR

A share-cropping contract (*muzāraʿa*) is valid if it fulfils six conditions. The partners to the contract must (1) specify the period of duration of the contract (*mudda*), (2) arrange for the separation (*takhliya*) between the land and its owner in a way that allows the working partner to till the soil without any direct, non-contractual interference by the landowner, (3) name the partner who contributes the seed (*ṣāḥib al-badhr*), (4) specify the kind of seed to be used, (5) specify the share of the crop or crops that falls due to the partner who does not contribute the seed, and (6) make sure that a partnership (*sharika*) with regard to the crop is established between the partners to the *muzāraʿa* contract. Any stipulation that leads to the dissolution of this partnership makes the share-cropping contract voidable.[41]

(a) Much as in the contract of tenancy (*ijāra*), the specification of the duration of the contract is justified on the grounds that it serves to define the value of the use of land or labour.[42] The second condition (*takhliya*) stipulates that the owner of the land delivers his land to the working partner and does not himself participate in the cultivation of the field. If the *takhliya*, the separation between the land and its owner, is not fulfilled, the contract of *muzāraʿa* is considered a voidable contract.[43] According to Qāḍīkhān, the contract is dissolved if the owner of the land works in his fields.[44] But the same author declares such a *muzāraʿa* to be valid, if it can be assumed that the owner who works in his own fields offers his help (*iʿāna*) or is asked by the working partner to give his help (*istiʿāna*).[45] Contrary to the conveyance of the land under the contract of tenancy (*ijāra*), the *takhliya* under the share-cropping contract does not imply that the cultivator has a free hand to treat the land as he sees fit. He may be bound to follow the contractual stipulations regarding the cultivation of the land imposed upon him by his partner if the work stipulated is of a quality that leads to an increase in the yield of agricultural production.[46] The tenant under a contract of tenancy (*ijāra*) may or may not use the land after it has been conveyed to him. The working partner under a share-cropping contract can be forced by the *qāḍī* to work and till the soil immediately after the land has been delivered to him.[47] In fact, it seems that under the contract of *muzāraʿa* the *takhliya* serves mainly as a necessary condition for the enforcement of the labour of the working partner in combinations (A) and (C) or as a means to secure the stronger partner's control over the land in combination (B).

The weaker partner in combinations (A) and (C) can be forced to work immediately after the conclusion of the contract and the conveyance of the land, whereas the owner of the seed can only be forced to work after the sowing of the seed. The *ẓāhir ar-riwāya*, the Hanafite legal tradition as embodied in the writings ascribed to Shaibānī, consistently defines work under the share-cropping contract as a production factor, i.e. as work that is necessary in order to produce the average amount (*muᶜtād*) of crops.[48] The working partner is under no obligation to perform labour that is not necessary in order to obtain the average yield[49] unless his partner stipulates this work in the contract.[50] Any stipulation of labour that constitutes a one-sided burden on the working partner to the exclusive advantage of the stronger partner is invalid. This holds true for all kinds of work whose effect would last longer than the contract of *muzāraᶜa* and would thereby constitute one-sided advantages for the non-working partner.[51] It also holds true for all kinds of work that have to be performed after the ripening of the crop. These tasks are not, according to the *ẓāhir ar-riwāya*, included among the duties of the working partner and cannot be the object of a share-cropping contract.[52] But many Hanafite jurists in Central Asia consider the work of harvesting, threshing, etc. to be included among the duties of the working partner.[53] It seems that the interest of early Hanafite law in defining labour as a production factor was gradually replaced by later jurists' interest in securing maximum advantages for the stronger partner.

On the other hand, the protection that the *ẓāhir ar-riwāya* grants to the working partner through defining labour as a production factor is effective only in short-term contracts of share-cropping. But jurists of Central Asia, such as Sarakhsī and Qāḍīkhān, discuss share-cropping contracts with terms ranging from five to 30 years.[54] Such a long-term *muzāraᶜa* is perfectly valid according to all Hanafite jurists who unanimously hold the opinion that the duration of the share-cropping (*muzāraᶜa*) should not, on the one hand, surpass the life expectancy of the partners to the contract and should not, on the other hand, be so short as not to allow the growing of a crop. But any duration of the contract that lies between this minimum and maximum period is legally valid.[55] This means that in combination (C), the dependency of the working partner could in fact last for a lifetime. In that case, his work could never produce effects that would last longer than the contract. He could legally be forced to do all agricultural work that would normally lead to an increase in the yield of the crop and, according to later jurists, all agricultural work that customarily has to be performed by the working partner. It is significant, I think, for the dependent status of the weaker partner to a *mu-*

zāraᶜa, that the jurists speak of the 'flight' (*hurūb*) of the working partner during the duration of the contract, an action which they carefully differentiate from his 'absence' (*ghaib*) after the end of the contract.[56] Under a long-term share-cropping contract, the peasant in combination (B) has to deliver his land to the stronger partner for a period of up to 30 years.[57] It is obvious that he thereby risks losing the ownership of his land. At the same time the jurists make it clear that, under a long-term share-cropping contract, the landowner's share of the crop may continually diminish.[58]

Contrary to the contract of tenancy, the valid share-cropping contract does not entitle the working partner to sublease the land in a *muzāraᶜa* unless the owner of the land in combinations (A) and (C) explicitly grants him this right.[59] In combination (B), the working partner, who also contributes seed and cattle, is entitled to sublease the land to a second working partner.[60] Again it is obvious that these legal ordinances are meant to strengthen the position of the partner who contributes most of the means of production to the *muzāraᶜa*.

(b) The hierarchical forms of the relations of production under the share-cropping contract (*muzāraᶜa*) are accentuated by the privileges granted to the owner of the seed. Quite naturally, the jurists stress the importance of the seed in agricultural production. Some jurists regard the seed as the capital in a partnership of work and capital.[61] Others try to justify the limitation of the legally valid combinations of labour and the means of production through a special theory according to which land and seed, on the one hand, and labour and cattle, on the other hand, are related species (*mutajānis*) because their nature causes a mutual reinforcement of their productive qualities. Therefore, the combination of elements that represent related species is legally valid and seed is considered to 'follow' the land, cattle is considered to 'follow' labour. To such a combination of related species a third means of production or labour may be added.[62]

In fact, the importance given to the seed may reflect older stages of agricultural production. But under the share-cropping contract it mainly serves as a symbol for the dominant position of the partner who contributes most of the means of production. The importance attributed to the contribution of seed is decisive for establishing an imbalance between the partners to the contract. Seed (just as cattle) can never be the object (*al-maʿqūd ʿalaihi*) of a share-cropping contract (*muzāraʿa*). Only in combination with land or labour is it recognised as a means of production that can legally form part of a share-cropping contract. In all three legally valid combinations of labour and the means of production it is used as an investment that indicates the dominant partner. As the jurists put it, it is always the owner of the seed who leases either land or labour.[63] Obviously, in two of the three legally valid combinations of labour and the means of production, i.e. combinations (B) and (C), the owner of the seed is the economically stronger partner who contributes most or all means of production. Through the special privileges conferred upon the owner of the seed, he also becomes the stronger partner in combination (A).

It is a natural fact that the owner of the seed decides which crop or crops[64] are to be cultivated under the share-cropping contract. But it is a social and legal fact that, in combination (B), the landowner is not entitled to ask for a guarantor to guarantee that the working partner will fulfill his duties, whereas in combinations (A) and (C) the landowner, who also contributes the seed, is entitled to ask for such a guarantor.[65] It is a social and legal, not a natural, fact that the contract is immediately binding for the partner who does not contribute the seed, whereas it is not binding for the owner of the seed.[66] In combinations (A) and (C) the working partner must prepare the soil for the sowing. The jurists expect him to plough the field, to dig irrigation ditches or to level the ground, if these tasks are necessary for the sowing of the seed and the growing of the crop.[67] If, after concluding the contract, the working partner refuses to execute such necessary work, the *qāḍī* may force him to work.[68]

For the owner of the seed, on the other hand, the contract of share-cropping (*muzāraʿa*) becomes binding only after the sowing of the seed. If he refuses to deliver the seed to the working partner after the ploughing of the field, the digging of the ditches and the levelling of the ground, the owner of the seed owes nothing to the working partner. This solution is justified by the following legal reasoning: the use of human labour has no value and is not warranted against damage except under a contract of tenancy (*ijāra*) or share-cropping (*muzāraʿa*). Before the sowing of the seed this contract is binding only for the working partner and not for the owner of the seed. Therefore the owner of the seed is under no legal obligation to pay a recompense to the working partner.[69] The owner of the seed may be religiously and morally obliged to pay the 'fair rent' to the labourer, but that is a matter between God and the owner of the seed and does not affect the legal solution.[70] In combinations (A) and (C), therefore, the contract of *muzāraʿa* before the sowing of the seed is a perfect legal basis for gratuitously exploiting peasant labour. At this stage the peasant who contributes labour (in combinations (A) and (C)) runs the risks of working without remuneration and the peasant who contributes only land to the *muzāraʿa* (combination (B)) runs the risk that his field will remain uncultivated because the stronger partner finds it more promising to invest his seed and cattle in other lands. Only after the sowing of the seed is the *muzāraʿa* contract equally binding for both partners.

The sixth condition for a valid share-cropping contract establishes the joint ownership of the partners with regard to the crop. The jurists leave the distribution of the shares of the crop to the stipulation of the partners to the contract.[71] In the case of partners who jointly contribute some of the means of production, Transoxanian authors, such as Sarakhsī and Qāḍīkhān, restrict this liberty of stipulation.[72] They base this restriction on a legal doctrine that is shared by all Hanafite jurists. According to this legal doctrine, a valid claim to a share in the crop may be based on one of two sources. One of these two sources is 'the growth of one's property' (*namāʾ milkihi*), the other one is the contract. The claim of the seed owner to a share in the crop is based on the fact that the crop is the result of the 'growth of his property'. In combinations (A) and (C) the claim of the working partner to a share in the crop is based only on the contract, as is the land owner's claim in combination (B).[73] Under a share-cropping contract between partners who jointly contribute some of the means of production, the difference between the two sources of a legally valid claim to a share in the crop has important legal consequences: it prohibits all stipulated ratios of sharing in the crop that do not correspond to the distribution of the seed among the partners. If the shares of the crop do not correspond to the contribution of land and cattle among the partners, the jurists try to legalise the stipulated ratios of sharing by explaining them in terms of 'offering gratuitous help' or 'gratuitous lending' of land.[74] But if the shares of the crop do not correspond to the distribution of the seed among the partners, the jurists declare the share-cropping contract to be voidable.[75]

Seed is considered to be the most important means of production.[76] It differs from land and cattle in that it cannot be used in the production process without being consumed. Seed being a commodity with a commodity value cannot, therefore, be offered gratuitously. If two partners jointly contribute the land to a share-cropping contract and the non-working partner contributes the seed, the partners are not allowed to stipulate an equal share in the crop. Such a stipulation makes the contract voidable and the whole crop falls to the partner who contributes land and seed. The working partner has a claim to the 'fair rent' (*ujrat al-mithl*) for his work and for his part of the land.[77] It is obvious that such a legal mechanism serves to dissolve forms of collective production, to create unequal relationships between the partners and to 'commercialise' the production process by considering the constituent elements of this process to be independent production factors that have to be remunerated according to their market value. The role of seed as the most important production factor serves as a means to restrict the autonomous application of the usages of mutual help among partners who jointly hold land and other means of production.

Under a valid *muzāraʿa* contract, in which none of the means of production is contributed jointly, the contributor of the seed of cereals enjoys a privileged position only with regard to the appropriation of straw. If the partners do not contractually stipulate the ratio of the shares of the straw, it falls to the owner of the seed because the straw is said to be the result of the 'growth of his property' and no contractual stipulation gives his partner a claim to it. On the other hand, it is impossible, according to the jurists, to insert a stipulation into the contract that gives the working partner, who did not contribute the seed, a claim to the whole yield of the straw. It is argued that the straw is the result of the growth of the seed owner's property and that no contractual stipulation can nullify his claim. The contractual claim can always be nullified if the contract is declared voidable, whereas the claim that results from the 'growth of one's property' can never be nullified.[78] The contract may support the claim that results from the 'growth of one's property'. It may, in the case of the straw, modify it. It can under no circumstances nullify it. At most, the working partner may have half of the straw if there is a contractual stipulation to this end.[79]

9. THE 'VOIDABLE' CONTRACT OF SHARE-CROPPING AND THE SEED OWNER'S DOMINANT POSITION

With regard to the voidable share-cropping contract (*muzāraʿa fāsida*), the teaching concerning the two sources of a legally valid claim to a share in the crop has the most important legal consequences. A contract becomes voidable (a) if it does not fulfil the six conditions mentioned above (3.8 above), and (b) if the combination of labour and the means of production does not follow the prescribed patterns of Hanafite law (3.5 above), and is not explainable in terms of 'gratuitous help' or 'gratuitous lending', (c) if partners who jointly contribute some of the means of production stipulate a ratio of sharing in the crop which does not correspond to their contribution of the seed (3.8 (b) above), and (d) if conditions are imposed on the labourer that serve solely the interest of the non-working partner (3.8 (a) above).[80] Under a voidable contract, the partner whose claim to a share in the yield of the crop is based only on the contractual stipulation loses the right to his share. The whole crop falls to the owner of the seed, because it is the result of the 'growth of his property'.[81] The partner with a contractual claim receives only the 'fair rent' (*ujrat al-mithl*) for his labour (combination (C)), for his labour and cattle (combination (A)) or for his land (combination (B)).[82] His claim to the 'fair rent' is based on the fact that land and labour were the objects of a voidable contract and, therefore, warranted against damage.[83]

The legal consequences of the voidable contract demonstrate that the teaching on the two sources of the legally valid claim to a share in the crop legitimises the dominance of the means of production over human labour. This is obvious with regard to the results of a voidable contract in combinations (A) and (C). It is impressively underlined by the jurists' special solution for a voidable contract in combination (B). The jurists stress the fact that in combination (A) and (C) it is the legal and the moral right (*yaṭību lahu*) of the partner who contributes land and seed to consume the whole yield of the crop after paying the 'fair rent' to the weaker partner.[84] In combination (B) the appropriation of the whole crop is the legal right of the partner who contributes seed, cattle and labour because the crop is the 'growth of his property'. Morally, however, he is not entitled to consume the whole crop (*wa-l-khāriju kulluhu lā yaṭību lahu*). It is his moral right to appropriate that amount of the crop which corresponds to the value of his seed and of the 'fair rent' that he paid to the owner of the land. The rest of the crop, according to the jurists, should be distributed as alms, 'because', as Kāsānī has it, 'even if it were the produce of his own seed it [was grown] on someone else's land under a voidable contract, so that it is possible to suspect it of being a dirty gain and therefore, the [correct] way is to distribute it as alms.'[85]

Obviously, the appropriation of gains that are legally acquired under a voidable contract may cause moral reprehensions. But in this respect, the use of land differs from that of human labour. Under a voidable contract of share-cropping, the use of land is morally reprehensible, the use of human labour is not. Under a voidable contract, the partner who contributes only his labour has neither a legal nor a moral claim to a share in the crop. The partner who contributes labour, seed and cattle acquires a legal claim to the appropriation of the crop under a voidable contract, but is not morally entitled to consume the crop. Only the partner who contributes seed and land or seed, land and cattle enjoys the legal and the moral right to appropriate the whole crop. Law and morality support the dominance of the means of production over labour.

10. QĀḌĪKHĀN'S NEW CONCEPT OF RENT

In discussing share-cropping relationships that are not based on a *muzāraʿa* contract, Qāḍīkhān introduces elements of a new doctrine on rent that, in later centuries, came to have a long-lasting and far-reaching influence on Hanafite law. He states that his teacher differentiates between lands that are held by their owners for the sole purpose of cultivating them through a share-cropping relationship and other lands that are not held for this purpose. He calls the first type of land 'lands that are held in order to be given over to share-croppers' (*al-arḍ al-muʿadda li-dafʿihā muzāraʿat^{an}*). It is obvious that this land is held by its owners in order to appropriate a rent in kind. According to Qāḍīkhān's teacher, every use of the 'lands that are held in order to be given over to share-croppers' should be regarded as establishing a share-cropping relationship between the user and the owner, even if no share-cropping contract has been concluded. This legal ordinance is subject to the condition that the share of the working peasant is fixed by custom and does not change.[86] Qāḍīkhān stresses that this legal ordinance does not apply to other forms of landed property.[87]

To the best of my knowledge, this is the first instance of legal reasoning suggesting that the contract is not a necessary condition of the obligation to pay rent. This type of legal reasoning clearly differentiates between the landed property of the rentier class and other forms of landed property. It amounts to saying that anyone who uses the landed property of a rentier enters into a share-cropping relationship with him, whereas anyone who uses the landed property of a peasant is *ghāṣib*, a person who makes unauthorised use of the land and does not have to pay rent. The rentier has a 'natural' claim to the rent that results from the fact that he holds his property for the sole purpose of appropriating rent. Therefore, his claim to rent is valid without a contractual basis. Qāḍīkhān applies the concept that gives a privileged legal position to the rentier's land also to urban real estate (*al-muʿadd li-l-istighlāl*).[88] But he is far from drawing all the logical and legal conclusions from this concept that, in later centuries, were to be incorporated into the Hanafite doctrine on rent. He knew that the privileged legal position granted to the rentier's property contradicted all analogical reasoning drawn from the pre-classical and classical traditions of the Hanafite school. He, therefore, based it on *istiḥsān*. He stated that the solution presupposes that the share of the labourer is fixed by custom and does not change. And he also made it dependent on the social standing and the intention of the person who makes unauthorised use of the land: 'If it is known', said Qāḍīkhān, 'that he cultivated it in an unauthorised way, for example if the cultivator admitted during the cultivation [of the field] that he cultivated it on his own account and not as part of a share-cropping [relationship], or if the man does not belong to those [social groups] who hold land under a share-cropping [relationship] and if he proudly refuses to do so, then he is considered to be a person who makes unauthorised use, the yield is [all] his and he is under the obligation [to pay the recompense for] the diminution of the value of the land. The same holds true if he admits after cultivating [the field] and says: I made unauthorised use [of the land] when I cultivated [the field]' (*fa-in ʿulima annahu zaraʿahā ghaṣb^un bi-an aqarra z-zāriʿu ʿinda z-zarʿi annahu yazraʿuhā li-nafsihi lā ʿala l-muzāraʿa au kāna r-rajulu mimman lā yaʾkhudhu l-arḍa muzāraʿat^an wa-yaʾnafu ʿan dhālika yakūna ghāṣib^un wa-yakūnu l-khāriju lahu wa-ʿalaihi nuqṣānu l-arḍ. wa-kadhā lau aqarra baᶜdamā zaraᶜa wa-qāla zaraᶜtu ghaṣb^an^).*[89]

In the work of Qāḍīkhān the concept of a privileged position of the rentier's landed property is still of minor importance. It is applicable only to a *muzāraᶜa* and subordinate to the condition that a general and unchanging custom fixes the labourer's share. It also presupposes the willingness of the labourer to enter into a share-cropping relationship and his being of an appropriate social status. It is true that Qāḍīkhān refers to jurists who apparently applied this principle in a more general way with regard to the *waqf* land and orphans' landed property, but Qāḍīkhān himself apparently does not yet consider this legal opinion to be binding for the mufti because, as he says, it contradicts the *ẓāhir ar-riwāya*, the literary Hanafite legal tradition.[90] Qāḍīkhān also applies the concept of giving privileged legal status to the rentier's property (*muᶜadd li-l-istighlāl*) to tenancy relationships concerning urban real assets. But again the application of the concept is not general and systematic. It remains restricted to individual instances. The general picture that emerges from Qāḍīkhān's *fatāwā* is that the concept of privileged legal status of the rentier's property was largely acknowledged among Hanafite jurists in Central Asia during the twelfth century and that its application started to gain ground, but that it was not yet systematically applied to all instances concerning the rentier's property and that the muftis were not yet obliged to follow this concept. When, in later centuries, Hanafite jurists in the Ottoman Empire systematically applied this principle, they contributed to diminishing the importance of the contractual element in tenancy and share-cropping relationships and helped to give a tributary character to the rent that made it largely impossible to differentiate between peasants' taxes and their rent.

11. A COMPARISON BETWEEN *IJĀRA* AND *MUZĀRAʿA*

It should be clear from the discussion of the *muzāraᶜa* above (3.1-9) that the status of the peasant who contributes only labour or land in the *muzāraᶜa* is much worse than the status of the tenant under a contract of tenancy (*ijāra*). With regard to the cultivation of the fields, the working partner is bound to follow, up to a certain degree, the stipulations inserted into the contract by the stronger partner. Before the sowing of the seed, the contract is unilaterally binding for the peasant who invests only labour and land. The labour that he performs at this time is lost to him, if the stronger partner decides not to deliver the seed to him. The land that he may deliver to the stronger partner in combination (B) may not be cultivated at all in that year and he may remain without any rent. The peasant who contributes only labour can be forced to work during the whole duration of the contract. Under a long-term *muzāraʿa* he may be forced to perform dependent labour throughout his life. He is not entitled to sublease the land unless the stronger partner explicitly grants him this right. The peasant who contributes only his land may, under a long-term *muzāraʿa,* lose the control of his land for decades. The sharing of the crop is largely determined by the distribution of the means of production between the partners to the contract. In addition, the Hanafite jurists teach that two sources for a valid claim to a share in the crop exist. The source of the peasant's claim, who contributes only land or labour, is the contract. The source of the economically stronger partner's claim is his ownership of the seed. Under all voidable share-cropping contracts, the owner of the seed, who is always the economically stronger partner, has a claim to the whole crop.

The concept of the privileged position of the rentier's property — apart from being the result of social and economic developments — seems to be a radical application of the principle of the two sources for a valid claim to a share in the crop. It makes the rentier's ownership of the means of production the source of a non-contractual claim to the rent. Under all conditions, the peasant who contributes only land or labour to the *muzāraʿa* is clearly in a dependent position *vis-à-vis* the stronger partner. In the Mamluk and Ottoman periods the peasant ceases to be regarded as a *kharāj* payer and an owner of landed property. He is more and more considered to be a share-cropper (*muzāriʿ*) on state, *iqṭāʿ* (*tīmār*) and *waqf* lands and on the private landed property of rentiers.

NOTES

1. Kāsānī, *Kitāb Badāʾiʿ aṣ-Ṣanāʾiʿ fī Tartīb ash-Sharāʾiʿ* (Cairo, 1328 A.H./910 A.D.), vol. 6. p. 177; see also Sarakhsī, *Kitāb al-*

Mabsūṭ, reprint edn (Beirut, n.d.), vol. 23, p. 86: '*wa-laisa lahu an yaghrisa fīhā karam*[an] *wa-lā shajar*[an] *... wa-ʿamalu l-gharsi ghairu ʿamali z-zirāʿati fa-t-tafāwutu bainahumā fī l-arḍi fāḥish*'. See ibid., p. 88. But it is obvious from Sarakhsī, ibid., pp. 41, 53, 61 that often contracts of *muʿāmala* and *muzāraʿa* were combined, especially under long-term contracts.

2. Ibid., vol. 23. pp. 41, 65; Qāḍīkhān, *Kitāb al-Fatāwā al-Khānīya* (Cairo, 1282 A.H.), vol. 3, p. 153. But see Qudūrī, *al-Kitāb*, printed on the margin of al-Ghanīmī, *al-Lubāb fī Sharḥ al-Kitāb*, reprint edn (Beirut, 1400 A.H./1980 A.D.), vol. 2, p. 234 and Samarqandī, *Tuḥfat al-Fuqahā*ʾ (Damascus, n.d.), vol. 3, pp. 366-7.

3. Kāsānī, *Badāʾiʿ aṣ-Ṣanāʾiʿ*, vol. 6, p. 178; Qāḍīkhān, *Kitāb al-Fatāwā*, vol. 3, pp. 155, 166, 176; Sarakhsī, *Mabsūṭ*, vol. 23, pp. 83-4.

4. Qāḍīkhān, *Kitāb al-Fatāwā*, vol. 3 p. 155; Samarqandī, *Tuḥfat al-Fuqahā*ʾ, vol. 3, p. 367.

5. Michael G. Morony, 'Landholding on Seventh-Century Iraq: Late Sasanian and Early Islamic Patterns', in A.L. Udovitch (ed.), *The Islamic Middle East 700-1900. Studies in Economic and Social History* (The Darwin Press Inc., Princeton, 1981), pp. 147-8; Ziaul Haque, *Landlord and Peasant in Early Islam* (Islamic Research Institute, Islamabad, 1977), pp. 169-71.

6. Ibid., ch. 4 *passim*.

7. Morony, 'Landholding', p. 163; E. Ashtor, *A Social and Economic History of the Near East in the Middle Ages*, (Collins, London, 1976), p. 38; Ziaul Haque, *Landlord and Peasant*, pp. 169-71.

8. Michael G. Morony, 'Landholding and Social Change: Lower al-ʿIraq in the Early Islamic Period' in Tarif Khalidi (ed.), *Land Tenure and Social Transformation in the Middle East* (Beirut, 1984), p. 214.

9. Michael G. Morony, 'Landholding', pp. 144, 163.

10. Ziaul Haque, *Landlord and Peasant*, pp. 290-1, 293, 299, 329.

11. Khaṣṣāf, *Kitāb Aḥkām al-Auqāf*, (Cairo, 1322 A.H./1904 A.D.), pp. 34-5; see Sarakhsī, *Mabsūṭ*, vol. 23, pp. 10, 12.

12. Khaṣṣāf, *Kitāb Aḥkām al-Auqāf*, pp. 207-8.

13. Sarakhsī, *Mabsūṭ*, vol. 23, pp. 12, 14.

14. Ibid., p. 12; Kāsānī, *Badāʾiʿ aṣ-Ṣanāʾiʿ*, vol. 6, p. 175; Marghīnānī, *al-Hidāya Sharḥ Bidāyati al-Mubtadi*ʾ, printed on the margin of Ibn al-Humām, *Sharḥ Fatḥ al-Qadīr* (Cairo, 1356 A.H.), vol. 8, pp. 33; Bābartī, *Sharḥ al-ʿInāya ʿalā al-Hidāya*, printed on the margin of Ibn al-Humām, *Sharḥ Fatḥ al-Qadīr*, vol. 8, p. 35. For a detailed discussion of the various arguments ascribed to Abū Ḥanīfa see Ziaul Haque, *Landlord and Peasant*, pp. 68-75 and note 31 below for some minor *mises au point*.

15. Ibid., ch. 2 *passim*; Ṭabarī, *Kitāb Ikhtilāf al-Fuqahā*ʾ, 2nd edn (Beirut, n.d., reprint edn. of F. Kern's edn. 1902), pp. 118-24.

16. Ibid., pp. 118-24; Sarakhsī, *Mabsūṭ*, vol. 23, pp. 13, 14, 17-8; Ziaul Haque, *Landlord and Peasant*, pp. 66, 79-80.

17. Ṭabarī, *Ikhtilāf*, pp. 120, 122, 123.

18. Sarakhsī, *Mabsūṭ*, vol. 23, p. 12: '*wa-l-murādu hāhuna l-intidābu ilā mā huwa min makārimi l-akhlāq*', see p. 13.

19. Ibid., pp. 20, 23, 44, 45, 47, 54, 58; Samarqandī, *Tuḥfat al-*

Fuqahāʾ, vol. 3, p. 363; Bābartī, *Sharḥ al-ʿInāya*, vol. 8, p. 41; Qāḍīzādeh, *Natāʾij al-Afkār fī Kashf ar-Rumūz wa-l Asrār* (printed as vols. 7 and 8 of Ibn al-Humām, *Sharḥ Fatḥ al-Qadīr*), vol. 8, p. 41; Qādīkhān, *Kitāb al-Fatāwa*, vol. 3, pp. 174, 175.

20. Sarakhsī, *Mabsūṭ*, vol. 23, pp. 18, 36, 37, 38, 40; Samarqandī, *Tuḥfat al-Fuqahāʾ*, vol. 3, p. 362; Kāsānī, *Badāʾiʿ aṣ-Ṣanāʾiʿ*, vol. 6, p. 179; Marghīnānī, *al-Hidāya*, vol. 8, p. 34; Bābartī, *Sharḥ al-ʿInāya*, vol. 8, pp. 34, 36, 37; Qāḍīzādeh, *Natāʾij al-Afkār*, vol. 8, pp. 34, 35, 36; Qāḍīkhān, *Kitāb al-Fatāwā*, vol. 3, p. 150.

21. Ziaul Haque, *Landlord and Peasant*, ch. 2 *passim*; Sarakhsī, *Mabsūṭ*, vol. 23, pp. 2-15; Kāsānī, *Badāʾiʿ aṣ-Ṣanāʾiʿ*, vol. 6, p. 175; Marghīnānī, *al-Hidāya*, vol. 8, p. 33; Bābartī, *Sharḥ al-ʿInāya*, vol. 8, p. 33.

22. Sarakhsī, *Mabsūṭ*, vol. 23, pp. 17, 18.

23. Qāḍīkhān, *Kitāb al-Fatāwā*, vol. 3, p. 150; Marghīnānī, *al-Hidāya*, vol. 8, p. 34; Bābartī, *Sharḥ al-ʿInāya*, vol. 8, p. 35; Sarakhsī, *Mabsūṭ*, vol. 23, pp. 17, 18, 36, 37, 38, 40.

24. Marghīnānī, *al-Hidāya*, vol. 8, p. 34: '*wa-l-qiyāsu yutraku bi-t-taʿāmul*'; Qāḍīzādeh, *Natāʾij al-Afkār*, vol. 8, p. 34.

25. Kāsānī, *Badāʾiʿ aṣ-Ṣanāʾiʿ*, vol. 6, p. 179; Samarqandī, *Tuḥfat al-Fuqahāʾ*, vol. 3, pp. 362, 364; Bābartī, *Sharḥ al-ʿInāya*, vol. 8, pp. 35-6, 37; Qāḍīzādeh, *Natāʾij al-Afkār*, vol. 8, p. 36.

26. This is implied in the six conditions mentioned above in chapter 3, section 8 of the text. See Sarakhsī, *Mabsūṭ*, vol. 23, pp. 19, 66. It is explicitly stated by Bābartī, *Sharḥ al-ʿInāya*, vol. 8, p. 36; Qāḍīzādeh, *Natāʾij al-Afkār*, vol. 8, p. 35 and Kāsānī, *Badāʾiʿ aṣ-Ṣanāʾiʿ*, vol. 6, pp. 177-8, 179.

27. Samarqandī, *Tuḥfat al-Fuqahāʾ*, vol. 3, p. 361; Marghīnānī, *al-Hidāya*, vol. 8, pp. 34, 35-6; Bābartī, *Sharḥ al-ʿInāya*, vol. 8, pp. 34, 36; Qāḍīzādeh, *Natāʾij al-Afkār*, vol. 8, pp. 35, 36; Qāḍīkhān, *Kitāb al-Fatāwā*, vol. 3, pp. 150, 151; Kāsānī, *Badāʾiʿ aṣ-Ṣanāʾiʿ*, vol. 6, pp. 177, 179.

28. This is implicit in the three legally valid combinations, see chapter 3, section 5 above. It is explicitly stated by Sarakhsī, *Mabsūṭ*, vol. 23, p. 20; Bābartī, *Sharḥ al-ʿInāya*, vol. 8, p. 38; Qāḍīzādeh, *Natāʾij al-Afkār*, vol. 8, p. 36. There are two forms of legal reasoning that justify the fact that seed can never be the object of a *muzāraʿa* contract: (a) The partner who contributes the seed is always considered to be the leaseholder of land or labour, Sarakhsī, *Mabsūṭ*, vol. 23, p. 86; Qāḍīzādeh, *Natāʾij al-Afkār*, vol. 8, p. 37. See also all references under note 27 above. If he contributes seed only, the separation between the land and its owner that is considered to be a necessary condition of the *muzāraʿa* contract is not realised. Therefore the *muzāraʿa* contract is voidable. Qāḍīkhān, *Kitāb al-Fatāwā*, vol. 3, p. 158; Kāsānī, *Badāʾiʿ aṣ-Ṣanāʾiʿ*, vol. 6, p. 180; Samarqandī, *Tuḥfat al-Fuqahāʾ*, vol. 3, p. 365. (b) The Prophet's example did not concern seed and cattle, but only labour. The business practice (*taʿāmul*) concerns only land and labour as objects of a share-cropping contract. Bābartī, *Sharḥ al-ʿInāya*, vol. 8, p. 35; See Qāḍīzādeh, *Natāʾij al-Afkār*, vol. 8, p. 24.

29. Qudūrī, *al-Kitāb*, vol. 2, p. 229; Sarakhsī, *Mabsūṭ*, vol. 23, pp. 19-20; Samarqandī, *Tuḥfat al-Fuqahāʾ*, vol. 3, pp. 363-4; Kāsānī, *Badāʾiʿ aṣ-Ṣanāʾiʿ*, vol. 6, p. 179; Qāḍīkhān, *Kitāb al-Fatāwā*, vol. 3, pp. 157-8; Marghīnānī, *al-Hidāya*, vol. 8, pp. 35-6; Bābartī, *Sharḥ al-ʿInāya*, vol. 8, pp. 35-6; Qāḍīzādeh, *Natāʾij al-Afkār*, vol. 8, pp. 35-6.

30. Sarakshī, *Mabsūṭ*, vol. 23, pp. 26, 85-6; Samarqandī, *Tuḥfat al-Fuqahāʾ*, vol. 3, pp. 361, 364; Kāsānī, *Badāʾiʿ aṣ-Ṣanāʾiʿ*, vol. 6, pp. 179-80; Marghīnānī, *al-Hidāya*, vol. 8, pp. 35-6; Bābartī, *Sharḥ al-ʿInāya*, vol. 8, p. 36; Qāḍīzādeh, *Natāʾij al-Afkār*, vol. 8, pp. 35-6. All jurists discuss — and reject — a fourth combination considered by Abū Yūsuf to be legally admissible and in which one partner contributes work and seed, the other one land and cattle.

31. Ziaul Haque, *Landlord and Peasant*, pp. 69, 70-3 who, on the authority of Zuhrī (Medina), stresses the fact that, according to Abū Ḥanīfa, the Jews of Khaibar were serfs and slaves of the Muslim state who, therefore, did not have the legal capacity to conclude contracts. This legal opinion is also transmitted within the Hanafite school, see Sarakhsī, *Mabsūṭ*, vol. 23, p. 2. But it is regarded as the 'weaker' of two legal opinions ascribed to Abū Ḥanīfa. It is said that, according to the 'stronger' of the two legal opinions ascribed to Abū Ḥanīfa, the Prophet imposed a *kharāj muqāsama* on a subject population granting them in turn the property of their lands and their life, see ibid., pp. 3, 6, 8. See also Marghīnānī, *al-Hidāya*, vol. 8, p. 33; Bābartī, *Sharḥ al-ʿInāya*, vol. 8, p. 33; Kāsānī, *Badāʾiʿ aṣ-Ṣanāʾiʿ*, vol. 6, p. 175, see p. 185, who says that, according to Abū Ḥanīfa, the Prophet took a share of the crop of the people of Khaibar as a *jizya*, a poll tax.

32. For *iʿāna* and *istiʿāna* see Sarakhsī, *Mabsūṭ*, vol. 23, pp. 23, 24, 28, 29, 30, 43, 44, 67; Qāḍīkhān, *Kitāb al-Fatāwā*, vol. 3, pp. 154, 159; Kāsānī, *Badāʾiʿ aṣ-Ṣanāʾiʿ*, vol. 6, p. 179 uses *istiʿāra* for 'help'. This may well be a printing mistake for *istiʿāna*.

33. For *iʿāra* see Sarakhsī, *Mabsūṭ*, vol. 23, pp. 23, 31, 44; Qāḍīkhān, *Kitāb al-Fatāwā*, vol. 3, pp. 154, 159.

34. For *qarḍ al-badhr* see Sarakhsī, *Mabsūṭ*, vol. 23, pp. 23, 24, 28, 44; Qāḍīkhān, *Kitāb al-Fatāwā*, vol. 3, pp. 154, 159.

35. Sarakhsī, *Mabsūṭ*, vol. 23, pp. 27-32, 107 ff; Qāḍīkhān, *Kitāb al-Fatāwā*, vol. 3, pp. 154, 159.

36. Sarakhsī, *Mabsūṭ*, vol. 23, pp. 23, 24; Qāḍīkhān, *Kitāb al-Fatāwā*, vol. 3, p. 154.

37. Kāsānī, *Badāʾiʿ aṣ-Ṣanāʾiʿ*, vol. 6, p. 179 uses *istiʿāra* in order to legalise two otherwise invalid forms of *muzāraʿa*. Qāḍīkhān, *Kitāb al-Fatāwā*, vol. 3, pp. 154, 179 uses the idea of mutual help to legalise the landowner's tilling of the soil which is not permissible under any of the three legally valid combinations of Hanafite law and which clearly contradicts the condition of *takhliya*, see below note 44. Sarakhsī, *Mabsūṭ*, vol. 23, pp. 23-4 uses the notion of *istiqrāḍ al-badhr* and *istiʿāna* in order to justify the landowner's obtaining the whole crop even if the seed and the labour is contributed by his partner. Ibid., p. 43, he uses the concept of *istiʿāna* in order to legalise a ratio of sharing under which the owner of land and seed gets the whole crop

and the working partner nothing. On p. 44 he uses the concept of *iʿāra* and *istiʿāna* and *istiqrāḍ* in order to legalise ratios of sharing which give the whole crop either to the working partner or to the owner of land and seed. See also pp. 27-32 and pp. 107-8 for other examples.

38. Ziaul Haque, *Landlord and Peasant*, pp. 323, 329, 360.

39. But according to Morony, 'Landholding', p. 163, the conditions of share-cropping among the Jews of Iraq did in many regards protect the working partner's interest.

40. Sarakhsī, *Mabsūṭ*, vol. 23, pp. 26-7, see p. 16 which underlines that in such a case, the working partner has the right to leave, because his slaves, hirelings and 'boys' (*ghilmān*) will work in his place. See also ibid., p. 69; Qāḍīkhān, *Kitāb al-Fatāwā*, vol. 3, p. 155. There are instances of the combinations (A) and (C) under which, according to the jurists, the working partner may employ salaried labour. See Sarakhsī, *Mabsūṭ*, vol. 23, p. 70. On the other hand ibid., pp. 127-8 and Qāḍīkhān, *Kitāb al-Fatāwā*, vol. 3, p. 182 declare it to be legally admissible that the working partner under combinations (A) and (C) is asked to nominate a guarantor (*kafīl*) for the labour, because the working partner incurs the obligation to perform enforceable work.

41. Special stress is placed on the specification of the term by Qudūrī, *al-Kitāb*, vol. 2, p. 230 and Samarqandī, *Tuḥfat al-Fuqahāʾ*, vol. 3, pp. 366-7. The list of six conditions is given by Sarakhsī, *Mabsūṭ*, vol. 23, p. 19. Marghīnānī, *al-Hidāya*, vol. 8, p. 34 adds that the land must be suitable for cultivation and that the partners to the contract should enjoy the capacity of concluding contracts. Bābartī, *Sharḥ al-ʿInāya*, vol. 8, p. 34 discusses only some of the conditions. Qāḍīzādeh, *Natāʾij al-Afkār*, vol. 8, pp. 150-6 offers the most extensive discussion of the six conditions. Kāsānī, *Badāʾiʿ aṣ-Ṣanāʾiʿ*, vol. 6, pp. 176-9 follows a different arrangement in discussing the conditions.

42. Sarakhsī, *Mabsūṭ*, vol. 23, p. 19; Marghīnānī, *al-Hidāya*, vol. 8, p. 34; Bābartī, *Sharḥ al-ʿInāya*, vol. 8, p. 34; Qāḍīkhān, *Kitāb al-Fatāwā*, vol. 3, pp. 150-1. It is important to note that all jurists mention the dissenting opinion of Transoxanian authorities who do not consider the specification of the term of the *muzāraʿa* to be a necessary condition under all circumstances.

43. Sarakhsī, *Mabsūṭ*, vol. 23, pp. 19, 21, 22, 109, 152, 153; Samarqandī, *Tuḥfat al-Fuqahāʾ*, vol. 3, pp. 365, 368; Marghīnānī, *al-Hidāya*, vol. 8, p. 34; Qāḍīkhān, *Kitāb al-Fatāwā*, vol. 3, p. 155; Kāsānī, *Badāʾiʿ aṣ-Ṣanāʾiʿ*, vol. 6, p. 178.

44. Qāḍīkhān, *Kitāb al-Fatāwā*, vol. 3, p. 151.

45. Ibid., pp. 154, 179.

46. Sarakhsī, *Mabsūṭ*, vol. 23, pp. 38-9, 65; Kāsānī, *Badāʾiʿ aṣ-Ṣanāʾiʿ*, vol. 6, p. 181; Bābartī, *Sharḥ al-ʿInāya*, vol. 8, p. 44; Qāḍīkhān, *Kitāb al-Fatāwā*, vol. 3, pp. 161, 164.

47. Sarakhsī, *Mabsūṭ*, vol. 23, p. 26 states that: 'the labourer is forced to cultivate it [i.e. the land] and it does not matter whether he wants to abandon agriculture in that year or not, because he is the hireling (*ajīr*) of the owner of the land and the hireling under a valid contract is under the obligation to fulfil [the duties] to which he committed himself', see also pp. 50-1. In these words Sarakhsī

abandons the old Hanafite tradition. Under the contract of tenancy, the tenant's intention to change his occupation constitutes a valid reason for the dissolution of the contract. The Hanafite tradition has it that all 'excuses' that constitute valid reasons for the tenant's dissolution of the contract of tenancy should also be considered valid reasons for the working partner's dissolution of the share-cropping contract (*muzāraʿa*). See Kāsānī, *Badāʾiʿ aṣ-Ṣanāʾiʿ*, vol. 6, p. 184, see also p. 182; Samarqandī, *Tuḥfat al-Fuqāhāʾ*, vol. 3, p. 369; Marghīnānī, *al-Hidāya*, vol. 8, p. 41; Bābartī, *Sharḥ al-ʿInāya*, vol. 8, p. 41. Samarqandī, *Tuḥfat al-Fuqahāʾ*, vol. 3, p. 369 and Kāsānī, *Badāʾiʿ aṣ-Ṣanāʾiʿ*, vol. 6, p. 184 state that the working partner's intention to travel and leave the countryside constitutes a valid reason for the dissolution of the contract. Sarakhsī, *Mabsūṭ*, vol. 23, p. 27 differs from their approach in that he does not regard the working partner's intention to give up agriculture as a valid reason for the dissolution of the contract. But, p. 27, he also insists that the intention of the working partner to travel (*safar*) may, in the case of *muzāraʿa*, but not in the case of *muʿāmala*, constitute a valid reason for the dissolution of the contract. Sarakhsī's discussion is not altogether clear except for the fact that the working partner who employs slaves and salaried labour may at any time leave the countryside.

48. Work is considered to be the decisive production factor. Sarakahsī, *Mabsūṭ*, vol. 23, p. 17:

> 'The proof for the fact that work influences the yield of the crop is that the person who makes unauthorised use of seed and land has a right to the crop if he cultivates [the field], because the crop is the result of his work'.

Sarakhsī considers it to be the 'capital' of the labourer that influences the yield of the crop, ibid., p. 36. On p. 61 he states: 'all this is obtained through his labour and the force of the land of his partner' (*li-anna hādhā kullahu ḥāṣil*[un] *bi-ʿamalihi wa-bi-quwati arḍi ṣāḥibihi*). See also p. 37. Only the kind of work that produces the crop and increases its yield is enforceable against the labouring partner, see ibid., pp. 37, 38, 39, 59; Samarqandī, *Tuḥfat al-Fuqahāʾ*, vol. 3, p. 368 (*muʿtād*); Bābartī, *Sharḥ al-ʿInāya*, vol. 8, p. 44, Qāḍīkhān, *Kitāb al-Fatāwā*, vol. 3, p. 163 (*muʿtād*), p. 164; Kāsānī, *Badāʾiʿ aṣ-Ṣanāʾiʿ*, vol. 6, pp. 180, 182.

49. Sarakhsī, *Mabsūṭ*, vol. 23, p. 38: 'Only the work that is necessary to obtain the [average] yield is obligatory upon him if the contract does not contain any further stipulations' (*fa-inna l-ʿamala lladhī la budda minhu li-taḥṣīli l-kharāji yaṣīru mustaḥaqq*[un] *ʿalaihi bi-muṭlaqi l-ʿaqd*). It is only through special stipulations that the working partner can be contractually obliged to perform work that improves the quality of the crop. Without such stipulations he is obliged to perform the work that is necessary to obtain the average crop. Samarqandī, *Tuḥfat al-Fuqahāʾ*, vol. 3, p. 368:

> . . . if the *muzāraʿa* contract has been concluded without further

stipulations, must the worker plough? If the situation is such that the land will produce an average yield (*zar^c mu^ctād*) without the ploughing: it is not obligatory on him [to plough], and if it does not produce an average yield [without ploughing], then he will be forced to do the ploughing, even if the land [without the ploughing] yields something (*shai' qalīl*), because he is obliged to perform the work of cultivation without any further stipulations (*li-annahu wajaba 'alaihi muṭlaqu ^camali z-zirā^ca*) and that applies to the lowest degree of average work (*fa-yaqa'u 'alā adnā ^camal^in mu^ctād*), but the trifling amount of a crop that is not the average is not considered (*fa-ammā ghairu l-mu^ctādi mina z-zar'i l-qalīli fa-lā ^cibrata bih*).

For the 'average yield' as the measure of the enforceable labour, see also Qāḍīkhān, *Kitāb al-Fatāwā*, vol. 3, p. 163; Kāsānī, *Badā'i^c aṣ-Ṣanā'i^c*, vol. 6, p. 182, see p. 180.

50. Sarakhsī, *Mabsūṭ*, vol. 23, pp. 38-9, see pp. 64, 65, 152, 153; Samarqandī, *Tuḥfat al-Fuqahā'*, vol. 3, pp. 367-8; Bābartī, *Sharḥ al-'Ināya*, vol. 8, p. 44 states that the working partner can be contractually obliged to perform all work that increases the yield of the crop. This is also the teaching of Qāḍīkhān, *Kitāb al-Fatāwā*, vol. 3, pp. 163-4, who insists that no contractual stipulation may be enforced against the working partner that does not increase the yield or damages the land, see also Kāsānī, *Badā'i' aṣ-Ṣanā'i^c*, vol. 6, p. 182 and Sarakhsī, *Mabsūṭ*, vol. 23, pp. 152-3.

51. Ibid., p. 39; Qāḍīkhān, *Kitāb al-Fatāwā*, vol. 3, pp. 161, 162, 164; Kāsānī, *Badā'i^c aṣ-Ṣanā'i'*, vol. 6, p. 181; Samarqandī, *Tuḥfat al-Fuqahā'*, vol. 3, p. 367.

52. Sarakhsī, *Mabsūṭ*, vol. 23, pp. 37, 46; Samarqandī, *Tuḥfat al-Fuqahā'*, vol. 3, p. 368; Kāsānī, *Badā'i' aṣ-Ṣanā'i'*, vol. 6, pp. 180, 181; Qāḍīkhān, *Kitāb al-Fatāwā*, vol. 3, p. 161; Marghīnānī, *al-Hidāya*, vol. 8, p. 44; Bābartī, *Sharḥ al-'Ināya*, vol. 8, p. 44.

53. Samarqandī, *Tuḥfat al-Fuqahā'*, vol. 3, p. 368 refers to the teaching of Abū Yūsuf and of the 'scholars (*mashāyikh*) of Khurāsān'. Kāsānī, *Badā'i^c aṣ-Ṣanā'i^c*, vol. 6, p. 181 refers to the muftis of Transoxania and to Naṣīr b. Yaḥyā and Muḥammad b. Salma whom he reckons among the '*mashāyikh* of Khurāsān'. Sarakhsī, *Mabsūṭ*, vol. 23, pp. 36-7 refers to Naṣīr b. Yaḥyā and Muḥammad b. Salma and Abū Bakr Muḥammad b. al-Faḍl. Sarakhsī's statement that: 'it is a valid practice in our region too' to shift this burden on the working partner's shoulders is often quoted by later jurists; see Marghīnānī, *al-Hidāya*, vol. 8, pp. 44-5 and Bābartī, *Sharḥ al-^cInāya*, vol. 8, pp. 44-5 as well as Qāḍīkhān, *Kitāb al-Fatāwā*, vol. 3, pp. 161-2, who extensively quotes Sarakhsī and adds other authorities that make the working partner liable for losses that occur because he did not perform these tasks in due time.

54. Sarakhsī, *Mabsūṭ*, vol. 23, pp. 41, 52-3, 61; Qāḍīkhān, *Kitāb al-Fatāwā*, vol. 3, pp. 152, 164.

55. Samarqandī, *Tuḥfat al-Fuqahā'*, vol. 3, pp. 366-7; Marghīnānī, *al-Hidāya*, vol. 8, p. 34; Bābartī, *Sharḥ al-^cInāya*, vol. 8, p. 34; Qāḍī-

khān, *Kitāb al-Fatāwā*, vol. 3, pp. 150-1.

56. Sarakhsī, *Mabsūṭ*, vol. 23, p. 48; Qāḍīkhān, *Kitāb al-Fatāwā*, vol. 3, p. 178.

57. Sarakhsī, *Mabsūṭ*, vol. 23, p. 41; Qāḍīkhān, *Kitāb al-Fatāwā*, vol. 3, p. 152.

58. Sarakhsī, *Mabsūṭ*, vol. 23, p. 64; Qāḍīkhān, *Kitāb al-Fatāwā*, vol. 3, pp. 152-3.

59. Sarakhsī, *Mabsūṭ*, vol. 23, pp. 70-1; Qāḍīkhān, *Kitāb al-Fatāwā*, vol. 3, p. 171. A sublease without such an explicit authorisation is considered to be a case of *ghaṣb*, 'unauthorised use' of the land, Sarakhsī, *Mabsūṭ*, vol. 23, pp. 70, 71, 72, 73; Qāḍīkhān, *Kitāb al-Fatāwā*, vol. 3, p. 171.

60. Sarakhsī, *Mabsūṭ*, vol. 23, pp. 75, 77; Qāḍīkhān, *Kitāb al-Fatāwā*, vol. 3, p. 171, because, it is argued, the partner who contributes seed, cattle and work leases the land. As a leaseholder of the land he enjoys the same rights as the tenant in a contract of tenancy (*ijāra*).

61. This is explicitly stated by Sarakhsī, *Mabsūṭ*, vol. 23, p. 17 who refers to land and seed as the equivalent of the capital (*māl*) in the *muḍāraba*. The analogy to the *muḍāraba* is rejected by Bābartī, *Sharḥ al-ʿInāya*, vol. 8, p. 33 on the grounds that under *ijāra* and *muzāraʿa* contracts, the period of duration of the contract must be specified (because this is the only way to evaluate the use of land and labour). Qāḍīzādeh, *Natāʾij al-Afkār*, vol. 8, p. 33 also rejects the analogy of the *muḍāraba*.

62. Sarakshī, *Mabsūṭ*, vol. 23, p. 20; Bābartī, *Sharḥ al-ʿInāya*, vol. 8, p. 36; Qāḍīzādeh, *Natāʾij al-Afkār*, vol. 8, p. 35; Qāḍīkhān, *Kitāb al-Fatāwā*, vol. 3, p. 158.

63. See notes 27 and 28 above.

64. Under combination (B) the owner may stipulate which seed shall be grown on his fields, but once the seed owner has signed the contract and sowed the seed, it is evidently the seed owner who decides which crops are to be grown on the field. It is possible to stipulate the sowing of more than one crop (and the use of more than one method of cultivation) under one *muzāraʿa* contract. The problems resulting from these stipulations are discussed under the term *tabʿīḍ*, see Sarakhsī, *Mabsūṭ*, vol. 23, pp. 40-3, 63-4. For *taḥwīl* see ibid., pp. 65-6. See Qāḍīkhān, *Kitāb al-Fatāwā*, vol. 3, pp. 151-2.

65. Sarakhsī, *Mabsūṭ*, vol. 23, pp. 126-7; Qāḍīkhān, *Kitāb al-Fatāwā*, vol. 3, p. 182.

66. Sarakhsī, *Mabsūṭ*, vol. 23, pp. 26, 40, 41, 42, 45, 46, 47, 54; Samarqandī, *Tuḥfat al-Fuqahāʾ*, vol. 3, p. 369; Marghīnānī, *al-Hidāya*, vol. 8, p. 41; Bābartī, *Sharḥ al-ʿInāya*, vol. 8, p. 41; Qāḍīzādeh, *Natāʾij al-Afkār*, vol. 8, p. 41; Qāḍīkhān, *Kitāb al-Fatāwā*, vol. 3, p. 174; Kāsānī, *Badāʾiʿ aṣ-Ṣanāʾiʿ*, vol. 6, p. 182.

67. Sarakhsī, *Mabsūṭ*, vol. 23, p. 47 describes the labour to be expected, see pp. 38, 40, 44; see also Samarqandī, *Tuḥfat al-Fuqahāʾ*, vol. 3, p. 369; Marghīnānī, *al-Hidāya*, vol. 8, p. 41; Bābartī, *Sharḥ al-ʿInāya*, vol. 8, p. 41; Kāsānī, *Badāʾiʿ aṣ-Ṣanāʾiʿ*, vol. 6, p. 182.

68. Sarakhsī, *Mabsūṭ*, vol. 23, p. 26; Samarqandī, *Tuḥfat al-Fuqahāʾ*, vol. 3, p. 368; Kāsānī, *Badāʾiʿ aṣ-Sanāʾiʿ*, vol. 6, p. 182;

Qāḍīkhān, *Kitāb al-Fatāwā*, vol. 3, p. 174; Marghīnānī, *al-Hidāya*, vol. 8, p. 41; Bābartī, *Sharḥ al-ʿInāya*, vol. 8, p. 41.

69. Sarakhsī, *Mabsūṭ*, vol. 23, p. 47 and for further risks at the unilateral stage of the contract, see p. 54; Bābartī, *Sharḥ al-ʿInāya*, vol. 8, p. 41; Qāḍīzādeh, *Natāʾij al-Afkār*, vol. 8, p. 41; Samarqandī, *Tuḥfat al-Fuqahāʾ*, vol. 3, p. 369.

70. Sarakhsī, *Mabsūṭ*, vol. 23, p. 47: 'this is the answer as far as the legal ordinance is concerned, but between him and his Lord it is right that he should pay the "fair rent" of the labourer's work to him ...' See also Qāḍīkhān, *Kitāb al-Fatāwā*, vol. 3, p. 174; Marghīnānī, *al-Hidāya*, vol. 8, p. 41.

71. Sarakhsī, *Mabsūṭ*, vol. 23, p. 20; Samarqandī, *Tuḥfat al-Fuqahāʾ*, vol. 3, p. 362; Marghīnānī, *al-Hidāya*, vol. 3, p. 39; Bābartī, *Sharḥ al-ʿInāya*, vol. 8, p. 39; Qāḍīzādeh, *Natāʾij al-Afkār*, vol. 8, pp. 39-41; Kāsānī, *Badāʾiʿ aṣ-Ṣanāʾiʿ*, vol. 6, pp. 177, 182.

72. Sarakhsī, *Mabsūṭ*, vol. 23, pp. 27-32, 107 *passim*; Qāḍīkhān, *Kitāb al-Fatāwā*, vol. 3, pp. 158, 159, 160.

73. For the two sources see Sarakhsī, *Mabsūṭ*, vol. 23, pp. 23, 67, 68; Samarqandī, *Tuḥfat al-Fuqahāʾ*, vol. 3, p. 362; Kāsānī, *Badāʾiʿ aṣ-Ṣanāʾiʿ*, vol. 6, p. 181; Qāḍīkhān, *Kitāb al-Fatāwā*, vol. 3, pp. 154, 158, 159, 160; Marghīnānī, *al-Hidāya*, vol. 8, pp. 39-40; Bābartī, *Sharḥ al-ʿInāya*, vol. 8, pp. 39-40. For the teaching according to which the partner who does not contribute the seed has only a contractual basis for his claim, see Sarakhsī, *Mabsūṭ*, vol. 23, pp. 23, 67, 87; Samarqandī, *Tuḥfat al-Fuqahāʾ*, vol. 3, p. 362; Marghīnānī, *al-Hidāya*, vol. 8, p. 34; Kāsānī, *Badāʾiʿ aṣ-Ṣanāʾiʿ*, vol. 6, p. 183.

74. Sarakhsī, *Mabsūṭ*, vol. 23, pp. 23, 28, 29, 43, 44, 107, 108; Qāḍīkhān, *Kitāb al-Fatāwā*, vol. 3, pp. 154, 159, 179.

75. Sarakhsī, *Mabsūṭ*, vol. 23, pp. 27-32, 107-8; Qāḍīkhān, *Kitāb al-Fatāwā*, vol. 3, pp. 154, 159, 179. The exception to this rule is the case under which the seed owner's contribution is interpreted as a 'gratuitous credit' (*qarḍ*) of seed to the partner, e.g. Sarakhsī, *Mabsūṭ*, vol. 23, pp. 23-4, 44. But, according to Sarakhsī, ibid., p. 28, such a credit has to be stated explicitly. See also Qāḍīkhān, *Kitāb al-Fatāwā*, vol. 3, p. 154.

76. In the classical period, some Ḥanafite jurists considered land to be the most important means of production and granted to the landowner the same privileged position that the seed owner enjoys in the prevailing legal doctrine of the Hanafite school of law, see Sarakhsī, *Mabsūṭ*, vol. 23, p. 22. The position of Bābartī, *Sharḥ al-ʿInāya*, vol. 8, p. 34 may well reflect this dissenting tradition.

77. Sarakhsī, *Mabsūṭ*, vol. 23, p. 28.

78. Ibid., pp. 60-1; Kāsānī, *Badāʾiʿ aṣ-Ṣanāʾiʿ*, vol. 6, p. 181; Marghīnānī, *al-Hidāya*, vol. 8, p. 39; Bābartī, *Sharḥ al-ʿInāya*, vol. 8, p. 39.

79. References as in note 78. This is one of the few instances in which the jurists of Balkh are reported to side with the working partner and to base his claim to an equal share of the crop and the straw on custom.

80. a) For instances in which the contract is considered to be

voidable because it does not fulfil one of the six conditions mentioned in chapter 3, section 8 above:

1. Condition 1 (*mudda*): Sarakhsī, *Mabsūṭ*, vol. 23, p. 19; Qudūrī, *al-Kitāb*, vol. 2, p. 230; Samarqandī, *Tuḥfat al-Fuqahāʾ*, vol. 3, pp. 366-7; Kāsānī, *Badāʾiʿ aṣ-Ṣanāʾiʿ*, vol. 6, p. 180; Qāḍīkhān, *Kitāb al-Fatāwā*, vol. 3, p. 150.
2. Condition 2 (*takhliya*): Sarakhsī, *Mabsūṭ*, vol. 23, pp. 19, 109, 152, 153; Qāḍīkhān, *Kitāb al-Fatāwā*, vol. 3, p. 155; Kāsānī, *Badāʾiʿ aṣ-Ṣanāʾiʿ*, vol. 6, p. 178; Samarqandī, *Tuḥfat al-Fuqahāʾ*, vol. 3, pp. 365, 368.
3. Condition 3 (*ṣāḥib al-badhr*): Sarakhsī, *Mabsūṭ*, vol. 23, pp. 19, 85; Kāsānī, *Badāʾiʿ aṣ-Ṣanāʾiʿ*, vol. 6, p. 179; Qāḍīkhān, *Kitāb al-Fatāwā*, vol. 3, p. 151; Marghīnānī, *al-Hidāya*, vol. 8, p. 34; Bābartī, *Sharḥ al-ʿInāya*, vol. 8, p. 34.
4. Condition 4 (*jins al-badhr*): Qāḍīkhān, *Kitāb al-Fatāwā*, vol. 3, pp. 151-2, 153; Kāsānī, *Badāʾiʿ aṣ-Ṣanāʾiʿ*, vol. 6, p. 177; Marghīnānī, *al-Hidāya*, vol. 8, p. 34; Sarakhsī, *Mabsūṭ*, vol. 23, pp. 19, 43, but pp. 85-6 he states that according to *istiḥsān*, custom (*ʿurf*) may replace the contractual stipulation. This opinion is shared by Bābartī, *Sharḥ al-ʿInāya*, vol. 8, p. 35.
5. Condition 5 (Specification of the respective shares of the crop): Sarakhsī, *Mabsūṭ*, vol. 23, pp. 19, 87, see also pp. 27, 30 with reference to ʿĪsā b. Abān; Qāḍīkhān, *Kitāb al-Fatāwā*, vol. 3, pp. 154-5; Kāsānī, *Badāʾiʿ aṣ-Ṣanāʾiʿ*, vol. 6, pp. 177-8; Marghīnānī, *al-Hidāya*, vol. 8, p. 34.
6. Condition 6 (*sharika* in the crop): Qudūrī, *al-Kitāb*, vol. 2, p. 230 who uses the term *mushāʿ*, undivided property; Sarakhsī, *Mabsūṭ*, vol. 23, pp. 19, 60, 62, 66; Qāḍīkhān, *Kitāb al-Fatāwā*, vol. 3, pp. 155-6; Kāsānī, *Badāʾiʿ aṣ-Ṣanāʾiʿ*, vol. 6, p. 177; Marghīnānī, *al-Hidāya*, vol. 8, p. 34, 38; Bābartī, *Sharḥ al-ʿInāya*, vol. 8, pp. 34, 38.

b) Instances of contracts that are declared to be voidable because under them labour and the means of production are combined in ways that the jurists judge to be inadmissible: Qudūrī, *al-Kitāb*, vol. 2, p. 329; Sarakhsī, *Mabsūṭ*, vol. 23, p. 20; Kāsānī, *Badāʾiʿ aṣ-Ṣanāʾiʿ*, vol. 6, pp. 179-80; Samarqandī, *Tuḥfat al-Fuqahāʾ*, vol. 3, pp. 364-5; Qāḍīkhān, *Kitāb al-Fatāwā*, vol. 3, p. 158; Marghīnānī, *al-Hidāya*, vol. 8, pp. 366-7; Bābartī, *Sharḥ al-ʿInāya*, vol. 8, pp. 35-6; Qāḍīzādeh, *Natāʾij al-Afkār*, vol. 8, pp. 35-8.

c) Ratios of sharing among partners who jointly contribute means of production: Sarakhsī, *Mabsūṭ*, vol. 23, pp. 27-32, 107-8; Qāḍīkhān, *Kitāb al-Fatāwā*, vol. 3, pp. 154, 158-60.

d) One-sided advantages for the land owner: see references under notes 51 and 52 above. See also Qudūrī, *al-Kitāb*, vol. 2, p. 233.

81. Sarakhsī, *Mabsūṭ*, vol. 23, pp. 16, 20, 28, 29-32, 35, 42-3, 60, 63, 68, 69, 72, 80, 107, 108; Samarqandī, *Tuḥfat al-Fuqahāʾ*, vol. 3, p. 362; Kāsānī, *Badāʾiʿ aṣ-Ṣanāʾiʿ*, vol. 6, pp. 179, 183; Qāḍīkhān, *Kitāb al-Fatāwā*, vol. 3, pp. 158-9; Marghīnānī, *al-Hidāya*, vol. 8,

pp. 39-40; Bābartī, *Sharḥ al-ʿInāya*, vol. 8, pp. 39-40.

82. Sarakhsī, *Mabsūṭ*, vol. 23, pp. 16, 20-1, 28, 30, 31, 32, 63, 68, 69, 72, 80, 107; Samarqandī, *Tuḥfat al-Fuqahāʾ*, vol. 3, p. 362; Qāḍīkhān, *Kitāb al-Fatāwā*, vol. 3, p. 160; Marghīnānī, *al-Hidāyā*, vol. 8, p. 40; Bābartī, *Sharḥ al-ʿInāya*, vol. 8, pp. 39-40. It is important to note that under the *muzāraʿa fāsida*, the payment of the 'fair rent' is a personal obligation of the seed owner, see Bābartī, *Sharḥ al-ʿInāya*, vol. 8, p. 39; Kāsānī, *Badāʾiʿ aṣ-Ṣanāʾiʿ*, vol. 6, p. 183; Sarakhsī, *Mabsūṭ*, vol. 23, p. 21.

83. Ibid., pp. 16, 20-1, 28, 30, 31, 32, 68, 69, 72, 80, 107; Bābartī, *Sharḥ al-ʿInāya*, vol. 8, p. 40.

84. Sarakhsī, *Mabsūṭ*, vol. 23, pp. 17, 30-2; Samarqandī, *Tuḥfat al-Fuqahāʾ*, vol. 3, p. 362; Kāsānī, *Badāʾiʿ aṣ-Ṣanāʾiʿ*, vol. 6, p. 183; Qāḍīkhān, *Kitāb al-Fatāwā*, vol. 3, p. 160; Marghīnānī, *al-Hidāya*, vol. 8, p. 40; Bābartī, *Sharḥ al-ʿInāya*, vol. 8, p. 40.

85. Kāsānī, *Badāʾiʿ aṣ-Ṣanāʾiʿ*, vol. 6, p. 183; for similar statements see also Samarqandī, *Tuḥfat al-Fuqahāʾ*, vol. 3, pp. 362-3; Sarakhsī, *Mabsūṭ*, vol. 23, pp. 16-7, 22, 28, 29, 30, 69, 73, 107-8; Qāḍīkhān, *Kitāb al-Fatāwā*, vol. 3, pp. 158-9, 160; Marghīnānī, *al-Hidāya*, vol. 8, p. 40; Bābartī, *Sharḥ al-ʿInāya*, vol. 8, p. 40.

86. Qāḍīkhān, *Kitāb al-Fatāwā*, vol. 3, pp. 168-9.

87. Ibid., p. 169.

88. Ibid., vol. 2, pp. 270, 274 and vol. 3, p. 335.

89. Ibid., p. 169.

90. Ibid., vol. 2, p. 281; see also vol. 3, pp. 331, 335.

4

The 'Death of the Proprietors'

1. HISTORICAL BACKGROUND

From the second half of the tenth century onwards the rural society of the Near and Middle East underwent fundamental changes. For a variety of reasons, army officers in many cases no longer received their pay from the public treasury. Instead, they were assigned districts where they collected taxes as remuneration for their services. This practice — already described by Khaṣṣāf in the ninth century (see chapter 1, section 3 above) — tended to obscure the difference between tax and rent.[1] Through it the peasant proprietors came to have a landlord who derived his revenue from the taxes they had to pay to him, of which only a part reached the public treasury.[2] The landlord was thus put in a position that allowed him to treat the taxes paid by the peasants as his private revenue. Furthermore, the landlord was often powerful enough to exercise coercion.[3] With reference to the situation in Iraq under the Buyids in the tenth and eleventh centuries, Ashtor says:

> Theoretically the fief holder had no judicial authority over the peasants, but in fact his position made him the patron in all respects ... The land tax being amalgamated with their rent was collected by the feudal lords. Many peasants surrendered their estates to them in order to redeem themselves from ever growing extortions and new taxes, and became simple tenants.[4]

The question as to whether or not this is feudal practice need not detain us here. What is important in this context is the fact that, with regard to the small peasant holdings, the difference between tax and rent ceased to exist. Indeed, the number of small peasant holdings consequently diminished,[5] a development which started in Iraq in the tenth century, but also became the outstanding feature of Egyptian agriculture from the twelfth century onwards.[6] The Hanafite legal doctrine on the *kharāj* payer as an owner of private landed property is hardly applicable to the Egyptian peasants of the Mamluk period (1250-1517 A.D.) The Hanafite legal doctrine of rent, according to which the obligation to pay rent can only result from use of land under a contract, is also not applicable to the relationship between landlord and peasant during the Mamluk and Ottoman periods. In the place of small peasant holdings large estates came into being through three factors: the transformation of tax assignments into private property,[7] the investment of capital in the buying of land from the public treasury either as tax assignments[8] or as proprietary rights with regard to state lands[9] and the granting of private ownership of state lands to members of the ruling dynasties.[10] The private landed property which thus came into being became one of the major sources for the formation of *waqf* land.[11] The transformation of state lands into *waqf* by members of the ruling dynasties gave rise to a special legal category, the *waqf irṣādī*.[12]

Beginning in the Fatimid period (tenth to twelfth centuries) at the latest, Muslim rulers tried time and again to confiscate the *auqāf* and to treat them as lands belonging to the state.[13] This tendency reached its climax under the Ottoman ruler Mehmed II who tried in the 1470s to 'sultanise' all arable lands including those of the *auqāf*. He recognised only orchards, vineyards and plantations as private property or pious foundations (*auqāf*). All arable lands were considered to be state property (*mīrī*). Mehmed II and his vizir were later murdered which may have in part resulted from their attempt to 'sultanise' *waqf* lands.[14] His successor restored part of the lands to their former status as pious foundations.[15] Nevertheless, until well into the second half of the sixteenth century the Ottoman system of land tenure was clearly based on the assumption that arable lands belonged in principle to the state. Ownership rights of private persons or pious foundations were recognised only if sufficient proof for them existed. Consequently, verifying the validity of property deeds became one of the strongest weapons which the public treasury had for controlling arable lands. In the course of verifying the deeds, the authorities could refuse to acknowledge the claims to private property or *waqf* rights on arable lands and instead incorporate the lands into the public domain.[16] This method was applied to the Arab countries that were taken over at the beginning of the sixteenth century, especially in Syria,[17] conquered in 1516, and in Egypt, conquered in 1517.

The attempt by the state to control arable lands and to incorporate private landed property and *waqf* lands into the public domain has always met with strong religious, social and economic resistance. Many religious scholars gave clear, persistent and unequivocal support to this resistance[18] and helped to make it successful in the long run. It is well known that a process of decentralisation accompanied by a process of political and economic fragmentation characterised the history of the Ottoman Empire during the seventeenth and eighteenth centuries.[19] In the course of these two centuries much of the domain lands seem to have reverted to *waqf* and private landed property (*milk*). Mouragea d'Ohsson, writing at the end of the eighteenth century, reports that the *auqāf* '... *embrassent une grande partie des terres, des immeubles, des richesses de l'Empire; qu'une infinité de citoyens en jouissent également* ...'[20] According to Afaf Lutfi al-Sayyid Marsot, one-fifth of all arable lands in Egypt were *waqf* lands at the end of the eighteenth century.[21] It is now generally accepted that many *waqf* lands existed in the Syrian countryside.[22] This is also the impression obtained from reading the Syrian *fatāwā* of the seventeenth and eighteenth centuries, that constantly speak of villages and fields as *waqf* lands.[23] The jurists' resistance to the 'sultanisation' of the *auqāf* and private landed property must have served as a strong ideological support to social groups engaged in reclaiming state land as *auqāf* or private property. It was the property of these groups that was above all defended and protected by the jurists.

2. THE DEATH OF THE KHARĀJ PAYER: A NEW DIMENSION TO AN OLD TEACHING

In defending the fiscal and legal privileges of *waqf* land and private landed property against the authorities' attempt to transform these lands into state property, the jurists of Egypt and Syria in the Mamluk and Ottoman periods made use of legal opinions that were first developed in Central Asia and that gave rentiers' and *waqf* property a privileged legal status. In order to apply these legal opinions in a systematic and coherent way, the jurists had to reinterpret the classical Hanafite doctrine on land tax (*kharāj*). This reinterpretation was discussed in terms of 'the death of the proprietors', a terminology which is by no means an invention of the Mamluk and Ottoman jurists. Hanafite jurists of all periods discuss the ruler's claims to lands that were formerly the property of *kharāj* payers who died without leaving heirs. This discussion forms part of the legal ordinances concerning the fiscal policy with regard to insolvent *kharāj* payers (see chapter 1, section 3 above). In tenth-century Syria the Hanafite scholar, Ṭaḥāwī, states that if a Muslim *kharāj* payer is not capable of cultivating his lands, the Imam is entitled to lease his land to other persons and to deduct the *kharāj* from the rent. The surplus that remains after the deduction of the *kharāj* from the rent should be returned to the insolvent *kharāj* payer.[24] It is obvious that, according to this legal opinion, the insolvent *kharāj* payer remains the proprietor of the land but loses his disposition of the immovable property. According to the twelfth century Transoxanian jurist, Qāḍīkhān, non unanimous legal opinion exists with regard to the *kharāj* payer who does not pay his land tax. Qāḍīkhān discusses three different cases:

(a) The case of the *kharāj* payers who fled (*harabū*) from the countryside. In their case Qāḍīkhān applied the teaching that Ṭaḥāwī developed with regard to the insolvent Muslim *kharāj* payer, i.e. the ruler is entitled to lease the land to third persons, to deduct the *kharāj* from the rent and to deliver the surplus to the *kharāj* payers if they return to the land. It is evident that, according to this legal opinion, the *kharāj* payers who fled from the countryside and then returned remained the proprietors of their land. But Qāḍīkhān informs his readers that, according to a legal opinion ascribed to Abū Ḥanīfa, the ruler has two other alternatives with regard to the land of *kharāj* payers who fled from the countryside: 1) he may have the land cultivated at the expense of the public treasury and appropriate the whole produce for the Muslim community; 2) he may hand over the land to other groups (*qaum*) for a fixed amount of levies (*muqāṭaʿatᵃⁿ ʿalā shaiʾ*). In this case nothing is said about the proprietary rights of the former *kharāj* payers.

(b) The second instance discussed by Qāḍīkhān is the case of the insolvent *kharāj* payer. Qāḍīkhān quotes Shaibānī's statement that, with regard to insolvent *kharāj* payers, the ruler is not entitled to take their land away from them and to deliver it to third persons. He is entitled only to lease the land and to deduct the *kharāj* from the rent. This amounts to confirming the proprietary rights of the insolvent *kharāj* payers. But if the ruler cannot find a tenant for the *kharāj* land he may sell it to persons 'who are strong enough to bear its *kharāj*' (*mimman yaqwī ʿalā kharājihā*). According to Qāḍīkhān, this solution is accepted by Abū Yūsuf and Shaibānī, but not by Abū Ḥanīfa who refuses the idea of selling the property of a tax payer in order to pay his tax arrears, because that would amount to legally incapacitating the proprietor.

(c) In one sentence only Qāḍīkhān mentions the death of the *kharāj* payers. It is said that, according to Abū Yūsuf, the ruler is entitled to appropriate the land of *kharāj* payers who die without heirs, to cultivate it or to lease it and assign the rent to the public treasury.[25] It would appear that, for Qāḍīkhān, the death of the *kharāj* payer is still a marginal notion with regard to the fiscal policy concerning the *kharāj* payers who do not pay the land tax. It is obvious that the Hanafite legal tradition grants the ruler the right to sequestrate insolvent *kharāj* payers' lands, to lease them, to cultivate them at the expense of the public treasury and — in the case of necessity — even to sell these lands. But under all these conditions, the insolvent *kharāj* payers retain a vague and ill-defined property right (see chapter 1, section 4 above and chapter 5, section 3 below). The public treasury enjoys a full and unrestricted ownership only with regard to the lands of the *kharāj* payers who die without heirs.

The notion of the *kharāj* payers' death acquires a new meaning and importance among Egyptian Hanafite jurists of the late Mamluk and early Ottoman periods. According to the Hanafite legal tradition, Egypt is a *kharāj*-paying country. The fifteenth-century Hanafite mufti, Ibn al-Humām, expresses his bewilderment over the legal conditions of his country, which he considers not to agree at all with the basic tenets of the Hanafite school regarding a *kharāj*-paying country. He says:

> ... truly, what is taken nowadays [from the peasants] amounts to payment for tenure (*badal al-ijāra*) and not to *kharāj*. Can't you see that the land is not the property of the cultivators (*zurrāʿ*)? This is so in spite of what we said about the lands of Egypt being *kharāj* lands. And God knows best.

> It is as if the proprietors died one after the other without leaving heirs so that the lands fell to the public treasury (*fa-inna l-maʾkhūdha al-āna badalu ijārat^{in} lā kharāj. A-lā tarā anna l-arḍa laisat mamlūkat^{an} li-z-zurrāʿ? Wa-hādhā baʿda mā qulnā anna arḍa miṣra kharājīya. Wa-llāhu aʿlam. Ka-annahu li-mauti l-mālikīna shaiʾ^{an} fa-shaiʾ^{an} min ghairi ikhlāfi warathat^{in} fa-ṣārat li-baiti l-māl*).[26]

Ibn al-Humām introduced the notion of the 'death of the *kharāj* payer' not in order to define the ruler's fiscal policy with regard to *kharāj* payers who do not pay their land tax, but with the purpose of explaining and legalising a historical situation which is irreconcilable with the basic tenets of the Hanafite legal tradition. It is true that, during the Mamluk period, the authorities' confiscation of private landed and urban property often took place at the death of the proprietors.[27] If we consider that during one epidemic more than 17,000 persons in Cairo lost life and property, it cannot be denied outright that such mortality might eventually have led to important changes in the socio-economic structure of the Cairene society.[28] But such changes seem to be more probable in big towns than in the countryside and obviously the loss of peasant proprietary rights is not reflected in a similar loss of property rights of other social classes which suffered equally from epidemics and confiscation. For Ibn al-Humām the notion of the 'death of the *kharāj* payer' served to explain and legalise the tenant status of peasants and the fact that they no longer enjoyed property rights with regard to their lands in spite of their paying their levies to the *muqṭaʿ* and the ruler.[29] In Egypt and Syria this notion became one of the cornerstones on which the reinterpretation of the Hanafite legal doctrine concerning tax and rent is based and Ibn al-Humām's statement is often quoted approvingly by the Hanafite jurists of the Ottoman period.[30]

3. IBN NUJAIM'S PAMPHLET AGAINST OTTOMAN FISCAL POLICY: THE 'DEATH OF THE KHARĀJ PAYER' AS THE LEGAL BASIS FOR THE FISCAL PRIVILEGES OF THE RENTIER CLASS

(a) Ibn al-Humām's notion of the 'death of the *kharāj* payer' is most skilfully and systematically used by the sixteenth-century

Egyptian mufti Ibn Nujaim in his important treatise on land tenure in Egypt, entitled *al-Tuḥfa al-Marḍīya fī al-Arāḍī al-Miṣrīya,* written in 959 A.H./1552 A.D. and of which a manuscript copy is available in the Staatsbibliothek Berlin.[31] Ibn Nujaim indicates the incident which led him to write the *Tuḥfa* in the introductory remarks of his treatise[32] and in his commentary on the *Kanz ad-Daqāʾiq.*[33] In 958 A.H./1551 A.D. the governor (*nāʾib*) of Cairo had ordered an examination of the legal status of all *rizqas*[34] that yielded rent for the upkeep of religious institutions and the salary of religious scholars or military officers. According to Ibn Nujaim, this led some people to question the legal validity of the treasury's sale of state lands to private persons. These people, as Ibn Nujaim says, aimed at 'annulling the *awqāf* and the charitable institutions' (*li-yatawaṣṣalū bi-dhālika ilā ibṭāli l-auqāfi wa-l-khairāt*). Shortly afterwards the Sultan sent an emissary who, in the words of Ibn Nujaim, 'required that *kharāj* be imposed on *awqāf* lands under the pretext (*mutamassik^{an}*) that *waqf* lands are subject to *kharāj*' (*fa-ṭalaba an yuḥdatha ʿalā arāḍi l-awqāfi kharāj^{an} mutamassīk^{an} bi-anna l-kharāja wājib^{un} fī arḍi l-waqf*).[35] A group of persons concerned with this development asked Ibn Nujaim to defend the status of the Egyptian *auqāf.* In reply to their request he wrote the *Tuḥfa* which he completed in one day, on Thursday the 27th Rabīʿ II 959 A.H./13th of April 1552 A.D.[36]

These remarks indicate that Ibn Nujaim wrote his *Tuḥfa* in order to defend *waqf* and private landed property against the imminent Ottoman *qānūnnāme* of 960/1553, which Stanford J. Shaw has aptly called 'The Land Law of Ottoman Egypt'.[37] Shaw has published a text and a translation of this *qānūnnāme.* This text shows that ʿAlī Pāshā, immediately upon his appointment as Ottoman governor of Egypt in 956 A.H./1549 A.D., prepared an investigation of the legal status of the Egyptian lands. In 957 (18 May 1550) he appointed a scribe '... to keep a record in Turkish in addition to several Arab scribes and two Qāḍīs known for their justice and piety'.[38] On the 27th of Jumāda II 959/21 May 1552, about a month after Ibn Nujaim had completed his *Tuḥfa,* 'it was decreed that there should be inspected all title deeds of the holders of *Vaqfs* and *Mulks* which had not been compared with the entries in the Mamluk registers ... and in addition all the papers of possession held by supervisors (*Nāẓir*) of *Vaqfs* ...'[39] In 960/1553 the Governor published the *qānūnnāme*. The years from 1550 to 1553 must therefore be seen as a period of legal and bureaucratic preparations for the *qānūnnāme*. We must assume that these preparations aroused the anxiety of all social circles and groups that had a vested interest in the safeguarding of *waqf* land, private landed property and the other remaining structures of the Mamluk system of land tenure. It is in defence of these groups that Ibn Nujaim wrote his *Tuḥfa* on the legal ordinances concerning Egyptian lands so that, as the mufti says, 'the rulers might apply them' (*laᶜalla an yaᶜmala biha l-ḥukkām*).[40] It is a jurist's defence of the fiscal and legal privileges of the landowning rentier class against the Ottoman attempt to turn their lands back into state property. The *Tuḥfa* also defines the basis for a compromise between the rentier class and Ottoman state power.

The anxiety of Ibn Nujaim and his collegues was well founded. Under the Ottoman *qānūnnāme* of 1553 *waqf* and private landed property were transformed into state property on an extensive scale. In Shaw's words: 'The end result of the Land Law of 1553 was to restore to the Treasury some 300 tax-producing *Muqaṭaᶜas* which had been alienated for various purposes in the late Mamluk and the early Ottoman times and to increase Treasury revenues by over 80 per cent during the last years of the century, with the result that it was able to send over twenty million paras to the Porte each year'.[41]

This fiscal success was achieved by verifying the existing property deeds and documents concerning the legal status of *milk* (private property), *waqf* and *rizqa* lands: '... the legality of each holding was to be determined not on the basis of its current status, but rather according to its legal status at the time the Mamluk registers were compiled'.[42] There were '... four legal types of evidence: ... the Mamluk cadastral registers ... the Ottoman cadastral registers ... the deeds and other legal documents held by the claimants themselves, and the records and certificates of the local judicial authorities'.[43] In the process of verifying these legal types of evidence, the Ottoman treasury took over lands that had been granted by the Mamluk rulers as military assignments and whose grantees had later changed the legal status of these lands into *waqf* or private landed property.[44] Private landed property, *waqf* and *rizqa* lands were confirmed only if their status dated from the Mamluk period[45] or if the owners or administrators were able to produce legal documentary evidence that the Mamluk treasury had sold these lands to them. Therefore, the documents proving the Mamluk treasury's sale of state lands were decisive in confirming the legal status of *waqf*, *rizqa* and private landed property.[46]

(b) The *Tuḥfa* is a mufti's pamphlet defending the fiscal and legal privileges of the Cairene rentier class against the Ottoman fiscal policy that led to the *qānūnnāme* of 1553. In the *Tuḥfa* Ibn Nujaim answers three questions: (1) Why is it legal that no *kharāj* is paid on many *auqāf* and much private landed property that was bought from the public treasury? (2) Why is it legitimate to constitute *waqf* from private landed property that had formerly belonged to the public domain? (3) How can the treasury's documents be used as proof for the claim that lands bought from the public treasury are tax exempt?

Ibn al-Humām's notion of the 'death of the peasant proprietors' is a key element in the answer to all three questions. Ibn Nujaim discusses the fiscal policy of the public treasury with regard to insolvent *kharāj* payers. He follows the classical Hanafite tradition in stating that *kharāj* payers lose the disposition of their landed property when they are not able to pay *kharāj* on the land or to cultivate it.[47] In the event that the ruler sequestrates the land of peasant proprietors for one of these two reasons he should act, according to Ibn Nujaim, as the proxy of the proprietors and either cultivate it at the expense of the public treasury or farm it out or sell it on their behalf. The *kharāj* owed to the public treasury should then be deducted from the yield of the crop or from the rent or the price of the land and the surplus should be given to the former owners.[48] It is obvious that in the first two cases a vague and precarious right of ownership is retained by the former *kharāj* payers. If the ruler sells the land, *kharāj* is deducted from the price and handed over to the public treasury. The surplus of the price will be given to the former owners. The public treasury does not lose its claim to *kharāj*, because the ruler acts only as a proxy of the former owners and the land does not change its status through the sale.[49] No fiscal privileges can result from the ownership of such lands.

But land reverts to the Sultan through 'the death of the *kharāj* payers', the ruler is entitled to lease it and have its rent paid to the public treasury.[50] He may also buy it himself, in which case he must first have it sold to a third person from whom he then buys it.[51] The ruler is entitled to sell these lands to private proprietors on the grounds that public interest requires it, that the public treasury is in need of money or simply because he wants to exercise his absolute and unquestionable right to sell state lands.[52] Land bought by private proprietors in this way is a privileged property and exempt from taxation.

Ibn Nujaim advances two legal reasons for this fiscal privilege. The first is the technical legal one that *kharāj* is a personal obligation. Once the person who is obliged to pay the *kharāj* dies, the obligation ceases to exist.[53] This legal opinion unequivocally contradicts the legal tradition of the Hanafite school according to which *kharāj muwaẓẓaf* is a *muʾna*, a burden on the productive land which has to be accepted as a personal obligation by any person enjoying property rights on such lands.[54] The second reason put forward by Ibn Nujaim is also very technical. He says that the ruler is entitled to sell either a thing itself or its use. If he receives a price for the land itself and hands that price over to the public treasury, he is no longer entitled to require an extra payment for the use of the land.[55] Consequently, the land ceases to be subject to *kharāj*. This reasoning clearly contradicts the classical Hanafite position on taxation according to which the payment of taxes proves the existence and continuity of proprietary rights. But both ways of reasoning were accepted by the Hanafite jurists of the Ottoman period and are quoted in legal compendia of the seventeenth century.[56]

The reason for this acceptance is obvious: Ibn Nujaim transforms the notion of the 'death of the *kharāj* payer' into a legal basis for the fiscal privileges of the landed property of the rentier class. As such it is accepted by other Hanafite jurists. And Ibn Nujaim quotes Ibn al-Humām verbatim in order to demonstrate that most Egyptian lands that reverted to the public treasury fell to it as a result of 'the death of the *kharāj* payer'.[57] Consequently, if the public treasury sold these lands, they were tax exempt.

Ibn Nujaim's definition of the legal consequences of 'the death of the *kharāj* payer' makes the ruler the most important seller of arable lands and fiscal privileges, because it entitles him to sequestrate peasant property, to inherit the lands of those proprietors who die without heirs and to dispose of the lands so acquired at his own discretion. Buying lands from the public treasury apparently was in many cases a means of acquiring fiscal privileges. Ibn Nujaim says that when the ruler sells arable lands he may either accord the buyer the fiscal privilege of exemption from taxes, an arrangement legitimised through the notion of the 'death of the *kharāj* payer', or he may treat the lands sold as taxable landed property on the basis that they were derived through the sequestration of the land of bankrupt peasant proprietors.

According to Ibn Nujaim these two types of sale can be distinguished from one another on the basis of two criteria. The first is of a technical legal character: if the documents prove that the price paid had been put into the public treasury without any deduction, then the land is exempt from taxes. Here, Ibn Nujaim follows the reasoning described above with regard to the legal consequences of the death of the *kharāj* payer and the sequestration of the land of the bankrupt *kharāj* payers.[58] The second criterion is the amount of the price paid for the land. According to Ibn Nujaim, no one would agree to pay a high price for arable lands which he has to till and on which he has to pay *kharāj*. Ibn Nujaim says:

> If the price is low this indicates that [the sale was effected] because of the proprietor's inability [to till the soil or pay the *kharāj*] and if the price is high this indicates that [the sale resulted] from the death of the proprietors [I read: *fa-qillatu th-thamani qarīnat*^{un} instead of *fa-qultu* as in the MS.] Because in this case, the buyer becomes an exclusive proprietor (*mālik*^{un} *lahā ʿalā l-khuṣūṣ*) of the land and he is not a share-cropper (*muzāriʿ*) or a peasant (*fallāḥ*). Therefore, he desires to purchase it at a high price. This is obvious and an established fact. It is generally known that the emirs [I read: *umarāʾ* instead of *umūr* as in the MS.] in the past used to be glad and proud if they bought land from the public treasury. Nobody reports that the Sultan ever asked them to pay *kharāj* after the sale or that the religious scholars demanded the payment of the *kharāj* from them or on the lands that were transformed into *waqf* [I read: *wa-lā ʿanna l-ʿulamāʾ* instead of *walāna l-ʿulamāʾ* as in the MS.] (*fa-qultu* [sic!] *ath-thamanu qarīnat*^{un} *ʿalā annahu li-ʿajzi arbābihā wa-kathratuhu qarīnat*^{un} *ʿalā annahu li-mauti arbābihā li-anna l-mushtariya fī hādhihi l-hālati mālik*^{un} *lahā ʿalā l-khuṣūṣi laisa bi-muzāriʿ*^{in} *wa-lā fallāḥ. wa-yarghabu fīhā bi-thaman*^{in} *kathīr. wa-hādhā ẓāhir*^{un} *mashhūr. fa-inna mina l-maʿlūmi l-mutawātiri anna l-umūra* [sic!] *fī z-zamani l-māḍī idha*

> *shtarau min baiti l-māli arāḍīya yafraḥūna bi-dhālika wa-yaftakhirūna bihā wa-lam yunqal ᶜan aḥadⁱⁿ anna s-sulṭāna ṭalaba minhumu l-kharāja baᶜda baiᶜihi lahum wa-lāna* [sic!] l-ᶜulamāʾ*a aujabū ᶜalaihimi l-kharāja wa-lā ᶜalā l-arāḍī l-mauqūfa*).[59]

The message is obvious. Persons of high rank pay a high price in order to acquire landed property which is exempt from taxation. By acquiring private landed property and the fiscal privileges connected with it, the prestige and social status of the purchaser are enhanced. Religious scholars and political authorities acknowledge this fact and regard the fiscal privileges as a valid legal symbol of social and political prestige. *Waqf* constituted from such a property is legally valid and is not subject to *kharāj* but to the much lower rate of *ᶜushr*.[60]

Fiscal privileges on landed property are, according to Ibn Nujaim, by no means restricted to top officers and the ruler's entourage who bought their land from the public treasury. The ruler may also exempt the private landed property of army officers and religious scholars from taxation. The ruler is entitled to assign waste lands to whomsoever he pleases. He may also grant arable lands forming his private property to third persons. He may exempt the assignee from the payment of *kharāj* if he is a member of the army or of the religious scholarly establishment (*ᶜulamāʾ*), i.e. if he belongs to one of those groups of persons who might legally receive part of the *kharāj* as salary, payment or donation.[61] The lands so assigned become the private property of those to whom they are granted and can be subjected to *kharāj* or exempted from it. They may be legally transformed into *waqf*.[62] The *waqf*, in this case, may be either subjected to *kharāj* or exempted from it.

A new concept of private landed property emerges from the legalisation of these various forms of fiscal privileges. Private landed property no longer comes into being through the confirmation of the primordial rights of the peasants by the ruler (see chapter 1, section 2a above). The channels of commodity exchange are recognised as sources of private landed property (see chapter 1, section 2b above) only if the land is bought from the ruler or the public treasury. Ibn Nujaim's defence of the fiscal privileges of the rentier class is based on the assumption that the ruler and the public treasury are the main sources of property rights and privileges and this assumption he shares with the authors of the Ottoman *qānūnnāme* of 960 A.H./ 1553 A.D.[63] The sales and assignments of arable lands by the Imam constitute the basis of most proprietary rights enumerated by Ibn Nujaim. Consequently, as he clearly states in the *Tuḥfa*, a hierarchy of different types of private landed property came into existence of which the following four can clearly be identified:

(1) the landed property of the power elite which is bought from the public treasury and, therefore, enjoys the privilege of tax exemption;
(2) the private property of religious scholars and army officers exempted from taxation by a decision of the ruler;
(3) the taxed property of the assignees;
(4) the *kharāj* property of the peasants and other owners who bought their lands from the ruler or the public treasury.

The social and political prestige of landed property owners of types (1) and (2) is clearly much greater than that of the *kharāj*-paying proprietors. Beneath these four ranks of proprietors the mass of cultivators and peasants who are regarded as tenants or share-croppers were to be found.

Ibn Nujaim's legalisation of the four forms of landed property and his analysis of their relationship to the ruler and the public treasury make it clear that the state became the most important source for the creation of *auqāf*. But it is important to note that the direct transformation of state land into *waqf* is invalid. According to Ibn Nujaim the direct transformation of state lands into *auqāf* was valid only if it was intended as a trust for a mosque. This direct transformation of state lands into *auqāf* led to the appearance of a new *waqf* category, the *waqf irṣādī*, which is treated in the *fatāwā* and the legal compendia of the Ottoman period.[64] But all other forms of *waqf* had to be constituted from lands that were private property. It is evident from the Ottoman *qānūnnāme* as well as from Ibn Nujaim's *Tuḥfa* that the ruler and the public treasury had become the most important source for private landed property that could legally be turned into *waqf*. *Waqf* constituted from the property of the first two privileged ranks was more favoured regarding taxation than other forms of *waqf*. Its administrators did not have to pay *kharāj* and still enjoyed the right to collect rent from their tenants. This seems to have been the main reason for

Ibn Nujaim's fervent defence of the legality of transforming this kind of property into *waqf*.[65] But also the existence of the private landed property of assignees of rank (3) was a good argument for recognising the transformation of lands that formerly belonged to the public domain into *auqāf* as being valid.[66] Finally, the transformation of peasant property into *waqf* was also considered to be legally valid but on such a *waqf* *kharāj* had to be paid, much as on the *waqf* resulting from category (3).[67] Only three forms of transforming state lands into *auqāf* were not considered to be legal: a ruler's making *waqf* of *arḍ al-ḥauz*,[68] sequestrated lands (see chapter 1, section 4 above and chapter 5, section 3 below), the *waqf* made by an assignee holding state lands which the ruler had not transformed into the assignee's private property,[69] and the *waqf* made by a peasant cultivator of lands on which he did not pay *kharāj* and who could not, therefore, be considered to be their proprietor.[70]

Most forms of private property which could be legally transformed into *waqf* and all fiscal privileges come into being through the ruler. The ruler is, therefore, the main purveyor of land and fiscal privileges through whom a constant supply of new lands, which could be transformed first into private property and then into *waqf*, is created. He is an indispensable source of income for the intermediary groups while also being their rival in the competition for the rent derived from the peasants. Obviously, the ruler has to take the supply of new lands from peasants and other proprietors. Their primordial property rights therefore become precarious.

NOTES

1. Hasanein Rabie, *The Financial System of Egypt, AH 564-741/AD 1169-1341* (Oxford University Press, London, New York, Toronto, 1972), pp. 26-7 for the *iqṭāᶜ* as described by Khaṣṣāf. For a different model developed under the Ayyubides which exempted the officer from the payment of *ᶜushr*, see ibid., p. 29 and Claude Cahen, 'Ayyubids', *The Encyclopaedia of Islam* (New Edition, Luzac & Co, London and E.J. Brill, Leiden, 1960).
2. Rabie, *Financial System*, pp. 41-5.
3. E. Ashtor, *A Social and Economic History of the Near East in the Middle Ages*, (Collins, London, 1976), pp. 182-3; Abdelaziz Duri, *Arabische Wirtschaftsgeschichte* (Artemis, Zurich and Munich, 1979), pp. 111, 120-1; Rabie, *Financial System*, p. 63.
4. Ashtor, *A Social and Economic History*, p. 182.

5. Duri, *Wirtschaftsgeschichte*, pp. 109-12 with regard to the Buyids in Iraq, p. 121 with regard to the Seljuqs; C. Cahen, *Der Islam I. Vom Ursprung bis zu den Anfängen des Osmanenreiches* (Fischer Taschenbuch Verlag, Frankfurt am Main, 1969), pp. 153-4 with regard to Egypt and Iran, p. 250 with regard to Turkish government and p. 293 for the Seljuqs. For a different development under Fatimid rule in Egypt see Duri, *Wirtschaftsgeschichte*, p. 95.

6. Ibid., pp. 127-33. It is interesting to note that according to Claude Cahen, Yūsuf Rāghib and Muṣṭafā Anouar Taher, 'L'achat et le waqf d'un grand domaine egyptien par le vizier fatimide Ṭalāī b. Ruzzīk contribution à une publication des waqfs egyptiens médiévaux', *Annales Islamologiques*, 14 (1978), p. 76 in Fatimid Egypt: '... *les cultivateurs, même s'ils sont en fait métayers/muzāri*ᶜ*ūn, sont juridiquement des propriétaires ayant comme tels à payer le kharādj, qu'ils versent en l'occurence au fermier*'.

7. Ashtor, *A Social and Economic History*, p. 273 and Duri, *Wirtschaftsgeschichte*, p. 127 with regard to Egypt. For the special development in pre-Ottoman Anatolia see Irene Beldiceanu-Steinherr, 'Fiscalité et formes de possession de la terre arable dans l'Anatolie préottomane', *Journal of the Economic and Social History of the Orient*, 19 pt. 3, pp. 267-8, 274, 296-8, 300; see Nicoara Beldiceanu and Irene Beldiceanu-Steinherr, 'Recherches sur la province de Qaraman au XVIe siècle', *JESHO* 11 (1968), pp. 15-6. For the general development see Cahen, *Der Islam I*, pp. 203-4, 250.

8. Ashtor, *A Social and Economic History*, p. 193 and Duri, *Wirtschaftsgeschichte*, p. 126 with regard to Egypt under the Fatimids. With regard to Ottoman rule see ibid., p. 143.

9. Cahen, Raghib and Taher, 'Le waqf d'un grand domaine egyptien', pp. 64-5, 67-8, 74; Stanford J. Shaw, 'The Land Law of Ottoman Egypt (960/1553): A Contribution to the Study of Landholding in the Early Years of Ottoman Rule in Egypt', *Der Islam* 38, nos. 1-2 (October 1962), pp. 115-6, 130, 132-3, 137.

10. Duri, *Wirtschaftsgeschichte*, p. 119. This practice was continued under the Ottomans, see Haim Gerber, 'The Waqf Institution in Early Ottoman Edirne', in Gabriel R. Warburg and Gad G. Gilbar (eds), *Studies in Islamic Society. Contributions in Memory of Gabriel Baer* (Haifa University Press, Haifa, 1984), pp. 29, 42-5; Oded Peri, 'The Waqf as an Instrument to Increase and Consolidate Political Power: The Case of Khāṣṣeki Sulṭān Waqf in Late Eighteenth-Century Ottoman Jerusalem', in Warburg and Gilbar (eds), *Studies in Islamic Society*, pp. 48-9.

11. Ashtor, *A Social and Economic History*, p. 261 for Iraq under the Mongols; W. Heffening, 'Waqf', *Die Enzyklopädie des Islam* (Leiden and Leipzig, 1936), vol. 4, p. 1189 on Egypt under the Mamluks; Ulrich Haarman, 'The Sons of Mamluks as Fief-Holders in Late Medieval Egypt', in Tarif Khalidi (ed.), *Land Tenure and Social Transformation in the Middle East* (American University of Beirut, Beirut, 1984), p. 145; Duri, *Wirtschaftsgeschichte*, p. 131 also discusses the transformation of peasant property into *waqf*.

12. Ibn ᶜĀbidīn, *al-ᶜUqūd ad-Durrīya fī Tanqīh al-Fatāwā al-Ḥām-*

idīya, 2nd edn (Bulaq, 1300 A.H. reprint edn, Beirut, n.d.), vol. 1, pp. 209, 210, 211; Ramlī, *Kitāb al-Fatāwā al-Khairīya li-Naf*[c] *al-Barrīya* (Bulaq, 1300 A.H., reprint edn, Beirut, 1974), vol. 1, pp. 100, 148; Ibn Nujaim, *at-Tuḥfa al-Marḍīya fī al-Arāḍī al-Miṣrīya*, ms, Berlin We 1724, fol. 135b.

13. Heffening, 'Waqf', p. 1189.

14. Nicoara Beldiceanu, 'Recherche sur la reforme foncière de Mehmed II' (article XII pp. 29-35), and Beldiceanu, 'Un paléologue inconnu de la region de Serres' (article XIII, pp. 11-12), in Beldiceanu (ed.) *Le monde ottoman des Balkans (1402-1566). Institutions, société, economie* (Variorum Reprints, London, 1976); Bistra Cvetkova, 'Sur certaines reformes du regime foncier au temps de Mehmet II', *Journal of the Economic and Social History of the Orient*, 6 (1963), pp. 105-20; Joseph Matuz, 'The Nature and Stages of Ottoman Feudalism', *Asian and African Studies. Journal of the Israel Oriental Society*, 16, no. 3 (November 1982), p. 287; Matuz, *Das Osmanische Reich, Grundlinien seiner Geschichte* (Wissenschaftliche Buchgesellschaft Darmstadt, Darmstadt, 1985), pp. 69-71.

15. Beldiceanu, 'Recherche'; Matuz, *Das Osmanische Reich*, p. 74.

16. M. Digeon, 'Canoun-namé ou édits de Sultan Soliman concernant la police de l'Egypte', in Digeon, *Nouveaux contes Turcs et Arabes* (Dupius, Paris, 1778), pp. 263-4, 267, 268-9, 273; H.A.R. Gibb and Harald Bowen, *Islamic Society and the West. A Study of the Impact of Western Civilization on Moslem Culture in the Near East* (Oxford University Press, London, 1950), vol. 1, pt. 2, pp. 172-3; Joseph von Hammer, *Des Osmanischen Reiches Staatsverfassung und Staatsverwaltung dargestellt aus den Quellen seiner Grundgesetze* (Vienna, 1815, reprint edn, Georg Olms Verlagsbuchhandlung, Hildesheim, 1963), vol. 1, p. 219.

17. Robert Mantran and Jean Sauvaget, *Règlements fiscaux ottomans. Les Provinces syriennes* (Institut Français de Damas, Paris, 1951). The impressive results of such a process of fiscal reorganisation are to be found in Wolf-Dieter Hütteroth and Kamal Abdulfattah, *Historical Geography of Palestine, Transjordan and Southern Syria in the Late 16th Century* (Selbstverlag der Fränkischen Geographischen Gesellschaft, Erlangen, 1977).

18. Heffening, 'Waqf', p. 1189. See chapter 4, section 3 below, and Ibn [c]Ābidīn, *Radd al-Muḥtār* [c]*alā ad-Durr al-Mukhtār. Sharḥ Tanwīr al-Abṣār fī Fiqh Madhhab al-Imām al-A*[c]*ẓam Abī Ḥanīfa an-Nu*[c]*mān* (Cairo, 1307 A.H.), vol. 3, p. 280.

19. Thomas Naff and Roger Owen (eds), *Studies in Eighteenth Century Islamic History* (Feffer & Simons, London and Amsterdam, 1977), *passim*; Matuz, *Das Osmanische Reich*, pp. 132-208.

20. Mouragea d'Ohsson, *Tableau générale de l'Empire ottoman* (Imprimerie de Monsieur, Paris, 1787), vol. 1, p. 320; see Gibb and Bowen, *Islamic Society and the West*, vol. 1, pt. 1, pp. 253-4.

21. Afaf Lutfi al-Sayyid Marsot, 'The Wealth of the Ulama in Late Eighteenth Century Cairo', in Naff and Owen (eds), *Studies*, p. 208.

22. Hütteroth and Abdulfattah, *Historical Geography*, pp. 102, 104 and map 4. The authors estimate (p. 106) the *waqf's* share of the

peasant taxes in Syria at the end of the sixteenth century at 25 per cent. See also Bernard Lewis, 'Ottoman Land Tenure and Taxation in Syria', *Studia Islamica* 50 (1979), p. 116. For the nineteenth-century situation in the Arab countries and the Ottoman Empire, see George Young, *Corps de droit Ottoman*, (Clarendon Press, Oxford, 1906) vol. 6, p. 113; Heffening, 'Waqf', p. 1191; Herwig Bartels, *Das Waqfrecht und seine Entwicklung in der libanesischen Republik* (Walter de Gruyter & Co, Berlin, 1967), p. 9; Eug. Clavel, *Le waqf ou habous d'aprés la doctrine et la jurisprudence (rites hanéfite et malekite)*, (Imprimerie Diemer, Cairo, 1896), p. 69.

23. Ramlī, *al-Fatāwā al-Khairīya*, vol. 1, pp. 100, 135, 145, 148, 161, 182, 203, 208, 209, 214, 215, 216; vol. 2, pp. 117, 126, 127, 135, 167, 211; Ibn ᶜĀbidīn, *ᶜUqūd*, vol. 1, pp. 9-10, 11, 12, 176, 182-3, 310; vol. 2, pp. 132, 181, 201, 202, 203.

24. Ṭaḥāwī, *Mukhtaṣar*, (Cairo, 1370 A.H.), p. 295.

25. Qāḍīkhān's discussion of these three alternatives is to be found in *Kitāb al-Fatāwā al-Khānīya* (Cairo, 1282 A.H.), vol. 3, p. 617. It is worth mentioning that the Ottoman *qānūnnāme* of 1525 leaves to the local Egyptian authorities the two alternatives mentioned under (c) with regard to the land of peasants who fled from the countryside; see Digeon, 'Canoun-namé', pp. 243-4.

26. Ibn al-Humām, *Sharḥ Fatḥ al-Qadīr* (Cairo, 1356 A.H.), vol. 4, p. 362. For a similar expression of perplexion with regard to European provinces of the Ottoman Empire, see al-Ḥaṣkafī, *Durr al-Muntaqā fī Sharḥ al-Multaqā*, printed on the margin of Ḍamād Afandī, vol. 1, p. 664.

27. Rabie, *Financial System*, pp. 127-9.

28. Ibid., pp. 130-1.

29. This is the way in which Ramlī, *al-Fatāwā al-Khairīya*, vol. 1, pp. 95-6 interprets Ibn al-Humām.

30. Ḥaṣkafī, *Durr al-Muntaqā*, vol. 1, pp. 662-3; Ramlī, *al-Fatāwā al-Khairīya*, vol. 1, p. 96.

31. Ibn Nujaim, *at-Tuḥfa*, fol. 132b.

32. Ibid., fol. 130a.

33. Ibn Nujaim, *al-Baḥr ar-Rāʾiq Sharḥ Kanz ad-Daqāʾiq* (Cairo, 1311 AH/1894 AD) vol. 5, p. 115.

34. On the development of the *rizqa* as 'a rent collected not from the cultivators ... but ... from the holders of the various kinds of muqātaᶜas over landed Imperial Possessions, who continued to pay in addition the taxes or services they owed to the Treasury', see Shaw, 'Land Law', p. 110.

35. Ibn Nujaim, *al-Baḥr ar-Rāʾiq*, vol. 5, p. 115.

36. Ibn Nujaim, *at-Tuḥfa*, fol. 142 and 130a.

37. Cahen, Rāghib and Taher, 'Le waqf d'un grand domaine egyptien', pp. 64-5, 67-8, 74; Shaw, 'Land Law', pp. 115-6, 130, 132-3, 137.

38. Ibid., p. 126.

39. Ibid., p. 134.

40. Ibn Nujaim, *at-Tuḥfa*, fol. 130a.

41. Shaw, 'Land Law', p. 116.

42. Ibid., p. 115.
43. Ibid.
44. Ibid., pp. 115-6, 130, 131, 132.
45. Ibid., pp. 115-6, 128-37.
46. Ibid., pp. 115-6, 128, 130, 132, 133, 137.
47. Ibn Nujaim, *at-Tuḥfa*, fol. 133a; Ibn Nujaim, *al-Baḥr ar-Rāʾiq*, vol. 5, p. 203.
48. Idem, *at-Tuḥfa*, fols. 133a, 133b.
49. Ibid.
50. Ibid., fols. 131a, 132b.
51. Ibid., fol. 131a.
52. Ibid., fols. 131b-132b. On the discussion of the ruler's right to sell state lands, see fols. 130a-133a, 135a-b, 136b, 138a-139a.
53. Ibid., fols. 133a, 133b, 134a, 137a.
54. Baber Johansen, 'Amwāl Ẓāhira and Amwāl Bāṭina. Town and Countryside as Reflected in the Tax System of the Hanafite School', in Wadad ad-Qāḍī (ed.) *Studia Arabica et Islamica, Festschrift for Iḥsān ʿAbbās on his Sixtieth Birthday* (American University of Beirut, Beirut, 1981), pp. 256-7.
55. Ibn Nujaim, *at-Tuḥfa*, fols. 133a, 133b, 136-137a, 138a, 138b.
56. Ḥaṣkafī, *Durr al-Muntaqā*, vol. 1, p. 663.
57. Ibn Nujaim, *at-Tuḥfa*, fol. 131b.
58. Ibid., fol. 138b.
59. Ibid., fols. 138b-139a.
60. Ibid., fols. 137a, 137b, 138a.
61. Ibid., fols. 135a, 139a. See also Ibn Nujaim, *ar-Risāla as-Sādisa ʿAshar fī Bayān al-ʿIqṭaʿāt* (Ms. Staatsbibliothek, Berlin 4832, Lbg. 526), fols. 305a-306. The differentiation between the fiscal privileges of the power elite and the privileges of the *muqṭaʿ* may well reflect the difference between the 'great amirs' with their *khaṣṣa* and 'the simple iqṭāʿ of ordinary soldiers' which Rabie, *Financial System*, pp. 42-4 (referring to Cahen) describes.
62. Ibn Nujaim, *at-Tuḥfa*, fols. 135a, 139a.
63. Shaw, 'Land Law', pp. 115-6, 128, 130, 133.
64. Ibn Nujaim, *at-Tuḥfa*, fols. 135b, 136a, 139b. For the *waqf irṣādī* see note 12 above and Ḥaṣkafī, *Durr al-Muntaqā*, vol. 1, pp. 664-5.
65. Ibn Nujaim, *at-Tuḥfa*, fols. 135a, 135b, 136b, 137a, 137b, 138a. See also the interesting remark of Hütteroth and Abdulfattah, *Historical Geography*, p. 101, according to which *milk* lands in Syria 'indicate land in the transitional stage between *mīrī* land ... and waqf'.
66. Ibn Nujaim, *at-Tuḥfa*, fols. 135a, 139a.
67. Ibid., fols. 132a, 134b, 136b.
68. Ibid., *al-Baḥr ar-Rāʾiq*, vol. 5, p. 203.
69. Ibid., *at-Tuḥfa*, fol. 135a; Ibn Nujaim, *al-Baḥr ar-Rāʾiq*, vol. 5, p. 203.
70. Ibn Nujaim does not state this explicitly, but it is implied in his argument.

5

The Ottoman Muftis' New Doctrine on Tax and Rent

1. THE OTTOMAN MUFTIS

The following analysis of the Ottoman muftis' new legal doctrine on tax and rent is mainly based on the writings of Ibn Nujaim and Syrian and Palestinian muftis of the seventeenth and eighteenth centuries, who constantly refer to Ibn Nujaim as one of the most important Hanafite authorities on tax, rent and landed property. Ibn Nujaim's writings constitute an important attempt to take stock of the problems connected with the changes in land tenure, tax and rent in the middle of the sixteenth century. He knew that he could not solve the problems he faced merely by continuing the old Hanafite legal tradition in dealing with them. The immense authority which his writings enjoyed in later centuries not only in Egypt but also in Syria and Palestine shows that his solutions were widely accepted. He was certainly not always the author of the legal opinions which he integrated into his solutions. In many respects his writings reflect the cumulative effects of a process of slow and cautious reformulation of the Hanafite legal tradition that had been going on since the tenth century and that had worked its way from Central Asia to Egypt and Syria during the Mamluk period. Ibn Nujaim was a capable synthetiser whose could integrate new notions and legal ordinances serving the interest of the rentier class. He shares with other Hanafite jurists of the Ottoman period the practical insights and economic and social interest that made the workable solution of new problems possible.

With regard to Syria and Palestine, I have mainly drawn on the *fatāwā* of Khair ad-Dīn Ramlī[1] and Ḥāmid b. ᶜAlī b. ᶜAbd ar-Raḥmān al-ᶜImādī. The *fatāwā* of Ḥāmid b. ᶜAlī al-ᶜImādī have been edited in an abridged version by the nineteenth-century Damascene jurist Ibn ᶜĀbidīn who also commented upon them.[2] Biographical information on Khair ad-Dīn Ramlī provided by Iḥsān ᶜAbbās[3] allows us to understand the social and economic situation of this important mufti. After completing his studies at al-Azhar, he returned to his native town, Ramla, in 1013/1605 where he became a renowned mufti and teacher. He was also a very successful agriculturist who is said to have owned more than 100,000 olive and fruit-trees from which he obtained a daily revenue of more than 100 *qurūsh*. Ḥāmid b. ᶜAlī al-ᶜImādī held the office of mufti of Damascus during the second quarter of the eighteenth century.[4] He came from a well-known family of Damascene muftis who inherited this office from father to son. Ḥāmid b. ᶜAlī was the last link in the long chain of muftis of the ᶜImādī family. He belonged to that stratum of high-ranking Damascene religious scholars about whom Rafeq reports that they bought, rented and speculated in land.[5] Ḥāmid b. ᶜAlī was once even accused of hoarding wheat for the purpose of speculation.[6]

Both muftis thus had a vested interest in the system of land tenure and land ownership as it developed in the seventeenth and eighteenth centuries. They had extensive knowledge of the economic problems connected with agriculture and those of taxes and rents and a first rate understanding of the economic and social consequences of their *fatāwā*. They belonged to a well-to-do social stratum that lived mainly from trade and rent of lands, but also owed their socio-economic, as well as their religio-cultural, standing to the fact that they guarded and defended the legal tradition of the Hanafite school. In order to be able to safeguard this tradition in a way that corresponded with their social and economic interest and the new political and socio-economic order under which they lived, they had to reinterpret this tradition. How they went about this is the subject matter of the last section of this study.

2. THE LAND TAX (KHARĀJ)

From Ibn Nujaim's *Tuḥfa* it is obvious that he abandoned the classical principle of '*nulle terre sans taxe*'. The private landed property of the power elite which is bought from the public treasury is exempt from taxation. The assignee may enjoy fiscal privileges through the ruler's decision. The *auqāf* that are constituted from these two forms of private property would also enjoy a privileged fiscal position. Only the proprietors of the third and fourth categories (see Chapter 4, section 3 above) are supposed to pay the *kharāj* regularly.

If neither the power elite nor the second rank of proprietors nor the peasants paid *kharāj*, where did the state's revenue come from? All jurists would agree that the peasants have to deliver a share of their crops and/or money to the public treasury for the use of the land. But what is the character of this payment? Ibn al-Humām (see Chapter 4, section 2 above) suggested that it was a kind of rent (*badal al-ijāra*). Ibn Nujaim and the Ottoman authorities of the early sixteenth century answer the question in the same way.[7] The jurists of the seventeenth century discuss the status of the tenant-cultivators on lands that are neither *kharāj* nor *ʿushr* lands but belong to the *mīrī* (also called *arḍ al-mamlaka*) and the land of the *ḥauz* (see Chapter 1, section 4 above and Chapter 5, section 3 below), i.e. they discuss the status of peasants on lands that are owned or administered by the state. They consider the peasant a tenant who has to pay rent. As the seventeenth-century Damascene mufti, Ḥaṣkafī, put it: '... as far as the Imam is concerned [the rent] that is collected (*al-maʾkhūdh*) is *kharāj* ... But with regard to the farm hands it is rent and nothing else, neither *ʿushr* nor *kharāj*' (*fa-yakūnu l-maʾkhūdhu fī ḥaqqi l-imāmi kharājᵘⁿ ... wa-ammā fī ḥaqqi l-akarati fa-ujratᵘⁿ lā ghaira lā ʿushra wa-lā kharāj*).[8]

However, Ibn Nujaim, Ḥaṣkafī and the famous seventeenth-century jurist Shaikhīzādeh (Ḍāmād) make it clear that the peasant pays rent under a voidable contract (*ijāra fāsida*)[9] (see Chapter 2, section 8 above). According to this reasoning, the amount of the rental of most peasants is unknown because most of the peasants have to deliver a share of their crop. If the rent is not specified under a contract of tenancy, the contract becomes voidable. If the peasant uses the land under a voidable contract, the 'fair rent' falls due. This legal doctrine clearly denies the peasant's proprietary rights with regard to the land he tills. But it also serves as a legal basis for safeguarding the peasant's personal liberty. In accordance with the classical legal tradition of Hanafite law, under a voidable contract of tenancy the tenant cannot be obliged to pay rent if he does not till the land (see Chapter 2, section 8 above). He cannot, therefore, become a debtor to the public treasury if he does not till the land. The Imam is entitled to sequestrate the peasant's property but cannot tie the peasant to the land. This is clearly expressed by Ibn Nujaim in his commentary on Nasafī's *Kanz ad-Daqāʾiq*:

> The land of Egypt is now no longer *kharāj* land. It is [leased] for rent. The *fallāḥ* does not owe anything if he leaves the land uncultivated (*lau ʿaṭṭalahā*). He is not a tenant of the land [because, according to the classical doctrine, the obligation to pay the 'fair rent' arises only from the actual use of the land rented under a voidable contract of tenancy]. No constraint may be imposed on him because of the land. Through this legal ordinance it becomes clear that if a cultivator gives up agriculture and lives in the cities, he owes nothing. The damage that the tyrants inflict upon him are forbidden, especially if he wants to dedicate himself to the study of the Koran and the pursuit of knowledge — as is the case of those who live in the protective neighbourhood of al-Azhar (*inna arḍa miṣra l-āna laisat kharājīyat*^an^ *innamā hiya bi-l-ujra. fa-lā shaiʾa ʿalā l-fallāḥi lau ʿaṭṭalahā wa-lam yakun mustaʾjir*^an^ *lahā wa-lā jabra ʿalaihi bi-sababihā wa-bihi ʿulima anna baʿḍa l-muzāriʿīna idhā taraka z-zirāʿata wa-sakana fī miṣrin fa-lā shaiʾa ʿalaih. fa-mā yafʿaluhu ẓ-ẓalamatu mina l-iḍrāri bihi fa-ḥarām*^un^ *khuṣūṣ*^an^ *idhā arāda l-ishtighāla bi-l-qurʾāni wa-l-ʿilmi ka-mujāwiri l-jāmiʿi l-azhar*).[10]

This legal opinion was upheld throughout the Syrian *fatāwā* of the seventeenth and eighteenth centuries.[11] In this relationship between the peasant and the state the last vestiges of the legal emancipation of the peasants that must have been connected with the old Hanafite doctrine on tax and rent can still be found.

It is obvious that the notion of the peasant as a tenant paying rent under a voidable contract of tenancy is a jurist's artifice for adapting elements of the legal tradition to new political and socio-economic circumstances under which the peasants could no longer be considered as *kharāj*-paying owners of their lands. But the artifice creates its own problems. In the classical tradition of Hanafite law, the tendency was to shift the burden of taxation from the lessor to the tenant as far as *kharāj muqāsama* was concerned (see Chapter 1, section 4 above). In the

Ottoman period *kharāj muqāsama* had become the most important form of *kharāj* in Syria and Egypt. It should, therefore, come as no surprise that the Palestinian and Syrian jurists of the seventeenth and eighteenth centuries often speak of tenants and share-croppers who pay the *kharāj.*[12] But there are many other instances in which the same jurists fervently defend the principle that it is always the lessor who has to pay the land tax[13] (*kharāj*). This confusion regarding legal principle is not completely eliminated but made less perplexing by examining the context in which the *fatāwā* are given.

In the Ottoman as well as in the Mamluk period different groups of persons competed with one another over the rents paid by the peasants of one village or tax district. The owners of private landed property and the *waqf* administrators, the representatives of the state administration and the *tīmārīs*, the military officers who were granted villages as remuneration for their military service, competed with each other over the rents paid by the peasants of the respective districts.[14] Obviously, in this competition those who collected the levies from the peasants had an advantage in disputes concerning the distribution of the rent. It was always possible for the collector not to honour the claim of his competitors and in the long run deprive them of their source of revenue. Many *fatāwā* deal with disputes ensuing from this competition. In all such disputes the legal principle that the lessor has to pay the taxes is upheld.[15] This principle serves as the major legal argument in safeguarding the *waqf* administrator's or freeholder's claim to priority over the *tīmār* holder with regard to collecting the rent from the peasants. The jurists make it clear that neither the ruler nor his representatives are entitled to collect the taxes from the tenants of the *waqf.*[16] The peasants are tenants. They do not pay taxes, they pay rent. The land tax is paid by the owner of the landed property or the *waqf* administrator. The land tax (*kharāj* or *ʿushr*) that the owner of landed property or the *waqf* administrator pays is a share of the rent that they have collected from the peasants. The state's claim to the land tax is a claim against *kharāj* payers, i.e. the *waqf* and the private proprietors. By paying the *kharāj* these proprietors prove their proprietary rights with regard to the land and safeguard their right to collect the rent from the peasants who till it. With regard to the tenants, the rent paid to the *waqf* cannot be distinguished from the tax. In fact, it includes the tax.[17] It is only through the proprietors' and *waqf* administrators' payment of the land tax that tax and rent are distinguished and that the tax that was included in the peasant's rent is separated from it. The division of tax and rent takes place through the tax payers' payment of the land tax. Paying the land tax had in fact become a privilege of land owners and *waqf* administrators, who thus became an intermediate group which, by paying *kharāj* or *ʿushr*, acquired the right to tax their tenants. Ḥaṣkafī is certainly right in underlining the fact that the peasant's rent is changed into a tax only when the representatives of the state receive it. In the relationship between the tenant-cultivator and the intermediate group of land owners no differentiation between tax and rent is possible.

This may be one of the main reasons for the bitter enmity that the muftis displayed towards the tax farmers, for the principle of tax farming threatens the rights of *waqf* administrators and private proprietors as intermediate tax collectors and tends to diminish their share of the rent. The muftis, therefore, declared tax farming to be invalid, 'a tenancy of consumption' (see Chapter 2, section 2 above), forbidden and null and void as far as legal consequences were concerned.[18]

With regard to the competition for the peasant's rent between the *waqf* and private proprietors on the one hand, and the state administration and the *tīmār* holders on the other hand, the jurists strictly upheld the principles that peasants paid rent and not the land tax and that it was always the lessor who paid the land tax. With regard to the relationship between landlord and peasant this principle was often completely neglected and it is by no means rare that we find the muftis speaking of the *kharāj* of tenants and share-croppers.

3. THE ARḌ AL-ḤAUZ: THE SEQUESTRATED LANDS

One of the devices that Hanafite jurists of the Mamluk period developed in order to reconcile their legal tradition with a new socio-economic and political order under which the peasants were not considered to be owners of landed property, was the legal fiction of the 'death of the *kharāj* payer'. Ibn al-Humām's tentative answer and its systematic application by Ibn Nujaim were so generally and so enthusiastically accepted by Hanafite lawyers of the Ottoman period because they served as a basis for the legalisation of the privileges of *waqfs* and private proprietors and of the expropriation of the peasants. But the conflict between a legal tradition that defines a legal person through his capacity to own property and a political and socio-economic order which *de facto* excludes the peasants from the ownership of landed property can clearly be discerned in the jurists' discussion of the *arḍ al-ḥauz*, the sequestrated landed property.

The term was already used as a technical legal term in the ninth century by Khaṣṣāf (see Chapter 1, section 3 above) who did not, however, give an explanation for its historical development nor a satisfactory legal definition of the term. All that can be deducted from Khaṣṣāf's use of the term is that it is land which is sequestrated by the Sultan and that the peasants who work it are not considered to be owners of the lands that they till. A much clearer definition was given at the end of the Mamluk period by Ibrāhīm aṭ-Ṭarābulsī in his work on the *auqāf*. Ṭarābulsī says:

> It is not legally valid to constitute as *waqf* the land of sequestration (*arḍ al-ḥauz*). This is land which the Sultan sequestrates when its proprietors (*aṣḥāb*) become unable either to use if for agriculture or to pay its levies. They give the land to him so that its use would fall to the [community of the] Muslims and replace the *kharāj* [which the peasants were unable to pay]. The land remains in the ownership of the proprietors (*wa-lā yaṣiḥḥu waqfu arḍi l-ḥauzi wa-hiya mā ḥāzaha s-sulṭānu ʿinda ʿajzi aṣḥābihā ʿan zirāʿatihā wa-adāʾi muʾanihā bi-dafʿihim iyāhā ilaihi li-takūna manfaʿatuhā li-l-muslimīna maqāma l-kharāji wa-raqabatu l-arḍi ʿalā milki arbābihā*).[19]

This definition corresponds to Qāḍīkhān's and Ibn Nujaim's definition of the ruler's sequestrating power with regard to the lands of the insolvent *kharāj* payers (see Chapter 4, sections 2 and 3 above). Ibn Nujaim uses the term *arḍ al-ḥauz* in the same way. He says that the ruler is not its proprietor and that he sequestrated it from its former owners so that its rent might replace the *kharāj*.[20] Syrian authors of the seventeenth century also clearly differentiate between state lands and *arḍ al-ḥauz*. They make it clear that with regard to these lands, the proprietary rights of the peasants continue to exist in principle without, however, invalidating the ruler's right to sequestrate the landed property and to dispose of it by farming it out under a *muzāraᶜa* or tenancy (*ijāra*), selling it or having it cultivated on behalf of the public treasury.[21] The precarious state of the peasant's landed property can clearly be seen in the *fatāwā* of Khair ad-Dīn Ramlī who said that:

> The sale of [the land] that the Sultan has sequestrated for the public treasury and farmed out to people under a *muzāraᶜa* ... is null and void, because they [i.e. the cultivators] do not own it. But the [land] that remained in its original state, is their property and they can sell it, transform it into *waqf* and bequeath it. And God knows best (*ammā mā ḥāzahu s-sulṭānu li-baiti l-māli wa-yadfaᶜuhu muzāraᶜat^an ila n-nāsi bi-r-rubᶜi wa-l-khumsi mathal^an fa-baiᶜuhum lahu bāṭil^un li-kaunihim lā yamlikūnahu wa-ammā mā baqiya ᶜalā aṣlihi fa-huwa milkuhum yajūzu baiᶜuhu wa-īqāfuhu wa-yakūnu mīrāth^an. Wa-llāhu aᶜlam*).[22]

Sequestration may at any time hit the peasant proprietor and transform his lands into *arḍ al-ḥauz*, sequestrated lands. He would then retain a precarious property right to his lands but lose the right to use them. As long as his lands were not sequestrated, he continued to be an owner of private landed property. After sequestration he was an owner of abstract proprietary rights.

Obviously, a legal situation, under which the former owners' proprietary rights with regard to his sequestrated lands are upheld, must lead to legal conflicts between the representatives of the state and the former land owners. We know of legal conflicts that have dragged on for more than a hundred years and ended with the land reverting into private property.[23] With regard to this kind of conflict, the jurists supported the ruler's right to sequestrate the land of insolvent tax payers. But they also upheld the principle that in such conflicts the law required the representative of the state to bring an action against the person in possession of the land who claimed proprietary rights with regard to it. Khair ad-Dīn Ramlī said:

> There is no pre-emption (*shufᶜa*) and no sale of lands that the Sultan sequestrated for the public treasury ... but if the actual possessor received it through sale or inheritance or in any other way in which ownership originates and if he claims

that the land is his property and that he pays the *kharāj* incumbent upon it, his testimony is valid. Whosoever wants to dispute his claim of proprietorship has to bring evidence (*burhān*). [This evidence shall only be admitted] if the action against him [i.e. the land owner] is legally valid and if all the conditions required for an action are fulfilled. I only mention this because this occurs very often in our lands and I want to be useful to the community of believers by clearly informing it about this legal rule which [persons at] all times are in need of. And God knows best (*wa-amma l-arāḍi llatī ḥāzaha s-sultānu li-baiti l-māli wa-yadfaᶜuhā li-n-nāsi muzāraᶜatan lā tubāᶜu wa-lā shufᶜata fīhā fa-idhā ddaᶜā wādiᶜu l-yadi lladhī talaqqāhā shirāᵓan au irthan au ghairahumā min asbābi l-milki annahā milkuhu wa-annahu yuᵓaddī kharājahā fa-l-qaulu lahu wa-ᶜalā man yukhāsimuhu fī l-milki l-burhānu in ṣaḥḥat daᶜwāhu ᶜalaihi sharᶜan wa-stūfiyat shurūtu d-daᶜwā wa-innamā dhakartu dhālika li-kathrati wuqūᶜihi fī bilādinā ḥarṣan ᶜalā nafᶜi hādhihi l-ummati bi-ifādati hādha l-ḥukmi sh-sharᶜiyyi alladhī yaḥtāju ilaihi kullu ḥīn. Wa-llāhu aᶜlam*).[24]

Ramlī's *fatwā* is quoted verbatim and approvingly by ᶜImādī.[25] The Ottoman muftis defined the procedure of sequestration in a way that protected the land owner's interest against state intervention. But they left no doubt that the *arḍ al-ḥauz* was an important and necessary fiscal institution. The *arḍ al-ḥauz* symbolised the unresolved conflict between the owner's right to their property and the state's claim to sequestration. It also helped to explain the fact that the cultivators did not own the lands that they tilled.

4. THE 'THREE EXEMPTED CATEGORIES' AND THE NEW CONCEPT OF RENT

The growing deterioration of the peasants' status *vis-à-vis* the rentier class can best be seen in the Ottoman Hanafite concept of rent and landed property. We have seen above (Chapter 2, section 11 and Chapter 3, section 10) that from the tenth century onwards prominent Hanafite jurists in Transoxania held the legal opinion that unauthorised use of *waqf* lands engendered the obligation to pay the 'fair rent' and that under certain conditions rentiers' lands (*al-arḍ al-muᶜadda li-*

daf^cihā muzāra^cat^{un}) and rentiers' urban property (*milk mu^cadd li-l-istighlāl*) enjoyed the same legal protection against unauthorised use (*ghaṣb*). But Qāḍīkhān's discussion of this special legal status of rentiers' property remained restricted to individual legal instances. Apparently, the Mamluk and Ottoman Hanafite jurists in Egypt and Syria accepted the new principle and the terminology in which it was expressed. In addition, by developing the notion of the 'death of the *kharāj* payer', they changed the classical Hanafite doctrine on taxation, legalised the expropriation of the peasants and supported the fiscal privileges of the rentier class. This change in the doctrine on taxation and on rent enabled them systematically to develop the concept of a special legal status of the rentier class property.

a) The protection of the rent-yielding property against unauthorised use

At the beginning of the Ottoman period, the jurists employed a well-defined concept of *mu^cadd li-l-istighlāl*, of 'property reserved for profitable use', that encompassed both urban and landed property. Objects which by definition fall under this category are shops, storage rooms[26] and baths[27]. According to the general rule all forms of property which are bought or built for the purpose of being put to profitable use or which are leased for more than three years in succession belong to this category.[28] By 'profitable use' (*istighlāl*) the authors mean the process of farming out the property or of using it for business purposes. A synonym that is widely used is *mu^cadd li-l-ujra*[29] or *mu^cadd li-l-ijāra*,[30] 'reserved for rent' or 'reserved for leasing'. According to the Syrian and Palestinian *fatāwā* of the seventeenth and eighteenth centuries 'property reserved for profitable use' may consist of houses, shops or lands that are farmed out[31] but also of tools used in the trade,[32] of camels[33] or donkeys[34]. All these may be leased for profit. In the case of landed property, the decisive criterion is whether the proprietor uses the land in order to satisfy his personal needs or in order to lease it to others. Only in the second case is the land considered to be 'private property reserved for profitable use'.[35] The term is also used with regard to means of production that are used for producing commodities, e.g. a soap factory is considered to be *mu^cadd li-l-istighlāl*, 'reserved for profitable use'.[36]

Waqf property, orphans' property and 'private property reserved for profitable use' (*milk muʿadd li-l-istighlāl*) are grouped together as the three forms of property enjoying a special legal status that clearly differentiates them from all other forms of private property.[37] A closer scrutiny of the *fatāwā* shows that the Syrian muftis treat *waqf* and state lands as enjoying the same protection against unauthorised use (*ghaṣb*) and the same legal privileges with regard to leasing.[38] It may indeed be so, that the whole concept of 'property reserved for profitable use' stems from an assimilation of the legal status of rentier property to that of state property. This assimilation is clearly discernible with regard to *waqf* property and orphans' property (*māl al-yatīm*). To a much lesser degree is the 'private property reserved for profitable use' granted the same status. Among the three forms of rent-yielding property that are not state property, the *waqf* clearly enjoys a privileged status since it is considered to be more dependent on 'profitable use' than private property. ʿImādī describes the difference between private property and *waqf* in the following words:

> The difference is that the proprietor may refrain from farming out his property. He may want to live on it or to sell it or not to use it at all (*yuʿaṭṭiluhu*) and in this respect his property differs from the *waqf* that is 'reserved to be farmed out' (*muʿadd li-l-ījār*). The administrator of the *waqf* must farm it out (*wa-l-farqu anna l-milka qad yamtaniʿu ṣāḥibuhu ʿan ījārihi wa-yurīdu an yaskunahu bi-nafsihi au yabīʿahu au yuʿattilahu bi-khilāfi l-mauqūfi l-muʿaddi li-l-ījāri fa-innahu laisa li-n-nāẓiri illā an yuʾajjirahu*).[39]

Only if the *waqf* is explicitly constituted for the personal use of its beneficiaries can it be said not to be *muʿadd li-l-ījār*, 'reserved to be farmed out'. In principle, the element of profitable use prevails for *waqf*. Consequently, all forms of *waqf* are considered to be rent-yielding property and the *waqf* is the rent-yielding property *par excellence.*[40]

According to the jurists, the three forms of rent-yielding property thus grouped together are legally united by the fact that unauthorised use (*manāfiʿ al-ghaṣb*) of these properties entails the obligation to pay the 'fair rent'. Ibn ʿĀbidīn calls these forms of rent-yielding property 'the three exempted ones' (*ath-thalāthu al-mustathnayāt*)[41] because they were exempted from the restrictions in the classical Hanafite doctrine on rent that made the contract a necessary condition for the obligation to pay the rent (see Chapter 2, sections 5-9 above). The Ottoman muftis regard non-contractual use of the 'three exempted ones' as entailing the obligation to pay the 'fair rent'. Ibn Nujaim states: 'Unauthorised use (*manāfiᶜ al-ghaṣb*) is not warranted except in three [cases]: The orphan's property (*māl al-yatīm*), the property of the *waqf*, and that which is "reserved for profitable use"'.[42] This position is upheld in the Syrian *fatāwā* of the Ottoman period.[43] Any person making unauthorised use of rent-yielding forms of property is liable to pay the 'fair rent' — even retroactively for many years. As Khair ad-Dīn Ramlī puts it: 'He has to pay the "fair rent" to the *waqf* on account of the choice made by the modern jurists (*al-mutaʾakhkhirīn*) concerning the liability for the use of the *waqf* without a contract of tenancy' (*ʿalaihi ujratu mithlihi li-l-waqfi ʿala khtiyāri l-mutaʾakhkhirīna fī ḍamāni manāfiʿi l-waqfi bi-ghairi ʿaqdi ijāratⁱⁿ fīh*).[44]

Use of the three forms of rent-yielding property that are 'reserved for profitable use' engenders the obligation to pay the 'fair rent'. But there is a clear differentiation between the *waqf* and the 'private property reserved for profitable use'. If someone uses private rent-yielding property on the grounds that he considers himself to be legally entitled to do so (*taʾwīl*), e.g. that he uses lands under an invalid contract of sale or if he wrongly thinks that he has a share in the property that entitles him to its use, he does not have to pay the 'fair rent' or in fact any rent. Private property, even if 'reserved for profitable use', is only partly covered by the protection that the post-classical law grants to rent-yielding property against unauthorised use. Only if a person consciously and intentionally makes 'unauthorised use of private property reserved for profitable use' is he bound to pay the 'fair rent'.[45]

This teaching does not agree with Qāḍīkhān's discussion of 'unauthorised use' of rent-yielding property (see Chapter 3, section 10 above). It is developed by the Mamluk and Ottoman jurists and strengthens the private rentier's claim to the 'fair rent'. But the private rentier's claim to the 'fair rent' is always weaker than that of the *waqf*. With regard to *waqf* property, the intention of the user is completely irrelevant. Whosoever uses such property is obliged retroactively to pay the 'fair rent'. To quote a few examples from the Syrian *fatāwā*: it may not come as a surprise that the man who transformed a mosque into a coffee house was held liable retroactively to pay the 'fair rent' to the *waqf*. At least he knew what he was doing.[46] The man who rents *waqf* land from a state representative whom he believes to be entitled to lease the land, is also held liable retroactively to pay the 'fair rent' to the *waqf*.[47] Peasants who reclaim waste *waqf* lands by building new irrigation systems are held liable to pay the 'fair rent' to the *waqf* retroactively.[48] If land is bought under a valid contract of sale and it later becomes known that it is *waqf* land, the buyer is held liable retroactively to pay the 'fair rent' to the *waqf*.[49] Peasants who live on lands that they consider to be their property and that the *waqf* administrator claims for the *waqf* and who cannot prove that the levies which they pay to the state are *kharāj*, are considered to be the *waqf*'s tenants and bound retroactively to pay the 'fair rent' to the *waqf*.[50] Retroactive payment may cover a period of several years. Such cases are by no means rare in the *fatāwā*.[51]

Holding the unauthorised user of *waqf* lands (and state lands) and orphans' lands liable under all circumstances to pay the 'fair rent' is certainly the most important change that the Hanafite jurists of the post-classical period introduced into the Hanafite legal doctrine concerning rent. The Ottoman jurists explicitly interpret this new concept of rent as the law of the 'modern jurists' (*al-muta'akhkhirūn*).[52]

The new doctrine on rent grants a privileged legal status to all forms of rent-yielding property and makes the *waqf* the rent-yielding property *par excellence*. With regard to the unauthorised use of *waqf* property, the contractual and consensual elements are conspicuously absent from the new doctrine on rent. Even if a *waqf*'s administrator offers a house or a room free of charge to a person who does not enjoy the right of benefit, the user is liable to pay the 'fair rent'. If the *waqf* administrator leases the *waqf* land for rent that falls far below the level of the 'fair rent', the tenant is liable retroactively to pay the 'fair rent'. This liability in no way depends on the will of the *waqf* administrator or the intention of the user. In fact, with regard to the *waqf*, the new concept of rent often comes very close to a concept of public law in which the *waqf* administrator is not entitled freely to waive his claims and the user is not entitled to accept special benefits.[53]

In the case of 'unauthorised use', the rent paid to the *waqf* can hardly be differentiated from a tax: the contract is no condition for the obligation to pay this rent; the *waqf* administrator has to defend the public interest, and were he to offer special advantages to the user, the user would not be entitled to accept them. The contractual and consensual element is virtually absent from this concept of rent. The tendency to give a dominant role to public law and to the *qāḍī* with regard to the leasing of *waqf* lands is already discernible in the ninth-century writings of Iraqi jurists (see Chapter 2, section 7 above). But it is only after the transformation of the peasants' taxes into rent and the introduction of the principle that 'unauthorised use' of rent-yielding property entails the obligation retroactively to pay the 'fair rent', that the rent paid to the *waqf* acquires the character of a tax.

With regard to 'unauthorised use' (*ghaṣb*), the post-classical Hanafite doctrine on rent differentiates between various forms of landed property. Someone making unauthorised use of state lands, *waqf* lands and orphans' property is held liable under all circumstances to pay the 'fair rent'. Someone using 'private property reserved for profitable use' is bound to pay rent only if he consciously and intentionally makes 'unauthorised use' of these lands. Someone making 'unauthorised use' of lands that are tilled by their owners and are not held in order to yield rent does not pay rent at all. With regard to the peasant owners who do not regularly lease their lands, but till them in order to satisfy their own needs, the classical Hanafite doctrine on rent (see Chapter 2, sections 5-9 above) applies. The post-classical Hanafite doctrine on rent in this way establishes a clear-cut difference between rent-yielding property of the rentier class and the property held by its owners for personal use. The classical concept of 'unauthorised use' remains meaningful only with regard to property that is not 'reserved for profitable use'.

b) The 'fair rent' as the yardstick of the 'contractually fixed rent'

A contract of tenancy or share-cropping concerning *waqf* lands or lands that are orphan's property (*māl al-yatīm*) that is concluded with a 'contractually fixed rent' (*musammā*) (see Chapter 2, sections 5, 7, 8 above) which falls far below the 'fair rent' is held by the Ottoman jurists to be a voidable contract. With regard to arable lands there is no unanimous agreement as to the difference that may legally exist between the 'contractually fixed' and the 'fair rent' without making the contract voidable. Some muftis think that the *laesio enormis* (*ghabn fāḥish*) results when this difference surpasses 20 per cent of the 'contractually fixed rent'.[54] Others think that 50 per cent is the limit.[55] The legal reasoning that makes such a *laesio enormis* sufficient grounds for the dissolution of a contract of tenancy is already implied in the classical doctrine (see Chapter 2, section 7 above). But according to the interpretation of the classical doctrine the 'fair rent' could only be levied after the dissolution of the old contract.[56] Transoxanian authors of the eleventh and twelfth centuries had discussed the question of whether such a contract was a voidable contract or a case of 'unauthorised use'.[57] The Syrian muftis of the seventeenth and eighteenth centuries held the tenant liable for retroactive payment of the 'fair rent' — beginning with the moment at which it was first possible for him to use the land. The muftis did not always follow their new principles. The *fatwā* did not, apparently, depend solely on the legal principle to be applied. Khair ad-Dīn Ramlī, for example, in one case applied the classical principle of *istiḥsān* according to which the 'fair rent' in such a case should not surpass the 'contractually fixed rent' (see Chapter 2, section 8 above).[58] In other cases he followed the 'modern' principle according to which retroactive payment of the 'fair rent' is due — whether it surpasses the 'contractually fixed rent' or not.[59] I consider these inconsistencies to be normal in the application of all legal systems. What is of importance to my argument is the fact that a new principle of retroactive payment of the 'fair rent' came into being and that it was generally acknowledged and partly applied.

The details of the jurists' rather theoretical argument about the definition of the 'fair rent' will not be discussed here. The muftis evidently wanted to maintain a rent market that was not completely determined by the tax/rent collected on state lands. They took great pains to establish a system of market rules[60] which took into account the coercive power of the Sultan and of the political elite which tended to jeopardise the rules and mechanisms of the rent market. The muftis, therefore, tried to ensure that the rent which the Sultan and the political elite obtained from their lands would not be considered as the basis for defining the 'fair rent'.[61] Also the outbidding which occurs for reasons of personal enmity between the tenant and the outbidder with the purpose of harming the interest of the tenant[62] should not be considered an indicator of the 'fair rent'. For, on the one hand, it is forbidden to do harm, and on the other, out-bidding does not reflect the general fluctuation of the market for rents.[63] In principle, only the general fluctuation of the market as represented through growing demand and the rising level of rents can legally be considered as determining the level of the 'fair rent'.[64] This rule is of practical importance only with regard to the dissolution of a contract of tenancy that was originally concluded with a 'contractually fixed rent' that corresponded to the 'fair rent'. Whether such a contract could be dissolved when the market level of the 'fair rent' rose was a question which the muftis had great difficulties in answering. In the end they agreed that dissolution was possible when the difference between the 'fair rent' and the 'contractually fixed rent' surpassed either 20 per cent or 50 per cent of the 'contractually fixed rent', and also that in this case the 'fair rent' could not be levied retroactively.[65] For all other practical purposes it would appear that the muftis followed the rule that the 'fair rent' was the highest attainable rent.[66]

c) The hierarchy of different forms of landed property

I should like to quote some examples from the *fatāwā* to show how in the eyes of the Syrian muftis of the seventeenth and eighteenth centuries the different forms of property and the different doctrines regarding rent were applied as a means of distinguishing between peasant ownership of land and rent-yielding forms of landed property. Ḥāmid b. ᶜAlī al-ᶜImādī was asked:

> If Zaid owns land he tills personally and which he does not [regularly] farm out under a share-cropping relationship and ᶜAmr tills the land and grows wheat on it with his own seed and without the permission of the landowner mentioned above and the crop is ready for harvesting, does the crop fall to the cultivator? The answer: Yes! (*suᵓila fīmā idhā kāna li-zaid^{in} arḍ^{un} yazraᶜuhā bi-nafsihi wa-lā yadfaᶜuhā muzāraᶜat^{an} fa-zaraᶜahā ᶜAmr^{un} bibadhrihi ḥinṭat^{an} bilā idhni mālikihā l-mazbūri wa-staḥṣada z-zarᶜu fa-hali z-zarᶜu l-iz-zāriᶜ? Al-jawāb: naᶜam*).[67]

In other words, the cultivator who makes unauthorised use of peasant lands that are not legally recognised as rent-yielding property (*muᶜadd li-l-ijār* or *muᶜadd li-l-muzāraᶜa*) appropriates the whole crop and is not obliged to pay any rent to the peasant.

The case is different when the cultivator makes unauthorised use of lands that are *muᶜadd li-z-zirāᶜa*, i.e. rent-yielding property. ᶜImādī is asked about the case of a cultivator who makes use of such village lands that are *muᶜadd li-z-zirāᶜa*, i.e. rent-yielding property, and for whose unauthorised use village custom fixes a ratio of crop-sharing between the owner and the user. The mufti accepts village custom as an adequate basis for settling the conflict. He adds, with reference to Ḥaṣkafī, that if no village custom fixes the ratio of crop-sharing the cultivator would have to pay the 'fair rent' and that a *waqf* would under all circumstances receive either the customary share or the 'fair rent'.[68] Ibn ᶜĀbidīn, commenting on this *fatwā*, points out that the sharing ratio of village custom does not necessarily represent the 'fair rent'.[69] Over two pages he discusses the different legal opinions on what constitutes a legally valid source of the claim to 'fair rent' and how to define the 'fair rent' with regard to different forms of landed property. He begins with a definition of the difference between a peasant proprietor and a proprietor who 'reserves his land for profitable use'. He says:

> [According to one legal opinion] it is said that if the land is prepared for profitable use, i.e. if the proprietor is among those persons who do not cultivate their lands in person and instead convey it [regularly to third persons] under a [contract of] share-cropping, then this [use] will be legally regarded as a share-cropping relationship and the proprietor of the land will receive his share according to the custom of that village (*wa-qīla lau kānati l-arḍu muᶜaddatᵘⁿ li-z-zirāᶜati bi-an kāna rabbuhā mimman la yazraᶜu bi-nafsihi wa-yadfaᶜuhā muzāraᶜatᵃⁿ fa-dhālika ᶜalā l-muzāraᶜati fa-li-rabbi l-arḍi ḥiṣṣatᵘⁿ ᶜalā mā huwa ᶜurfu tilka l-qarya*).[70]

He adds that according to this legal opinion, which is apparently the legal opinion that was already held by Qāḍīkhān in the twelfth century (see Chapter 3, section 10 above), the customary share falls due only if it is not known at the time of the cultivation of the land that the user consciously and intentionally makes 'unauthorised use' of the land. If, for example, the landowner refuses to lease the land to him and he cultivates it in spite of this refusal, the classical doctrine applies and no rent falls due, even if the land is *muᶜadd li-l-istighlāl*, rent-yielding property. Only the *waqf*'s claim to a customary share or the 'fair rent' is valid even under these circumstances.[71] He then goes on to say that 'unauthorised use' of the land does not engender any obligation to pay rent if the owner of the land is a peasant who tills the soil personally (*lau kāna ṣāḥibuhā yazraᶜuhā bi-nafsih*).[72]

Ibn ᶜĀbidīn makes it clear that these legal opinions are obsolete. They represent only the beginning of the 'modern' doctrine on rent. Ibn ᶜĀbidīn does not accept the legal opinion that makes the payment of the 'fair rent' or of the customary share of the crop dependent on the intention of the person who makes unauthorised use of the land. He clearly defends the principle that the legal status of rent-yielding property is the source of the obligation to pay the 'fair rent' or the customary share of the crop. He says: 'But the legal opinion that is generally held (*al-mashhūr*) and according to which the *fatwā* is given is that 'unauthorised use' is not warranted except in the [cases of] *waqf*, orphans' property and '[private] property reserved for profitable use ...'[73] After discussing the various legal opinions on the question, Ibn ᶜĀbidīn reaches the following conclusion:

> The result is that, if someone tills someone else's land without his permission even by way of 'unauthorised use' then [the following will apply] (1) if the land was private property and the proprietor reserved it for agricultural use [on a share-cropping basis], the customary rate of sharing, if there is one, will be taken into account; (2) if there is no such custom and he [i.e. the landowner] reserved it for the purpose of farming it out, the whole crop will fall to the cultivating peasant upon whom the payment of the 'fair rent' to the proprietor falls due; (3) if not [i.e. if it was not prepared for the purpose of being farmed out] and the land diminished in value [through its cultivation] the cultivator owes the diminution of the value. If it did not diminish [in value], he owes nothing; (4) if it is a *waqf* and a custom [about rates of crop-sharing] exists and if it proves to be more beneficial to the *waqf* [than the fair rent], then it is the custom that is

legally relevant; otherwise, the fair rent [applies]. This rule holds also if the lands are orphan's property or belong to the sultan ... (*fa-l-ḥāṣilu anna man zaraʿa arḍa ghairihi bilā idhnihi wa-lau ʿalā wajhi l-ghaṣbi fa-in kānati l-arḍu milkᵃⁿ wa-aʿaddahā rabbuhā li-z-zirāʿati ʿtabara l-ʿurfu fī l-ḥiṣṣati in kāna thammata ʿurf. Wa-illā fa-in aʿaddahā li-l-ījāri fa-l-khāriju kulluhu li-z-zāriʿi wa-ʿalaihi ajru mithlihā li-rabbihā. Wa-illā fa-in intaqaṣat fa-ʿalaihi n-nuqṣān. Wa-illā fa-lā shaiʾa ʿalaih. Wa-in kānat waqfᵃⁿ fa-in thammata ʿurfᵘⁿ wa-kāna anfaʿa ʿtabar. Wa-illā fa-ajru l-mithl. Wa-kadhā lau kānat māla yatīmⁱⁿ au sulṭāniyya* ...).[74]

This summary conclusion of a legal discussion that began in the classical and continued throughout the post-classical period of Hanafite law clearly underlines the existence of a hierarchy of different forms of landed property. At the top level state lands, *waqf* lands and orphans' landed property always receive the biggest obtainable amount of rent. The private rent-yielding property is much more dependent on custom. In the case of 'unauthorised use' it will receive the 'fair rent' only if no customary rate of crop-sharing exists. Otherwise, it will receive the customary share. In the case of 'unauthorised use' of his lands the peasant proprietor will receive no rent at all. This also holds true for the peasant cultivator who is a tenant on state lands, *waqf* lands or the landed property of private owners.[75]

Different concepts of rent and property are expressed in the classical and the post-classical Hanafite doctrine on rent. In the Ottoman period they existed side by side. They are evidently used as a means of differentiating between different forms of landed property. The classical doctrine with all its restrictions applies to the peasant proprietors. The modern law is applied to the 'exempted categories', i.e. to those rent-yielding forms of property that are the source of revenue of the rentier class.

The many difficulties that result from the coexistence of an old and a modern doctrine and of various legal opinions within each of these doctrines find their clearest expression in the basic rule concerning litigations dealing with *waqf*. It is held throughout the post-classical period that, whenever differences of legal opinions exist, the muftis must follow the legal opinion most useful (*anfaʿ*) for the *waqf*.[76]

5. THE MODERN LEGAL DOCTRINE

It is commonly assumed that the conservative idealism of Islamic law finds its expression in the deep-rooted conviction of the jurists that the prescriptions of Islamic law are unchanged and unchangeable. But until well into the nineteenth century this was not how muftis and jurists viewed their legal tradition. Beginning in the eleventh century and continuing until the period of the Tanzimat (1839-76), the jurists were aware of differences in conceptions and doctrines that separated the Hanafite doctrine of the 'modern jurists' (*al-muta'akhkhirūn*) from that of the 'classical jurists' (*al-mutaqaddimūn*). Time and again they tell their readers that they follow a legal doctrine that was developed by the 'modern jurists'. This modern doctrine by no means dealt with only those cases that had not been settled by the old doctrine. The muftis and jurists openly acknowledged that their doctrine differs from the legal opinions of the classical school of Hanafite law[77] and stressed the point that the *fatwā* has to be given according to the legal opinion of the 'modern jurists'.[78] Such an attitude is indeed not surprising in a situation in which the old doctrine dealt with only the peasant proprietors whereas the 'modern doctrine' supported and protected the interests of classes who drew their revenue from rent-yielding property.

NOTES

1. Ramlī, *Kitāb al-Fatāwā al-Khairīya li-Naf' al-Barrīya* (Bulaq, 1300 A.H., reprint edn, Beirut, 1974), vol. 1, pp. 98, 215, vol. 2, pp. 13, 154; Ibn ʿĀbidīn, *al-ʿUqūd ad-Durrīya fī Tanqīh al-Fatāwā al-Ḥāmidīya* (2nd edn, Bulaq, 1300 A.H., reprint edn, Beirut, n.d.), vol. 1, pp. 182-3.

2. Ibid., p. 352 states that he completed the first volume in Ramadan 1236 A.H./June 1821 A.D., and vol. 2, p. 336 that he completed the second volume in Rabīʿ 1238 A.H./December 1822 A.D.

3. Iḥsān ʿAbbās, 'Khair ad-Dīn ar-Ramlī's Fatāwā: A New Light on Life in Palestine in the Eleventh/Seventeenth Century', in Ulrich Haarmann and Peter Bachmann (eds), *Die islamische Welt zwischen Mittelalter und Neuzeit. Festschrift für Hans Robert Roemer zum 60. Geburstag* (Beiruter Texte und Studien. Band 22. Franz Steiner Verlag, Wiesbaden, 1979).

4. According to Ibn ʿĀbidīn, *ʿUqūd*, vol. 2, p. 335, Ḥāmid b. ʿAlī al-ʿImādī held office from 1136-55 A.H./1724/5 — 1742/3 A.D. According to Linda Schatkowski Schilcher, *Families in Politics.*

Damascene Factions and Estates of the 18th and 19th centuries (Berliner Islamstudien Band 2, Franz Steiner Verlag, Stuttgart 1985), p. 119, he held office from 1725-58 with only ten months' interruption. It is likely that this interruption occurred in 1155 A.H./1742-3 A.D. because otherwise it is unexplainable why Ibn ᶜĀbidīn should give this date as the end of the *iftāʾ* of Ḥāmid b. ᶜAlī. On the ᶜImādī family, see H.A.R. Gibb and Harold Bowen, *Islamic Society and the West, A Study of the Impact of Western Civilization on Moslem Culture in the Near East* (Oxford University Press, London, 1950), vol. 1, part 2, p. 136.

5. Abdul-Karim Rafeq, 'Economic Relations between Damascus and the Dependent Countryside, 1743-71', in A.L. Udovitch (ed.), *The Islamic Middle East 700-1900. Studies in Economic and Social History* (The Darwin Press Inc., Princeton, 1981).

6. Ibid., p. 656.

7. Ibn Nujaim, *at-Tuḥfa al-Marḍīya fī Arāḍī al-Miṣrīya* (MS Staatsbibliothek, Berlin, WE 1724), fols 131b, 132b. For the Ottoman authorities, see Joseph Matuz, *Das Osmanische Reich, Grundlinien seiner Geschichte* (Wissenschaftliche Buchgesellschaft Darmstadt, Darmstadt, 1985), pp. 107-8, 147. It would appear that already under the Ayyubids the tax-paying peasant was regarded as a tenant on state lands, see Claude Cahen, 'Le régime des impôts dans le Fayyūm Ayyūbide', *Arabica*, 3 (1956), p. 24.

8. Ḥaṣkafī, *Durr al-Multaqā fī Sharḥ al-Multaqā*, printed on the margin of Ḍamād Afandī, *Majmaᶜ al-Anhur fī Sharḥ Multaqā al-Abḥur*, vol. 1, p. 663.

9. Ḍamād Afandī, *Majmaᶜ al-Anhur fī Sharḥ Multaqā al-Abḥur* (Dār Iḥyāʾ at-Tūrath al-ᶜArabī, n.pl., 1316 A.H.), vol. 1, p. 663.

10. Ibn Nujaim, *al-Baḥr ar-Rāʾiq Sharḥ Kanz ad-Daqāʾiq* (Cairo, 1311 A.H./1894 A.D.), vol. 5, p. 118.

11. Ramlī, *al-Fatāwā al-Khairīya*, vol. 1, pp. 99-100, 151, 196; vol. 2, p. 233; Ibn ʿĀbidīn, *ʿUqūd*, vol. 1, p. 310; vol. 2, p. 112.

12. Ramlī, *al-Fatāwā al-Khairīya*, vol. 1, pp. 96, 100, 167; Ibn ᶜĀbidīn, *ʿUqūd*, vol. 2, p. 199.

13. Ramlī, *al-Fatāwā al-Khairīya*, vol. 1, pp. 97, 98, 99-100, 206, 215-6; vol. 2, p. 136; Ibn ᶜĀbidīn, *ᶜUqūd*, vol. 1, pp. 9-10; vol. 2, pp. 132, 141. See also Ṭarābulsī, *al-Isʿāf fī Aḥkām al-Awqāf* (Beirut, 1401 A.H./1981 A.D.), p. 71, and Ibn Nujaim, *al-Ashbāh wa-n-Naẓāʾir ᶜalā Madhhab Abī Ḥanīfa an-Nuʿmān* (Beirut, 1400 A.H./1980 A.D.), p. 271 and see p. 414.

14. On the various groups of rentiers that had claims on the peasants of the same villages and tax districts in Mamluk Egypt, see Heinz Halm, *Ägypten nach den mamlukischen Lehensregistern*, vol. 1, *Oberägypten und das Fayyum* (Dr Ludwig Reichert Verlag, Wiesbaden, 1979), *passim*. On the competition for rent in Palestine and Syria during the seventeenth and eighteenth centuries see Ramlī, *al-Fatāwā al-Khairīya*, vol. 1, pp. 99, 148, 206; Ibn ᶜĀbidīn, *ᶜUqūd*, vol. 1, pp. 9, 12, 176, 182, 313; vol. 2, pp. 28, 103-4, 132, 201.

15. Ramlī, *al-fatāwā al-Khairīya*, vol. 1, pp. 99, 206; Ibn ᶜĀbidīn, *ʿUqūd*, vol. 1, pp. 9-10, 176, 313. In cases in which the administrator's right to collect the *waqf*'s share of the peasant's levies is not disputed,

the jurists do not hesitate to impose the obligation to pay the *kharāj* to the soldier on the peasant, see Ramlī, *al-Fatāwā al-Khairīya*, vol. 1, p. 146.

16. Ibid., pp. 99, 148, 206; Ibn ᶜĀbidīn, *ᶜUqūd*, vol. 1, pp. 9-10, 176, 313. It is only in the nineteenth century that a jurist like Ibn ᶜĀbidīn pleads for a return to the legal opinions of Abū Yūsuf and Shaibānī in order to shift the burden of taxation on the tenant, see ibid., p. 10.

17. Ibid.

18. Ramlī, *al-Fatāwā al-Khairīya*, vol. 1, pp. 185-6, vol. 2, pp. 117, 119, 126, 127, 129, 135, 136; Ibn ᶜĀibidīn, *ᶜUqūd*, vol. 2, pp. 111, 132. It is worth mentioning that Ibn ᶜĀbidīn in his commentary on ᶜImādī tends to regard it as admissible, see ibid., p. 111.

19. Ṭarābulsī, *al-Isᶜāf*, pp. 24-5.

20. Ibn Nujaim, *al-Baḥr ar-Rāʾiq*, vol. 5, pp. 203, 240.

21. Ḥaṣkafī, *Durr al-Muntaqā*, vol. 1, pp. 663-4. See also Ḍamād Afandī, *Majmaᶜ al-Anhur*, vol. 1, p. 668.

22. Ramlī, *al-Fatāwā al-Khairīya*, vol. 1, p. 239.

23. Ibrahim el-Mouelhy, 'Nouveaux documents sur le fallah et le régime des terres sous les Ottomans', *Annales Islamologiques*, 11 (1972), pp. 254-5.

24. Ramlī, *al-Fatāwā al-Khairīya*, vol. 2, p. 154; see Ibn ᶜĀbidīn, *ᶜUqūd*, vol. 1, p. 182.

25. Ibid., *ᶜUqūd*, p. 182, see. vol. 2, p. 199.

26. Ibid., pp. 104, 157 on shops, magazines and other *musaqqafāt* (rentable buildings (with roofs) as opposed to lands).

27. The bath seems to have been the classical example for illustrating the real property 'reserved for profitable use'. The fact that Shaibānī in the *Aṣl* does not differentiate between a house and a bath is quoted by Qāḍīkhān, *Kitāb al-Fatāwā al-Khānīya* (Cairo, 1282 A.H.) vol. 2, p. 270 as indicating that Shaibānī did not yet differentiate between the two forms of property. According to the new doctrine a bath is always 'reserved for profitable use'.

28. Ibn Nujaim, *al-Baḥr ar-Rāʾiq*, vol. 5, p. 221 and Ḍamād Afandī, *Majmaᶜ al-Anhur*, vol. 2, p. 467.

29. Ṭarābulsī, *al-Isᶜāf*, p. 38.

30. Qāḍīzādeh, *Natāʾij al-Afkār fī Kashf ar-Rumūz waʾl-Asrār*, printed as vols 7 and 8 of Ibn al-Humām, *Sharḥ Fatḥ al-Qadīr* (Cairo 1356 A.H.), vol. 7, p. 396; Ramlī, *al-Fatāwā al-Khairīya*, vol. 2, p. 119.

31. Ibid., vol. 1, pp. 95, 99, 195; Ibn ᶜĀbidīn, *ᶜUqūd*, vol. 1, p. 196; vol. 2, p. 129.

32. Ibid., p. 109.

33. Ibid., p. 130.

34. Ibid., p. 136.

35. Ibid., pp. 156-8.

36. Ibid., p. 130.

37. Ibid., vol. 1, pp. 181, 196; vol. 2, pp. 102, 103, 109, 114, 115, 136, 141, 158. They are constantly treated as one unity. Ramlī on the other hand tends to underline the difference between *waqf* and *milk*

muʿadd li-l-istighlāl.

38. Ramlī, *al-Fatāwā al-Khairīya*, vol. 1, pp. 95, 99, 100, 123; vol. 2, p. 78; Ibn ʿĀbidīn, *ʿUqūd*, vol. 1, p. 176; vol. 2, pp. 102, 158. Occasionally the muftis display the tendency to restrict the retroactive payment of the 'fair rent' to *waqf* land and to exclude state land from this legal ordinance, e.g. ibid., vol. 2, p. 208.

39. Ibid., p. 200, see also p. 101.

40. Ibn Nujaim, *al-Baḥr ar-Rāʾiq*, vol. 5, p. 235; Ibn ʿĀbidīn, *ʿUqūd*, vol. 1, pp. 180, 184, 193; Ramlī, *al-Fatāwā al-Khairīya*, vol. 2, p. 118.

41. Ibn ʿĀbidīn, *ʿUqūd*, vol. 2, pp. 103, 115.

42. Ibn Nujaim, *al-Ashbāh*, p. 284.

43. See note 37 above.

44. Ramlī, *al-Fatāwā al-Khairīya*, vol. 1, p. 195.

45. Ibn Nujaim, *al-Ashbāh*, pp. 284-5; Ramlī, *al-Fatāwā al-Khairīya*, vol. 2, pp. 130-1; Ibn ʿĀbidīn, *ʿUqūd*, vol. 2, pp. 102, 130, 138.

46. Ibid., vol. 1, p. 181.

47. Ramlī, *al-Fatāwā al-Khairīya*, vol. 1, p. 199.

48. Ibn ʿĀbidīn, *ʿUqūd*, vol. 2, p. 132.

49. Ramlī, *al-Fatāwā al-Khairīya*, vol. 1, pp. 131, 194-5; Ibn ʿĀbidīn, *ʿUqūd*, vol. 1, p. 172.

50. Ibid., vol. 1, p. 183.

51. Ibid., pp. 175, 181, 182-3; vol. 2, pp. 99, 134; Ramlī, *al-Fatāwā al-Khairīya*, vol. 1, pp. 121, 195, 197; vol. 2, pp. 121, 130.

52. Ibn Nujaim, *al-Ashbāh*, p. 284; Ramlī, *al-Fatāwā al-Khairīya*, vol. 1, pp. 121, 195; vol. 2, pp. 118, 119, 130-1; Ibn ʿĀbidīn, *ʿUqūd*, vol. 1, pp. 184, 224; vol. 2, pp. 102, 115, 136, 158. Similarly, the right of the Imam, the muezzin, etc. to a contractually fixed salary is a 'modern' regulation, see Baber Johansen, 'The Servants of the Mosques', *The Maghreb Review*, 7, nos. 1-2 (January-April 1982), p. 28. Other forms of 'modern' legal ordinances collected at random from the *fatāwā* concern the sale of the orphan's property, Ramlī, *al-Fatāwā al-Khairīya*, vol. 1, p. 95; the obvious appearances as a valid form of evidence that carries greater weight than the testimony of one or two witnesses, ibid., vol. 1, p. 217; the principle that the mufti always has to choose the legal opinion that is most useful to the *waqf*, ibid., p. 218; special liabilities resulting from the destruction of *waqf* buildings, ibid., vol. 2, p. 122; the legal ordinance that land should revert to its former owner if it has been sold at too low a price, ibid., vol. 2, p. 143; the liability of the informer for the damage that the authorities might inflict on the denounced person, ibid., pp. 151, 153, and Ibn ʿĀbidīn, *ʿUqūd*, vol. 1, p. 310; vol. 2, pp. 164-5; the liability of the plaintiff before a secular court for the damage that might be inflicted upon the defendant, ibid., vol. 1, p. 310; the repartition of the levies collected on the villages so that those landowners who left the villages and were living in towns were obliged to pay the levies on the lands only and not the levies on persons, ibid., vol. 2, pp. 182-3.

53. Ramlī, *al-Fatāwā al-Khairīya*, vol. 1, p. 148, see p. 197 and vol. 2, p. 130; Ibn ʿĀbidīn, *ʿUqūd*, vol. 1, p. 224; vol. 2, pp. 100, 121, 131, 157-8.

54. Ramlī, *al-Fatāwā al-Khairīya*, vol. 1, p. 219; Ibn ʿĀbidīn, *ʿUqūd*, vol. 2, p. 101.

55. Ibid., vol. 1, p. 225; vol. 2, p. 101.

56. Kāsānī, *Kitāb Badāʾiʿ aṣ-Ṣanāʾiʿ fī Tartīb ash-Sharāʾiʿ* (Cairo, 1328 A.H./1910 A.D.), vol. 4, p. 200.

57. Qāḍīkhān, *Kitāb al-Fatāwā*, vol. 2, p. 281; vol. 3, p. 331.

58. Ramlī, *al-Fatāwā al-Khairīya*, vol. 1, p. 213.

59. Ibid., pp. 177, 197; vol. 2, pp. 129-30.

60. See the detailed discussion in Ibn ʿĀbidīn, *ʿUqūd*, vol. 1, pp. 224-6.

61. Ibid., vol 2, p. 104.

62. Such outbidding for reasons of personal enmity creates problems for *waqf* administrations until this very day, see for example Georg Stöber, '"Habous Public" in Chaouen: Zur wirtschaftlichen Bedeutung religiöser Stiftungen in Nordmarokko', *Die Welt des Islams*, 25 (1985), note 11.

63. Ramlī, *al-Fatāwā al-Khairīya*, vol. 1, pp. 212-3; vol. 2, pp. 124, 230; Ibn ʿĀbidīn, *ʿUqūd*, vol. 1, pp. 224, 225, 226; vol. 2, pp. 114, 200.

64. Ibid., vol. 1, pp. 224-6.

65. Ibn Nujaim, *al-Ashbāh*, p. 268; Ramlī, *al-Fatāwā al-Khairīya*. vol. 1, p. 213; Ibn ʿĀbidīn, *ʿUqūd*, vol. 1, pp. 224-6; vol. 2, pp. 101, 116, 134.

66. Ibid., pp. 101, 117.

67. Ibid., p. 156.

68. Ibid., p. 157.

69. Ibid., pp. 114, 157, 158.

70. Ibid., p. 157.

71. Ibid.

72. Ibid., p. 158. I should not like to pass in silence over the fact that among the legal opinions mentioned by Ibn ʿĀbidīn and characterised as being irrelevant to the *fatwā*, he quotes one legal opinion as stating that if a village custom of crop-sharing exists it may apply to peasants' lands also, see ibid., p. 157.

73. Ibid., p. 158.

74. Ibid.

75. Ibid., vol. 2, pp. 114, 132, 157, 209; Ramlī, *al-Fatāwa al-Khairīya*, vol. 2, pp. 150, 166, 167; see also p. 168.

76. Ibid., vol. 1, pp. 120, 161, 190, 197, 199, 203, 218; vol. 2, pp. 121, 138; Ibn ʿĀbidīn, *ʿUqūd*, vol. 2, p. 158. This principle is already applied by Qāḍīkhān, *Kitāb al-Fatāwā*, vol. 3, pp. 330, 335.

77. Ramlī, *al-Fatāwā al-Khairīya*, vol. 2, p. 130; Ibn ʿĀbidīn, *ʿUqud*, vol. 2, pp. 102, 136; see also note 52 above.

78. Ramlī, *al-Fatāwa al-Khairīya*, vol. 1, p. 218; vol. 2, p. 119; Ibn ʿĀbidīn, *ʿUqūd*, vol. 1, p. 184; vol. 2, pp. 102, 136, 157.

6

Summary and Conclusion

SUMMARY

1. The pre-classical and classical Hanafite doctrine on tax and rent defines the payment of land taxes as a proof of proprietary rights with regard to arable lands. It states that taxation is universal and applicable to all lands and (almost) all social groups and strata.

2. With regard to the productive use of land, classical Hanafite law developed a new dimension for the notion of property. It would appear that the Hanafite notions of commodity (*māl mutaqauwim*) and commodity value (*taqawwum*) are based on the idea that the ownership of exchangeable commodities, *res in commercio* (*amwāl mutaqauwima*), is an ownership of things. Commodities in this sense can be either exchanged or used by their owners. But the productive use of such commodities by third persons does not constitute a commodity. In order to legalise the land owners' appropriation of rent from their tenants, Hanafite jurists had to develop the idea that through the contract of tenancy or share-cropping the productive use of land is transformed into a commodity. Consequently, Hanafite law of the pre-classical and classical periods considers the contract to be a necessary (but not a sufficient) condition for the obligation to pay rent. The contract, thereby, becomes the clearest criterion for the differentiation between tax and rent.

3. In the post-classical period of Hanafite law, the majority of peasants are excluded from the payment of the land tax. The

levies collected from them are considered to be rent that does not prove ownership rights. This development is symbolised and legalised in terms of the discussion of 'the death of the *kharāj* payer' and the *arḍ al-ḥauz*, the sequestrated lands. In this way, the payment of the land tax becomes a privilege that proves the rentier classes' proprietary rights to their lands and guarantees their right to collect rent from the peasants who till these lands. Fiscal privileges of members of the rentier class are generally acknowledged.

4. The legal status of rent-yielding landed property is assimilated to that of state lands in that the rent paid for its use falls due in the way of taxes. With regard to rent-yielding landed property, the contract is no longer considered to be a necessary condition for the obligation to pay rent. The relationship between the rentier and his peasants is no longer based mainly on contract and consent. In all cases of non-contractual use and in many cases of contractual use, the amount of rent to be paid does not depend on the agreement between tenant and lessor nor on the intention of the *waqf* administrator. The assimilation of the rent on rent-yielding landed property to a tax is obvious with regard to *waqf* lands and to lands administered in the interest of orphans (i.e. falling under the special jurisdiction of the *qāḍīs*). To a lesser degree the tendency is also discernible with regard to 'private property reserved for profitable use' (*milk mu'add li-l-istighlāl*). With regard to these three forms of property, the contract ceases to be a necessary condition for the obligation to pay rent. This also holds true for state lands. All forms of the rentier classes' landed property are thereby clearly differentiated from the peasants' ownership of landed property to which the classical doctrine of contractual rent continues to apply.

5. The notion that the levies collected from the peasants are rent and not taxes gives the *waqf* and the private owners of rent-yielding landed property the right of priority over the state and its representatives with regard to the collection of the rent from their tenants. The state's claim to tax *waqf* and private landed property can only be enforced against the tax payer, i.e. the *waqf* or the private owner of rent-yielding property. The peasants are tenant cultivators who pay rent, not taxes. This amounts to saying that their rent to the *waqf* and the private

owner of rent-yielding landed property includes the tax and cannot be distinguished from it. It is only through the tax payer's payment of the land tax that the private revenue accruing to the rentier is differentiated from the tax that is paid to the state. In the relationship between landlord and peasant the tax cannot be distinguished from the rent.

6. The notions and concepts of the new doctrine on rent were first developed in Balkh and Bukhara during the classical period. How and when the new doctrine became the prevalent legal doctrine in Mamluk and Ottoman Syria and Egypt remains a matter for investigation. It seems clear, however, that the disappearance of peasant ownership of small holdings as an important structural characteristic of the rural society of the Near East was one of the conditions that made the new doctrine so convincing to the jurists and the rentiers in Egypt and Syria and encouraged the systematic elaboration of the new doctrine by Ottoman Hanafite jurists.

7. It is noteworthy that throughout the post-classical period the Hanafite jurists were aware of the fact that they applied new legal doctrine and they did not make the slightest attempt to conceal this awareness.

CONCLUSIONS

1. It seems impossible to maintain the notion, equally cherished in East and West, that *fiqh* after the tenth century is an unchanging structure of legal ordinances. After the tenth century, Muslim jurists found it impossible simply to adhere to the old legal ordinances without sacrificing the economic interest of the social stratum to which they belonged. The law had to be adapted to a new political and socio-economic order. The knowledge that was required for this adaptation had to be acquired in a process of trial and error which eventually led to the introduction of new notions, concepts and doctrines. Indeed, the whole history of Islamic law may be studied as a slow process of accumulating legal opinions which diverge from the old doctrine. Such a study should follow the development in time and space of legal opinions with regard to interrelated key concepts of the law. In the light of research along these lines a re-interpretation of the relationship between *ijtihād* and *taqlīd*

seems desirable. Far from being a historical reality at all levels of legal activities, *taqlīd* often seems to be a pious wish rather than the actual practice of the jurists. It is a conscious attempt to maintain important elements of the legal tradition in the face of social and legal change that threatened the unity of Hanafite legal teaching.

2. Researchers should pay more attention than in the past to the relationship between the different levels of legal literature. This subject is often treated by the Ottoman jurists who clearly assigned different functions to the different layers of *mutūn*, *shurūḥ* and *fatāwā* in the context of upholding the venerated tradition and changing it. A systematic comparison of the results obtained from the analysis of these layers of legal literature with the *qāḍīs' sijillāt* seems highly desirable. From the jurists' discussion of tax and rent it seems evident that, at the level of the *fatāwā*, new legal opinions are introduced and that it is easily acceptable to the jurists that the *fatwā* has to be given in the light of the 'modern jurists' legal opinions. When new legal opinions are accumulated at the level of the *fatwā*, they exert their influence on the commentaries (*shurūh*). In the Ottoman period it is by no means rare to find references to collections of *fatāwā* and their new ways of legal reasoning in the commentaries (*shurūḥ*). The *mutūn* largely represent the unchanging tradition, but it is clearly understood by the jurists that they are not always to be followed.

The *uṣūl*, finally, offer a means of stabilising the relationship between the legal opinions of the 'modern jurists' and the concept of an unchanging legal tradition as embodied in the concept of *taqlīd* and the literary genre of *mutūn*. At the level of the *uṣūl*, all the questions discussed in this essay boil down to the relationship between *istiḥsān* and *qiyās* — both of them equally acceptable within the framework of the legal tradition of Islamic law. Islamic law, in my opinion, should be studied by comparing the development of the different layers of the legal literature and defining their interrelationship. It seems to me that such a way of studying Islamic law would allow us to see wide-ranging changes at certain levels of the legal literature and it should also allow us to understand the functioning of Islamic law as a tradition in change and one of the ways in which Near Eastern society reconciled its awareness of change with its preservation of a normative tradition.

Bibliography

ARABIC SOURCES

Abū Yūsuf Yaʿqūb, *Kitāb al-Kharāj* (3rd edn, Cairo, 1382 A.H.), tr. E. Fagnan as *Le livre de l'impôt foncier* (Librairie Orientaliste Paul Geuthner, Paris, 1921)

al-Azdī, Abū ʿUbaid al-Qāsim b. Salam, *Kitāb al-Amwāl* (Cairo, 1968)

al-Bābartī, Muḥammad b. Maḥmūd, *Sharḥ al-ʿInāya ʿalā al-Hidāya*, printed on the margin of Ibn al-Humām, *Sharḥ Fatḥ al-Qadīr* (Cairo, 1356 A.H.)

Ḍamād Afandi (ʿAbd Allah b. ash-Shaikh Muḥammad b. as-Sulaimān), *Majmaʿ al-Anhur fī Sharḥ Multaqā al-Abḥur* (Dār Iḥyā' at-Tūrath al-ʿArabī, n.pl., 1316 A.H.)

al-Ḥaṣkafī (Muḥammad b. ʿAlī b. Muḥammad b. ʿAlī), *Durr al-Muntaqā fī Sharḥ al-Multaqā*, printed on the margin of Ḍāmād Afandī, *Majmaʿ al-Anhur fī Sharḥ Multaqā al-Abḥur* (Dār Thya' at-Tūrath al-ʿArabī, n.pl., 1316 A.H.)

—— *ad-Durr al-Mukhtār Sharh Tanwir al-Abṣār*, printed on the margin of Ibn ʿĀbidīn, *Radd al-Muḥtār ʿalā ad-Durr al-Mukhtār* (Cairo, 1307 A.H.)

Ibn ʿĀbidīn, *Radd al-Muḥtār ʿalā ad-Durr al-Mukhtār. Sharh Tanwīr al-Abṣār fī Fiqh Madhhab al-Imām al-Aʿẓam Abī Ḥanīfa an-Nuʿmān* (Cairo, 1307 A.H.)

—— *al-ʿUqūd ad-Durrīya fī Tanqīḥ al-Fatāwā al-Ḥāmidīya* (Būlāq, 1300 A.H., reprint 2nd edn, Beirut, n.d.)

Ibn al-Humām, *Sharḥ Fatḥ al-Qadīr* (Cairo, 1356 A.H.)

Ibn Nujaim, Zain, *at-Tuḥfa al-Marḍīya fī al-Arāḍī al-Miṣrīya*, MS, (Staatsbibliothek Berlin, We 1724)

—— *al-Ashbāh wa-n-Naẓā'ir ʿalā Madhhab Abī Ḥanīfa an-Nuʿmān* (Beirut, 1400 A.H./1980 A.D.)

—— *ar-Risāla as-Sādisa ʿAshar fī Bayān al-Iqṭaʿāt*, (MS, Staatsbibliothek, Berlin 4832) Lbg. 526

—— *al-Baḥr ar-Rā'iq Sharḥ Kanz ad-Daqā'iq* (Cairo, 1311 A.H./1894 A.D.)

al-Jazīrī, ʿAbd ar-Raḥman, *Kitāb al-Fiqh ʿalā al-Madhāhib al-Arbaʿa*, 6th edn, (Beirut, n.d.)

al-Kāsānī, Abū Bakr b. Masʿūd, *Kitāb Badā'iʿ aṣ-Ṣanā'iʿ fī Tartīb ash-Sharā'iʿ* (Cairo, 1328 A.H./1910 A.D.)

al-Khaṣṣāf, Abū Bakr Aḥmad b. ʿAmr ash-Shaibānī, *Kitāb Aḥkām al-Auqāf* (Cairo, 1322 A.H./1904 A.D.)

al-Marghīnānī, Burhān ad-Dīn ʿAlī b. Abī Bakr, *al-Hidāya, Sharḥ Bidāyat al-Mubtadi'*, printed on the margin of Ibn al-Humām, *Sharḥ Fatḥ al-Qadīr* (Cairo, 1356 A.H.)

an-Nasafī, Najm ad-Dīn b. Ḥafṣ, *Ṭalibat aṭ-Ṭalaba fī al-Iṣṭilāḥāt al-Fiqhīya* (n.p., 1311 A.H.)

Qāḍīkhān, Fakhr ad-Dīn al-Ḥusain b. Manṣūr al-Ūzjandī al-Farghānī,

Kitāb al-Fatāwā al-Khānīya (Cairo, 1282 A.H.)
Qāḍīzādeh (Aḥmad b. Qaudar), *Nata'ij al-Afkār fī Kashf ar-Rumūz wa-l-Asrār*, printed as vols 7 and 8 of Ibn al-Humām *Sharḥ Fatḥ al-Qadīr* (Cairo, 1356 A.H.)
al-Qudūrī, Abū al-Ḥusain Aḥmad b. Muḥammad, *al-Kitāb*, printed on the margin of ᶜAbd al-Ghanī al-Ghanīmī ad-Dimashqī al-Maidānī, *al-Lubāb fī Sharḥ al-Kitāb*, reprint edn (Beirut, 1400 A.H./1980 A.D.)
ar-Ramlī, Khair ad-Dīn, *Kitāb al-Fatāwā al-Khairīya li-Nafᶜ al-Barrīya* (Bulaq, 1300 A.H.; reprint edn, Beirut, 1974)
as-Samarqandī, *Tuḥfat al-Fuqahā'* (Damascus, n.d.)
as-Sarakhsī, Abū Bakr Muḥammad b. Abī Sahl, *Kitāb al-Mabsūṭ*, reprint edn (Beirut n.d.)
as-Sarakhsī, Abū Bakr Muḥammad b. Aḥmad, *Sharḥ Kitāb as-Siyar al-Kabīr*, edited by Ṣalāḥ ad-Dīn Munajjid (Cairo, 1971)
ash-Shaibānī, Abū ᶜAbd Allāh Muḥammad b. al-Ḥasan, *Kitāb al-Aṣl* (Hyderabad, 1969)
aṭ-Ṭabarī, Abū Jaᶜfar Muḥammad b. Jarīr. *Kitāb Ikhtilāf al-Fuqahā'*, 2nd edn (Beirut, n.d.); reprint of F. Kern's edn (1902)
aṭ-Ṭaḥāwī, Abū Jaᶜfar Aḥmad b. Muḥammad b. Salāma, *Mukhtaṣar* (Cairo, 1370 A.H.)
aṭ-Ṭarābulsī, Burhān ad-Dīn Ibrāhīm b. Mūsā b. Abī Bakr b. ash-Shaikh ᶜAlī, *al-Isᶜāf fī Aḥkām al-Awqāf* (Beirut, 1401 A.H./1981 A.D.)

BOOKS IN EUROPEAN LANGUAGES

Aghnides, N.P. (1916) *Mohammedan Theories of Finance*, AMS Press, New York
Ashtor, E. (1976) *A Social and Economic History of the Near East in the Middle Ages*, Collins, London
Bartels, Herwig (1967) *Das Waqfrecht und seine Entwicklung in der libanesischen Republik*, Walter de Gruyter & Co, Berlin
Becker, C.H. (1924) *Islamstudien. Vom Werden und Wesen der islamischen Welt*, Quelle und Meyer Leipzig; reprint edn, Georg Olms Verlagsbuchhandlung Hildesheim, 1967
Cahen, Claude (1969) *Der Islam I. Vom Ursprung bis zu den Anfängen des Osmanenreiches*, Fischer Taschenbuch Verlag Frankfurt am Main
Chehata, Chafik (1969) *Théorie générale de l'obligation en droit musulman hanéfite*, Editions Sirey, Paris
—— (1971) *Droit musulman. Applications au proche-orient*, Librairie Dalloz, Paris
—— (1971-3) *Etudes de droit musulman*, 2 vols., Presses Universitaires de France, Paris
Chitty, J. (1983) *On Contracts*, 25th edn, Sweet & Maxwell, London
Clavel, E. (1896) *Le waqf ou habous d'après la doctrine et la jurisprudence (rites hanéfite et malekite)*, Imprimerie Diemer, Cairo

Coulson, Noel J. (1964) *A History of Islamic Law*, Edinburgh University Press, Edinburgh

D'Ohsson, Mouragea (1787) *Tableau générale de l'empire ottoman*, vol. I, Imprimerie de Monsieur, Paris

Duri, Abdelaziz (1979) *Arabische Wirtschaftsgeschichte*, Artemis. Zurich and Munich

Eisenman, Robert H. (1978) *Islamic Law in Palestine and Israel*, E.J. Brill, Leiden

Gibb, H.A.R. and Bowen, Harold (1950) *Islamic Society and the West. A Study of the Impact of Western Civilization on Moslem Culture in the Near East*, Oxford University Press, London

Halm, Heinz (1979) *Ägypten nach den mamlukischen Lehensregistern*, vol. 1: *Oberägypten und das Fayyum*, Dr Ludwig Reichert Verlag, Wiesbaden

Haque, Ziaul (1977) *Landlord and Peasant in Early Islam*. Islamic Research Institute, Islamabad

Hütteroth, Wolf-Dieter and Abdulfattah, Kamal (1977) *Historical Geography of Palestine, Transjordan and Southern Syria in the Late 16th Century*, Selbstverlag der Fränkischen Geographischen Gesellschaft, Erlangen

Issawi, Charles (1982) *An Economic History of the Middle East and North Africa*, Methuen, New York

Khadduri, Majid and Liebesny, Herbert J. (eds) (1955) *Law in the Middle East*, Washington

Krüger, Hilmar (1978) *Fetwa und Siyar — Zur international-rechtlichen Gutachterpraxis der osmanischen Şeyh ül -Islam vom 17.-19 Jahrhundert*, Wiesbaden

Mantran, Robert and Sauvaget, Jean (1951) *Réglements fiscaux ottomans. Les provinces syriennes*, Institut Français de Damas, Paris

Matuz, J. (1985) *Das Osmanische Reich. Grundlinien seiner Geschichte*, Wissenschaftliche Buchgesellschaft, Darmstadt

Naff, Thomas and Owen, Roger (eds) (1977) *Studies in Eighteenth Century Islamic History*, Feffer & Simons, London and Amsterdam

Owen, Roger (1981) *The Middle East in the World Economy, 1800-1914*, Methuen, London and New York

Rabie, Hasanein (1972) *The Financial System of Egypt, AH 564-741/ AD 1169-1341*, Oxford University Press, London, New York, Toronto

Ruedy, John (1967) *Land Policy in Colonial Algeria. The Origins of the Rural Public Domain*, University of California, Los Angeles

Schacht, Joseph (1950) *The Origins of Muhammadan Jurisprudence*, Clarendon Press, Oxford

—— (1964) *An Introduction to Islamic Law*, Clarendon Press, Oxford

Schatkowski-Schilcher, Linda (1985) *Families in Politics. Damascene Factions and Estates of the 18th and 19th Centuries*, Franz Steiner Verlag, Stuttgart

Schmucker, Werner (1972) *Untersuchungen zu einigen wichtigen bodenrechtlichen Konsequenzen der islamischen Eroberungsbewegungen*, Orientalisches Seminar, Bonn

Von Hammer, Joseph (1815) *Des Osmanischen Reiches Staatsverfassung und Staatsverwaltung dargestellt aus den Quellen seiner Grundgesetze*, reprint Georg Olms Verlagsbuchhandlung, Hildesheim, 1963, Vienna

Young, George (1906) *Corps de droit ottoman*, Clarendon Press, Oxford

ARTICLES

'Abbās, Iḥsān (1979) 'Khair ad-Dīn ar-Ramlī's Fatāwā: A New Light on Life in Palestine in the Eleventh/Seventeenth Century', in Ulrich Haarmann and Peter Bachmann (eds), *Die Islamische Welt zwischen Mittelalter und Neuzeit. Festschrift für Hans Robert Roemer zum 60. Geburstag*, Beiruter Texte und Studien, Band 22, Franz Steiner Verlag, Wiesbaden

Beldiceanu, Nicoara (1976) 'Recherche sur la reforme foncière de Mehmed II', in Beldiceanu (ed.) *Le monde ottoman des Balkans (1402-1566). Institutions, Société, Économie*, Variorum Reprints London, 1976

—— (1976) 'Un paléologue inconnu de la region de Serres', in Beldiceanu, *Le monde ottoman des Balkans (1402-1566). Institutions, Société, Économie*, London, 1976

Beldiceanu, Nicoara and Beldiceanu-Steinherr, Irene (1968) 'Recherches sur la province de Qaraman au XVIe siècle', *Journal of the Economic and Social History of the Orient*, 2

Beldiceanu-Steinherr, Irene (1976) 'Fiscalité et formes de possession de la terre arable dans l'Anatolie pré-ottomane', *Journal of the Economic and Social History of the Orient*, 19

Belin, M. (1861) 'Etudes sur la propriété foncière en pays musulmans, et spécialement en Turquie (rite Hanéfite)', *Journal Asiatique*, August 1861-May 1862

Cahen, Claude (1954) 'Fiscalité, propriété, antagonismes sociaux en Haute-Mésopotamie au temps des premiers "Abbásides d'après Denys de Tell-Mahré"', *Arabica*, 1

—— (1956) 'La régime des impôts dans le Fayyūm', *Arabica*, 3

—— (1962) 'Contribution à l'etude des impôts dans l'Egypte médiévale', *Journal of the Economic and Social History of the Orient*, 5

—— (1972) 'Al-Makhzūmī et Ibn Mammātī sur l'agriculture egyptienne médiévale', *Annales Islamologiques*, 11

—— (1975) 'Aperçu sur les impôts du sol en Syrie au moyen age', *Journal of the Economic and Social History of the Orient*, 18

Cahen, Claude, Rāghib, Yusuf and Taher, Mustafa A. (1978) 'L'achat et le waqf d'un grand domaine egyptien par le vizier fatimide Ṭalāī b. Ruzzīk — contribution à une publication des waqfs egyptiens médiévaux', *Annales Islamologiques*, 14

Cvetkova, Bistra (1963) 'Sur certaines reformes du regime foncier au temps de Mehmet II', *Journal of the Economic and Social History of the Orient*, 6

Die Enzyklopädie des Islam, 1936 edn, s.v. 'Waqf', by W. Heffening, E.J. Brill, Leiden and Otto Harrassowitz, Leipzig
Digeon, M. (1778) 'Canoun-namé ou édits de Sultan Soliman concernant la police de l'Egypte', in Digeon, *Nouveaux contes Turcs et Arabes*, Dupuis, Paris
Encyclopaedia of Islam, new edn, s.v. 'Ayyubids', by C. Cahen and E.J. Brill, Leiden and Luzac & Co, London
Encyclopaedia of Islam, new edn, s.v. 'Kharādj', by C. Cahen and E.J. Brill, Leiden and Luzac & Co, London
Forand, Paul G. (1971) 'The Status of the Land and Inhabitants of the Sawad during the First Two Centuries of Islam', *Journal of the Economic and Social History of the Orient*, 14
Gerber, Haim (1984) 'The Waqf Institution in Early Ottoman Edirne', in Gabriel R. Warburg and Gad G. Gilbar (eds) *Studies in Islamic Society. Contributions in Memory of Gabriel Baer*, The Institute of Middle Eastern Studies, University of Haifa, Haifa
Haarmann, Ulrich (1984) 'The Sons of Mamluks as Fief-Holders in Late Medieval Egypt', in T. Khalidi (ed.) *Land Tenure and Social Transformation in the Middle East*, American University of Beirut, Beirut
Hammoudi, Abdellah A. (1985) 'Substance and Relation: Water Rights and Water Distribution in the Ḍrā Valley', in A.E. Mayer (ed.) *Property, Social Structure and Law in the Modern Middle East*, State University of New York Press, Albany
Johansen, Baber (1981) 'Amwāl Ẓāhira and Amwāl Bāṭina. Town and Countryside as Reflected in the Tax System of the Hanafite School', in W. al-Qāḍī (ed.) *Studia Arabica et Islamica. Festschrift for Iḥsān ʿAbbās on his Sixtieth Birthday*, American University of Beirut, Beirut
—— (1981) 'Secular and Religious Elements in Hanafite Law — Function and Limits of the Absolute Character of Government Authority', in E. Gellner and J.C. Vatin (eds) *Islam et Politique au Maghreb*, Centre National de la Recherche Scientifique, Paris
—— (1982) 'The Servants of the Mosques', *The Maghreb Review* 7, nos. 1-2 January-April
Lewis, Bernard (1979) 'Ottoman Land Tenure and Taxation in Syria', *Studia Islamica*, 50
Marsot, A.L. al-S. (1977) 'The Wealth of the Ulama in Late Eighteenth Century Cairo', in Thomas Naff and Roger Owen (eds) *Studies in Eighteenth Century Islamic History*, Feffer & Simons, London
Matuz, Joseph (1982) 'The Nature and Stages of Ottoman Feudalism', *Asian and African Studies*, 16, no. 3, November
Meron, Yaʾakov (1969) 'The Development of Legal Thought in Hanafi Texts', *Studia Islamica*, 30
Morony, Michael G. (1981) 'Landholding in Seventh-Century Iraq: Late Sasanian and Early Islamic Patterns', in A.L. Udovitch (ed.) *The Islamic Middle East 700-1900. Studies in Economic and Social History*, The Darwin Press Inc., Princeton, N.J.
—— (1984) 'Landholding and Social Change: Lower al-ʿIrāq in the Early Islamic Period', in T. Khalidi (ed.) *Land Tenure and Social*

Transformation in the Middle East, American University of Beirut, Beirut

el-Mouelhy, Ibrahim (1972) 'Nouveaux documents sur le fallah et le régime des terres sous les Ottomans', *Annales Islamologiques*, 11

Peri, Oded (1984) 'The Waqf as an Instrument to Increase and Consolidate Political Power: The Case of Khāṣṣeki Sultan Waqf in Late Eighteenth-Century Ottoman Jerusalem', in Gabriel R. Warburg and Gad G. Gilbar (eds) *Studies in Islamic Society. Contributions in Memory of Gabriel Baer*, The Institute of Middle Eastern Studies, University of Haifa, Haifa

Pritsch, Erich and Spies, Otto (1953) 'Der islamische Werklieferungsvertrag', *Zeitschrift für vergleichende Rechtswissenschaft*, 56

Rafeq, Abdul-Karim (1981) 'Economic Relations between Damascus and the Dependent Countryside 1743-1771', in A.L. Udovitch (ed.) *The Islamic Middle East 700-1900. Studies in Economic and Social History*, The Darwin Press Inc., Princeton, N.J.

Shaw, Stanford J. (1962) 'The Land Law of Ottoman Egypt (960/1553): A Contribution to the Study of Landholding in the Early Years of Ottoman Rule in Egypt', *Der Islam*, 38, nos 1-2

Shimizu, Makoto (1966) 'Les finances publiques de l'etat abbaside', *Der Islam*, 42

Sourdel-Thomine, Janine, and Sourdel, Dominique (1972) 'Biens fonciers constitués waqf en Syrie fatimide pour une famille de šarīfs damascains', *Journal of the Economic and Social History of the Orient*, 15

Stöber, Georg (1985) '"Habous public" in Chaouen: Zur wirtschaftlichen Bedeutung religiöser Stiftungen in Nordmarokko', *Die Welt des Islams*, 25

Talbi, Mohamed (1981) 'Law and Economy in Ifrīqīya (Tunisia) in the Third Islamic Century: Agriculture and the Role of Slaves in the Country's Economy', in A.L. Udovitch (ed.) *The Islamic Middle East 700-1900. Studies in Economic and Social History*, The Darwin Press Inc., Princeton, N.J.

Udovitch, A.L. (1981) 'Technology, Land Tenure and Plural Society: Aspects of Continuity in the Agricultural History of the Pre-Modern Middle East', in A.L. Udovitch (ed.), *The Islamic Middle East 700-1900. Studies in Economic and Social History*, The Darwin Press Inc., Princeton, N.J.

Watson, Andrew M. (1981) 'A Medieval Green Revolution: New Crops and Farming Techniques in the Early Islamic World', in A.L. Udovitch (ed.) *The Islamic Middle East 700-1900. Studies in Economic and Social History*, The Darwin Press Inc., Princeton, N.J.

Name Index

This index lists only the names of persons who are mentioned in the text, or whose legal opinions are either quoted verbatim or discussed in the notes.

ᶜAbbās, Iḥsān 99
Abū Bakr Muḥammad b.al-Faḍl 75n.53
Abū Ḥanīfa 7, 15, 16, 17, 27, 35, 40, 41, 53, 56, 70n.14, 72n.31, 83
Abū Ḥifṣ al-Bukhārī 48n.51
Abū al-Laith Naṣr al-Samarqandī 48n.51
Abū Yūsuf 7, 8, 15, 16, 19n.2, 27, 35, 53, 75n.53, 84
Aghnides, N.P. 8
ʿAlā' al-Dīn M. b. Aḥmad b. Abī Aḥmad al-Samarqandī (author of the tuḥfa) 41, 47n.41, 74n.49
ᶜAlī Bāšā (Ottoman governor) 86
ʿAlī al-Sughdī 48n.51
Ashtor, Eliahu 17, 80

Bābartī 41, 50n.72
Becker, C.H. 8
Belin, M. 8
Bowen, H. 8
al-Bukhārī *see* Abū Ḥifs

Cahen, Claude 8, 16, 17, 18, 20n.8
Chehata, Chafik 1, 4, 5
Coulson, N.J. 1, 2

Ḍamād Afandī (Shaikhīzādeh) 22n.30, 100

Forand, Paul 8

Gibb, H.A.R. 8

v. Hammer, Joseph 8
Hammoudi, Abdellah 28, 29
Haque, Ziaul 51, 57, 58
Ḥaṣkafī 100, 114

Ibn ᶜĀbidīn 99, 114, 115
Ibn al-Faḍl *see* Abū Bakr Muḥammad b. al-Faḍl
Ibn al-Humām 10, 84, 85, 89, 100
Ibn Nujaim 10, 85-6, 87, 88, 90, 91, 92, 98, 99, 100, 104, 109
Ibn Yaḥyā *see* Naṣīr b. Yaḥyā
al-ᶜImādī 98-9, 106, 108 113, 114, 117n.4
Ismāᶜīl al-Zāhid 50n.81
Issawi, Charles 3

Kāsānī 35, 36, 38, 41, 46nn.29 & 32, 47n.41, 49n.56, 51
Khair al-Dīn *see* Ramlī
Khaṣṣāf 9, 13, 14, 21n.10, 27, 33, 37, 52, 93n.1, 104

Lutfi as-Sayyid Marsot, Afaf 82

Mālik Ibn Anas 53
Marghīnānī 10, 21n.26, 45n.26
Meḥmed II (Ottoman sultan) 81
Morony, M. 8, 11, 52
Muḥammad, the Prophet 54, 55, 56
Muḥammad Ibn al-Faḍl *see* Abū Bakr Muḥammad b. al-Faḍl
Muḥammad Ibn Salma 75n.53
Muḥammad al-Shaibānī *see* al-Shaibānī

Naṣīr Ibn Yaḥyā 75n.53

d'Ohsson, Mouragea 82

Qāḍīkhān 36, 42, 47nn.40 & 41, 56, 60, 66-8, 83-4, 104, 107, 109, 114
Qaḍīzādeh 45n.26
al-Qudūrī 9

Rafeq, ᶜAbd al-Karim 99
al-Ramlī, Khair al-Dīn 98, 99, 105, 106, 109, 112

al-Samarqandī *see* ʿAlā' al-Dīn M. b. Aḥmad b. Abī Aḥmad al-Samarqandī
al-Samarqandī *see* Abū al-Laith Naṣr al-Samarqandī
al-Sarakhsī 8, 9, 10, 21nn.24 & 25, 27, 28, 30, 32, 35, 36, 40, 41, 42, 44n.11, 45n.25, 47n.41,

49n.56, 54, 56, 60, 69n.1, 70n.18, 73n.47, 74n.48, 75n.53, 77n.70
Schacht, Joseph 1, 25, 32, 35, 44n.12
Schmucker, W. 9, 11, 13
al-Shāfiʿī 53
al-Shaibānī, M. 8, 16, 27, 35, 37, 41, 47n.40, 53, 84
Shaikhizādeh *see* Ḍamād Afandī
Shimizu, Makoto 15
al-Sughdī *see* ʿAlī al-Sughdī

al-Ṭabarī 27
al-Ṭaḥāwī 9, 83
al-Ṭarābulsī, Ibrāhīm 104
Thaurī 53

Udovitch, Abraham 2
ʿUthmān Ibn ʿAffān (the third caliph) 16

al-Zāhid *see* Ismaʿīl al-Zāhid
al-Zuhrī 72n.31

Subject Index

âfa *see force majeure*
ajr (synonym *ujra*), rent
see also ghaṣb, ijāra and *rent*
a price or equivalent paid for the use of land or labour (*see also* land use) 45n.18
under a valid tenancy contract (*see ijāra* and *contracts*) paid for the 'possibility to use' the land or labour 27, 31, 32, 34, 64
under a voidable tenancy contract paid for the actual use of land or labour 34-5, 100-1
to be paid in money, kind or services 27
religious opposition against (*see also ijāra*) 27-8
its amount determined by the time during which land or labour are used 31-2, 47n.41
al-ajr al-musammā (synonym: al-musammā), i.e. the contractually fixed rent 31-6, 111 always binding under a valid tenancy contract 32, 34, 48n.46
ajr al-mithl (synonym: *ujrat al-mithl*) i.e. the average or 'fair rent' obtainable for lands or labour of the same quality and kind 33, 62, 77n.70
payable under a voidable contract of tenancy (*see ijāra fāsida*) or share-cropping (*see muzāra' a fāsida*) 35-6, 64-5
Ottoman jurists' definition of *ajr al-mithl* 112-13
al-ajr al-musammā and *ajr al-mithl* under a voidable tenancy contract 35-6, 48n.46, 49n.62
both kinds of *ajr* result from contracts 30, 38, 39, 62
legal protection of *waqf* and orphans' property against tenants through
1. shorter periods of tenancy contracts 34
2. declaring the tenancy contract to be voidable 36, 111-12
3. dissolution of the tenancy contract 33
4. defining tenancy as a case of 'unauthorized use' (*see ghaṣb*) which engenders the obligation to pay *ajr al-mithl* 42, 112
Central Asian jurists on *ghaṣb* and *ajr* with regard to *waqf* lands 40-1, 42, 67, 68
Ottoman jurists on *ghaṣb* and *ajr* with regard to *waqf* lands and other forms of rent-yielding property 114-15
analogy (*qiyās*) *see also istiḥsān*
establishes the contract of sale (*bai'*) as the model of all bilateral and commutative contracts 27
analogies drawn from the basic rules of the contract of sale contradict basic rules of the tenancy and the share-cropping (*see* muzāra'a) contracts 30, 46n.31, 53
attempts to construe the *muzāra'a* contract as an analogy to the *muḍāraba* (*see* sub verbo) contract 76n.61
business practice as a valid reason for abandoning analogy 54, 71n.24
Qāḍikhān's new concept of *muzāra'a* without contract contradicts analogical reasoning 67
Anatolia 94n.7
arḍ al-ḥauz, sequestrated lands with regard to which private proprietary rights still exist 14, 15, 17, 19, 52, 93, 104-6, 123
assignments *see land assignment, tax assignment* and *iqṭā'*
al-Azhar 99, 101

badhr, *see muzāraʿa, jins al-badhr* and *qarḍ al-badhr*
baiʿ, contract of sale 27
  model for all bilateral and commutative contracts 27
  the tenancy contract (*see ijāra*) cannot be construed in analogy to the contract of sale 30, 32-3, 49n.57
bait al-māl *see public treasury*
Balkh, jurists of 40, 41, 42, 50n.78, 77n.79, 124
Bukhara, jurists of 42, 124
Buyids, dynasty in Iraq 94n.5
Byzantine Empire
  share-cropping in (*see also muzārʿa*) 52

Central Asia
  development of legal doctrine in 34, 36, 40, 41, 42, 48n.51, 60, 68, 82, 98
classical period *see periodization*
commodity
  defined as *māl mutaqauwim* (res in commercio) 27, 122
  commodity value (*taqauwum*) 30, 122
  something that can be accumulated and stored until times of need 29, 45n.25
  rent as an equivalent for a commodity 27
  land use as a non-commodity 29-30
  land use transformed into a commodity through the tenancy contract (*see ijāra*) 30, 31, 32, 122 or the share-cropping contract (*see muzāraʿa*) 54, 122
  see also juʿl
  see also kirāʾ
contracts
  bilateral contracts 27
  contract of sale (*see baiʿ*) 27, 49n.57
  tenancy contract (*see ijāra*) 25 ff
    valid tenancy contract 26, 49n.56
    voidable tenancy contract 34-6, 48n.52, 49n. 56
  valid and voidable tenancy contracts transform the use of land and labour into a commodity 30, 31, 32, 38, 46n.29, 49n.58
  contract of *kirāʾ*, i.e. the renting of land 25
  contract of *juʿl*, i.e. locatio conductio operis 25
  contract of *muzāraʿa*, *see muzāraʿa*
  classical doctrine on contractual character of rent 32, 34, 100-1
  post-classical doctrine questions the contractual character of rent 66-7
corpus juris of Islamic Law
  development of 1, 2
  role of state administration for 3
  role of social traditions for 3, 6n.12
crops
  cereals 3
  summer crops 26, 43nn.6 & 7, 44n.12, 51
  legal differences between contracts for agriculture on fields and for the planting of plantations 69n.1

Damascus 99
dihqān, Iranian landowner and notable 16
doctrine
  classical doctrine on tax and rent 2, 4
  equally applicable to all forms of landed property 4, 18
  recognizes peasant ownership (*see also peasants*) of arable lands, 4, 17-19
  defines the source of the obligation to pay rent (*see rent* and *ajr*) 30, 32-3, 38-9
  discusses the period of duration of the tenancy contract (*see ijāra*) 26, 34
  defines the payment of *kharāj* as a proof of the tax payer's ownership of his landed property 7, 8, 9, 10, 11, 15, 16, 18, 21n.25, 26, 30, 40, 69, 83, *see also* 102-3
  classical doctrine obsolete in the Mamlūk period 81
  protection of *waqf* and orphans' property at the origins of the *post-classical doctrine* 39-42, 66-8, 124

post-classical doctrine on
peasants' ownership of arable lands (*see also peasants*) 4
defines peasants' levies as rent 84-5, 102-3
legitimizes the fiscal privileges of the *rent-yielding landed property* (*see rent-yielding property*) through the doctrine of the 'death of the *kharāj* payer' 83, 84, 85, 88, 89, 90, 91, 99-100, 103-4
characterized by the co-existence of different legal concepts with regard to the sources of the obligation to pay rent 116-17

Egypt 81
a *kharāj* paying country according to the classical doctrine 84
no longer a *kharāj* paying country according to jurists of the sixteenth century 89, 101
waqf lands in 82
development of legal doctrine in 82-3, 85-93
land tenure in 89
Ottoman *qānūnnāme* of 1525 95n.22
Ottoman *qānūnnāme* of 1553 86, 87, 88, 92
the jurists' interpretation of the peasants' status in the Mamlūk and Ottoman periods 85, 124, 96n.25

fai', doctrine of, a legal concept that legitimizes state ownership of arable lands on historical grounds 9
fair rent *see ajr al-mithl*
Fatimid period 81, 94n.5
fatwā (pl. fatāwā)
legal opinion (*see also mufti*) 2, 42, 68, 92, 98, 99, 101, 102
a special kind of legal literature 125
Syrian *fatwā-s* 101, 106, 107, 109
Palestinian *fatwā-s* Ch. 5 *passim*
Egyptian *fatwā-s* 2 *see also* Ch. 4 *passim*

relationship to *mutun* (*see* sub verbo) and *shurūh* (*see sharh*) 125
fiqh, the science of Islamic Law 1, 124-5
fiscal privileges *see privileges*
force majeure (*āfa*) 31, 47n.40

ghabn fāḥish, laesio enormis, the 'outrageous economic disadvantage' that justifies the dissolution of the contract 33
the big difference between *ajr musammā* and *ajr mithl* (*see ajr*) 33, 112
ghaṣb, unauthorized use of lands or labour 31, 36, 37, 67
engenders the obligation to pay a compensation for the loss of the land's value 37, 38, 39
methods of evaluation of the compensation 40-1
breach of contract defined as *ghaṣb* 45n.15
ghaṣb does not engender the obligation to pay rent according to the classical doctrine 32, 37, 38, 50n.72
assimilation of *ghaṣb* and tenancy (*see ijāra*) in the post-classical doctrine 40-1, 50n.81, 68, 106-7
ghaṣb of state lands, *waqf* lands and orphans' lands engenders the obligation to pay rent in the post-classical doctrine 111, 115-16
classical doctrine on *ghaṣb* applies only to peasants in the Ottoman period 111, 113-14, 115

ḥamām, classical example for *rent-yielding property* (*see* sub verbo) 119n.27
hauz *see arḍ al-ḥauz*
hurūb, the tax payer's and share-cropper's flight from the land 14, 61, 83

iʿāna, the offering of gratuitous labour under a *muzāraʿa* contract (*see muzāraʿa*) 56, 59, 72n.32
ʿibra, the unit in which the fiscal

value of lands is evaluated 23n.48
iğtihād, the rational deduction of legal rules from the sources of the law (*uṣūl al-fiqh*) 124
ijāra, the contract of tenancy
originally the hiring of labour (locatio conductio operarum) 25
a combination of three contracts: *kirā'* (the renting of land, *see* sub verbo) *ijāra* (i.e. the hiring of labour) and *ju'l* (*see* sub verbo) 25
with regard to arable lands a tenancy contract referring to agriculture on fields 3, 25, 26
in principle not applicable to gardens, plantations and pastures 26
the forbidden *ijāra*: *ijārat al-istihlāk* 26, 103
the tenancy contract's period of duration in the classical period
a. general 26
b. concerning *waqf* and big estates 34, 44n.13
the tenancy contract's conditions of validity 26, 34
a bilateral contract 27
legitimized on the basis of *istiḥsān see* sub verbo 30-1, 46n.32
the tenancy contract transforms the land use into a commodity 30, 31, 32, 38
religious opposition against this transformation 27, 28
the tenancy contract as a condition for the obligation to pay rent 32
sources of the obligation to pay rent 31, 34-5, 100-1
time (*waqt*) as a factor that determines the amount of rent and salary 31-2, 47n.41, 59
the tenancy contract as an instrument of social and economic integration 38-9
the contractual and consensual element more important in the contract of tenancy than in the contract of sale 32-3
ijāra fāsida, a voidable contract of tenancy 32, 34 is validated through the tenant's land use 34-5, 100-1
rent under a voidable contract of tenancy 35, 36
voidable tenancy contract and *ghaṣb* in the post-classical doctrine 42
Imām, the ruler of the Muslim political community 10, 11, 12, 15, 18-19, 83-4, 92, 100 *see also Sulṭān*
iqṭā', i.e. the Imām's assignment of lands or tax districts to individuals *see qaṭī'a*, land *assignment* and *tax assignment*
Iran 94n.5
Iraq
arable lands in Iraq pay *kharāj* 9
kharāj lands as *private property* 9-11, 18
legal doctrine during the classical period 34, 37, 41, 53, 111
muzāra'a in Iraq before Islam 52
situation of peasants in the Buyid period 80 and under the Mongols 94n.11
irṣādī, *see waqf irsādī*
isti'āna i.e. 'asking for gratuitous labour' in a *muzāra'a* relationship 56, 59, 72n.32
istighlāl *see mu'add li-l-istighlāl*
istiḥsān, *see also analogy*, admitting for practical and moral purposes legal solutions that contradict conclusions drawn on the basis of analogical reasoning from the basic rules of the legal system 30-1, 125
legitimizes the tenancy contract (*see ijāra*) 30-1, 46n.32
legitimizes the contract of share-cropping *see muzāra'a* 54, 55
based on the Prophet's example 54, 55, 56
based on Koran, sunna and consensus 46n.32
based on general business practice and custom ('*urf*) 54, 55, 56
legitimizes Qāḍīkhān's new

concept of *muzāraʿa* without contract 67
determines the amount of rent to be paid under a voidable tenancy contract 35, 112
justifies the solution according to which general practice (*ʿurf*) may replace contractual stipulation 77n.80

Jews
of Khaibar 54, 56, 72n.31
of Iraq 73n.39
jins al-badhr, the specification of the kind of seed to be used under a *muzāraʿa* contract, one of the six prerequisites of a valid share-cropping contract 59, 77n.80
juʿl, locatio conductio operis (Werkvertrag) (*see also ijāra*) 25

kafīl, suretyship 73n.40
Khaibar, oasis of 54, 56, 72n.31
kharāj, land tax (*see also taxation*) 7, 8, 9, 10, 11, 14, 15nn.4 & 8, 18, 21nn.17, 24 & 25, 39, 40, 81, 83, 84, 85, 86, 88, 89, 90, 91, 100, 101, 102, 103, 106, 110, 123
western definitions of 8, 20nn.3-11
classical Hanafite doctrine holds that the payment of *kharāj* proves the tax payer's ownership of his landed property 9-11, 18, 21n.25, 26, 30, 40, 69, 83
kharāj muwaẓẓaf (synonym: *kharāj waẓīfa*) *see also taxation*, a fixed tax on arable lands 3, 15, 16, 18, 19
kharāj muwaẓẓaf as a personal obligation 15
according to the classical doctrine payable by the owner of the landed property 7, 8, 9, 10, 11, 16, 102-3
kharāj muqāsama, see also taxation, a proportional share of the land's produce up to 50% 13, 15, 16, 19, 94n.6
an obligation in re 15
payable by the tenant 16, 17, 101, 119n.16
a tax on lands of aristocratic owners 16
spread of after the tenth century 16, 19
most important form of *kharāj* in Egypt and Syria 102
classical *kharāj* doctrine obsolete under Mamlūks 81
the doctrine of the 'death of the *kharāj* payers' and the loss of the peasants' property rights 83, 84, 85, 88, 89, 90, 107, 123
kharāj waẓīfa *see kharāj muwaẓẓaf*
Khorasan, the jurists of 75n.53
kirāʾ *see also ijāra*, the contract of renting real property 25

laesio enormis *see ghabn fāḥish*
land assignment, the Imām's assignment of lands to persons who are in charge of its mise-en-valeur (*see also qaṭīʿa* and *iqṭāʿ*) 8-9, 12, 19n.2, 69,86, 99-100
land tax *see kharāj, taxation* and *ʿushr*
land tenure, forms of
milk (private property) 2
milk muʿadd li-l-istighlāl (*see rent-yielding property*) 67
mal al-yatīm, orphan's property whose administration is (usually) supervised by the *qāḍī* 42, 68, 108, 109, 110, 111, 115, 116, 123
waqf, see sub verbo
arḍ al-ḥauz, see sub verbo
arḍ al-mamlaka or *mīrī*, i.e. state lands 69, 81, 100, 108
land assignments held in *milk* 8-9, 12, 69
ijāra, see sub verbo
muzāraʿa, see sub verbo
tax assignments 13, 16, 69, 80-1, 93n.1, 97n.61, 102
land use
as a commodity 27
as a non-commodity 29-30, 45n.26
transformed into a commodity through the contracts of tenancy (*see ijāra*) and share-cropping (*see muzāraʿa*) 30, 38
religious opposition against this

transformation 27, 28
contractual land use is the source of the obligation to pay rent, 31, 38
unauthorized land use engenders the obligation to pay compensation, not rent 37-8
legal consequences of the land use of '*rent-yielding property*' (*see* sub verbo) 42, 67, 68, 111, 114

māl, *see commodity*
māl al-yatīm, the orphan's property whose administration is normally supervised by the *qāḍī* 111
considered to be *rent-yielding property, see* sub verbo
Mamlūk period (1250-1517)
development of legal doctrine in 69, 82, 84-5, 103, 124
socio-economic development in 81, 85
cadastral registers of 86, 87
al-ma'qūd 'alaih, the object of the contract, that which is sold or farmed out under a contract 55
mawāt, waste lands 12, 19
milk, *see private property*
mīrī, state lands *see land tenure*
mu'add li-l-ījār (synonym for *mu'add li-l-istighlāl*)
mu'add li-l-istighlāl, property reserved for business purposes and not for personal use, *see also mu'add li-l-ījār, mu'add li-l-muzāra'a* and *rent-yielding property*
a form of rent-yielding property 67-8, 107-9, 111, 113-16, 123
mu'add li-l-muzāra'a, lands held for the purpose of farming them out under a share-cropping contract 66-7, 106-7, 114
mu'āmala, a contract for the planting of plantations 51
muḍāraba, a partnership, a commenda 76n.61
mudda, the period of duration of the contracts of *ijāra* (*see* sub verbo) or *muzāra'a*, (*see* sub verbo) 58, 59, 73n.42, 77n.80
mufti, a jurist who gives authoritative legal opinions on legal and religious matters (*see also fatwā*) 1, 2, 75n.53, 98-9, 117
mufti-s of Central Asia 2
Egyptian *mufti-s* 2 see also chapter 4 passim
Palestinian *mufti-s* 98, 102
Syrian *mufti-s* 2, 98, 102, 112, 113
muqāṭa'a, unit of taxation 87
muqṭa', the person who holds a land or tax assignment *see also iqṭā', qaṭī'a* 17, 80-1, 85, 97n.61, 100
musāqāt, a contract for the planting of trees 51
musaqqafāt, roofed rentable buildings as opposed to rentable lands 119n.26
muta'akhkhirūn, the 'modern jurists' as opposed to the 'classical jurists' (*mutaqaddimūn*) 4, 109, 110, 117, 120n.52, 124
mutajānis, 'related species' of production factors in *muzāra'a* contract 61
mutaqaddimūn, the 'classical jurists' as opposed to the 'modern jurists' (*muta'akhkhirūn*) 4, 109, 117
mutūn, law texts studied and learned by heart by students 125
muzāra'a, the contract of share-cropping with regard to agriculture (*see also share-cropping, mu'add li-l-muzāra'a* and *rent-yielding property*) 3, 38, 51, 52
a contract between unequal partners 43, 52, 57-63, 65-6, 68-9, 73nn.40 & 47
transforms land use into a commodity 54
practised on big estates 52
rejected on religious and juridical grounds 27, 52, 53
contradicts the basic rules that govern synallagmatic contracts 53, 54
is legitimized on the basis of *istiḥsān* (*see* sub verbo) 54-5
begins as a tenancy contract and ends as a contract of partnership (*sharika*) 55
that which is farmed out under this contract is land or labour 55, 61, 71n.28

the three legally valid combinations of the four elements of agricultural production 55, 56, 61-2
peasant usages integrated into the *muzāraʿa* contract 56-7, 72n.37
special importance of seed investment 57, 61, 62, 63, 69
the six conditions of a valid *muzāraʿa* contract 58-9, 73nn.41 & 42, 77n.80
the voidable contract of *muzāraʿa* 59, 63-4, 65, 77n.80
the legal consequences of a voidable contract of share-cropping 64, 65, 69, 78n.82
time of land use determines amount of rent 59, 76n.61
work defined as a production factor 60, 74nn.48 & 49
long-term and short-term contracts 60-1, 69
sublease under a *muzāraʿa* contract 61, 69, 76n.59
namāʾ milkih (*see* sub verbo) and the contract of share-cropping 63-5, 69
differences between a tenant and a share-cropper 68-9, 76n.60
the mobility of the working partner 73n.47
Qāḍīkhān's *muzāraʿa* without contract 66-7, 106-7

namā'milkih, *see muzāraʿa*, a doctrine that favours the seed contributor under a voidable *muzāraʿa* contract 63-5, 69

Ottoman
period (13th century to 1924)
qānūnnāme of Egypt 1525 96n.25
qānūnnāme of Egypt 1553 86, 87, 88, 92
mufti-s 98
system of *land tenure* 81-2 *see also tīmār*
Ottoman Empire 68, 69, 92, 96n.26
development of legal doctrine in 85, 89, 91-2, 107, 111, 124
socio-economic development in 81
waqf lands in 82
Ownership *see* private property

peasants
classical Hanafite doctrine protects peasant ownership 3, 4, 17-19, 38, 80-1
peasants not attached to soil 10-11
cultivators of *arḍ al-ḥauz* (*see* sub verbo) are not considered proprietors 14
peasant usages and contracts 56-7
the decline of small peasant holdings 80-1, 94n.11
the peasant proprietor transformed into a tenant 80-1
the jurists' interpretation of this transformation 69, 84-5, 96n.25
the doctrine of the 'death of the *kharāj* payer' 83-5, 88-90, 103-4
peasant's taxes defined as rent 84, 100, 101, 123
peasants enjoy personal liberty 100-1
classical doctrine of *ghaṣb* (*see* sub verbo) applies only to peasants in Ottoman period 111, 113, 115-16
the peasants' rent includes the land tax 102-3, 118n.15, 123-4
village custom as a legal factor 114
periodization of Islamic Law
early or formative period 1
pre-classical period 1, 3, 4
classical period 1 *see also doctrine*
post-classical period 2, 4 and chapters 4-6 *passim*
pre-emption *see shufʿa*
privileges, fiscal *see also doctrine, rent-yielding property* and *taxation*
based on the doctrine of the 'death of the *kharāj* payer' 87-91, 99-100, 103-4, 106-7
private property
(*milk*) of arable lands *see also rent-yielding property, peasants, land tenure* and

mu' add li-l-istighlāl
sources of ownership 11-12, 18-19, 81, 91-2
relationship to taxation and rent 2, 3, 7-11, 102-3
bought from the treasury 87-8
sequestration of 105-6
differentiation between peasants' *private property* and '*rent-yielding property*' 107-9, 111, 113-16, 123-4
public treasury (*bait al-māl*)
the main seller of state lands, fiscal privileges and property rights 81, 89-93

qānūnnāme *see Ottoman*
qarḍ al-badhr, a gratuitous credit of seed that is to be restored after harvesting 56, 72n.34, 77n.75
qaṭī'a, a piece of land assigned by the *Imām* to individual persons 8, 19n.2
cultivated by slaves and salaried labour 12, 17 *see also iqṭā'* and *muqṭa'*
qiyās *see* analogy

Ramla 99
rent *see also ajr* and *ijāra*
contractually fixed rent *see ajr musammā*
fair rent, average rent *see ajr al-mithl*
contractual character of 3, 25, 30, 31, 38-9
does not result from a delict 30
differentiated from taxes by its contractual character 38, 62
non-contractual rent 40-2, 67-8, 80-1, 84-5, 102-3, 123
peasants' taxes considered to be rent 103, 106-7, 123
peasants not entitled to collect rent for the 'unauthorized use' (*see ghaṣb*) of their lands 111, 113-14
competition for rent 102, 103, 118nn.14 & 15
rent-yielding property
see also mu' add li-l-istighlal, *mu' add li-l-muzara' a*, *waqf* and *māl al - yatim*
enjoys privileged legal and fiscal status if compared to peasants' lands 67-8, 83, 87-92, 99-100, 106-11, 114-16, 123
waqf lands, orphans' lands and *milk mu' add li-l-istighlāl* as the three forms of *rent-yielding property* 108-9, 115-17, 123
their relationship to state lands 108, 120n.38
every use of *waqf* and orphans' lands engenders the obligation to pay rent 42, 67-8, 109-10, 114-15
rizqa, rent collected from the holders of *muqāṭa' -a-s* (*see* sub verbo) 86, 96n.34

ṣāhib al-badhr, the person who contributes the seed in a *muzāra' a* (*see* sub verbo) relationship 59, 77n.80
sawād, the rural districts of Iraq 10, 11, 21n.26, 22n.30
ṣawāfī, crown lands 9, 16
Seljuqs, dynasty of 84n.5
sijillāt, the court registers 125
Sulṭān 13-14, 81, 88-90, 104-6, 116
Syria
arable lands pay *kharāj* 10
waqf lands during Ottoman period 82, 95n.22
milk lands during Ottoman period 97n.65
jurists of and legal doctrine in 34, 41, 82-3, 85
share-cropping
contract of *see muzāra' a*
as a form of taxation (*see also kharāj muqāsama* and *taxation*) 14, 56, 58, 72n.31
among the Jews of Iraq 73n.39
sharḥ (pl. shurūḥ), glosses and commentaries of *mutūn* (*see sub verbo*) 125
sharika, partnership 59, 63, 77n.80
shuf'a, the right of pre-emption 12, 105-6

tab'īḍ, the sowing of more than one seed and the use of more than one method of cultivation under one *muzara' a* contract 76n.64
takhliya, the land owner's delivering of the land to the working partner under a *muzāra' a* (*see*

sub verbo) contract 58-9, 71n.28, 72n.37, 77n.80
tamlīk, the transfer of property rights 27
tamlīk al-manāfiʿ, the transfer of the right to use land or labour 27
tanẓīmāt, the period of Ottoman reforms in the nineteenth century (1839-1876) 117
taqlīd, reliance on the transmitted legal opinions of a school of law 124-5
taslīm, the conveyance of the (rented) property to the tenant 31
tax assignment, (*iqṭaʿ*) the *Imām*'s assignment of a tax district to a *muqṭaʿ* who appropriates part of the taxes as his due 13, 69, 80-1, 87
taxation
of arable lands universal 7, 18, 122
no longer universal in post-classical doctrine 87, 89-92, 99-100
relationship to *rent* and *private property* 2, 3, 7-11, 38, 102-3
land tax consists of either *kharāj*, (*see* sub verbo) or *ʿushr* (*see* sub verbo) 7, 18
kharāj is a heavier burden than *ʿushr* and has less religious undertones 12, 18, 19
ʿushr (*see* sub verbo) is a tax on the Muslim's agricultural produce 7
taxation of *auqāf* lands 12, 86
kharāj on *qaṭīʿa-s* 19n.2
the sequestration of the insolvent tax payer's lands (*see also arḍ al-ḥauz*, *kharāj* and *doctrine*) 14, 15, 83-4, 88
fiscal privileges sold by the public treasury 87-91, 99-100, 106-7
mīrī, the Ottoman levy on state lands 81, 97n.65
kharāj and the competition for rent according to Ottoman doctrine 102-3, 123
peasant's taxes defined as rent 84, 100-1, 106-7, 123
tax farmers, opposed by the *mufti-s* 103
tenancy *see ijāra*
tīmār, the lands assigned to an officer or official in the Ottoman system of land tenure 69, 102
tīmārī, the *tīmār* holder 102
Transoxania, jurists of 33, 63, 73n.42, 75n.53, 83, 106, 112

ujra, *see ajr*
unauthorized use, *see ghaṣb*
ʿurf, the legally recognized custom 54, 114
use (*manfaʿa*)
of land and labour *see land use*
ʿushr, *see also taxation* the dime 7, 18
a proportional share of the agricultural produce that is levied on the Muslim's harvest 12, 40, 100, 103
an obligation in re 15
payable by the tenant or the share-cropper according to Abū Yūsuf 16
uṣūl al-fiqh, the sources of law 1, 125

waqf, a foundation. Only to be constituted from *private property*, *see* sub verbo
kharāj lands can be transformed into *waqf* 9-12, 81, 23n.42, 93
tax assignments may not be transformed into *waqf* 13
fiscal privileges for *waqf* lands in the Ottoman period 88, 91-3
slave labour and salaried labour on *waqf* lands 12, 17
special rules for the tenancy contract that concerns *waqf* lands 33-4, 36, 44n.13
ghaṣb, *see* sub verbo of *waqf* lands 42, 68
waqf as the *rent-yielding property* (*see* sub verbo) par excellence 108-10, 119n.37
entitled to maximum rent from all *unauthorized users* 109-10, 115-16
the verification of property deeds as a means for the confiscating of *waqf* lands 81-2, 86-7
taxation of *waqf* lands in Ottoman Egypt 86

extension of *waqf* lands in Egypt, Syria and the rest of the Ottoman Empire during the seventeenth and eighteenth centuries 82
competition for rent between the *waqf* administrator and the *tīmārī* (*see* sub verbo) 102-3
waqf irṣādī, a *waqf* constituted by rulers from public property 81, 92, 97n.64
waste lands, *see mawāt*

Ẓāhir ar-riwāya, the six books by *Shaibānī* which embody the classical Hanafite *doctrine* and its *corpus juris* 41-2, 50n.80, 59-60, 68